D0209683

Sociology and the demystification of the modern world

International Library of Sociology

Founded by Karl Mannheim

Editor: John Rex, University of Warwick

Arbor Scientiae
Arbor Vitae

A catalogue of the books available in the **International Library of
Sociology** and other series of Social Science books published by
Routledge & Kegan Paul will be found at the end of this volume.

Sociology and the demystification of the modern world

John Rex
Professor of Sociology,
University of Warwick

Routledge & Kegan Paul
London and Boston

First published in 1974
by Routledge & Kegan Paul Ltd
Broadway House, 68–74 Carter Lane,
London EC4V 5EL and
9 Park Street,
Boston, Mass. 02108, USA
Set in Times Roman, leaded
and Printed in Great Britain by
Unwin Brothers Limited
The Gresham Press
Old Woking, Surrey
© John Rex 1974
No part of this book may be reproduced in
any form without permission from the
publisher, except for the quotation of brief
passages in criticism

ISBN 0 7100 7858 7
Library of Congress Catalog Card No. 73–93637

Dedicated to Saint Augustine and Franz Fanon,
both of whom worked in North Africa and
faced up in different ways to the fact
of living in collapsing empires

Contents

Part four **Social structures and moral perspectives**

Preface

This book is written out of a deep conviction that sociology is a subject whose insights should be available to the great mass of the people in order that they should be able to use it to liberate themselves from the mystification of social reality which is continuously provided for them by those in our society who exercise power and influence. This is not to say that doing sociology is an entirely simple business. It does involve some very difficult philosophical questions, particularly in the theory of knowledge. Whatever doubts the philosophers may have had in the past about their capacity to know the physical world, these are as nothing compared with those which arise in connection with knowledge of the social world. Precisely because of this uncertainty, however, it is possible for ideological distortions to pass as truth. On the other hand, professional sociologists in the last few years have got so bogged down in having philosophical doubts that they rarely rise to the level on which they can say much that isn't trivial.

This book's perspective is based upon a recognition that a great many sociologists simply take the value assumptions of the powerful for granted and devote themselves to policy-oriented research. Such policy-oriented research, however, usually involves a manipulative attitude towards people. We, therefore, suggest that it is the positive duty of the sociologist, *qua* sociologist, not to commit himself to policy-oriented research, at least before he makes a prior analysis of the actual policies being pursued by the powerful.

Still more fundamentally, writing in the second half of the twentieth century, we are able to see how foolhardy and misleading were the assumptions of the Enlightenment about industrial society. Just as it is important for sociologists not to take governments at their word when they say they are pursuing a particular policy, so also it is important that they should dissociate themselves from the

A*   ix hysterical optimism of the Enlightenment about the new world which came into being in the wake of the political and industrial revolutions of the eighteenth century and early nineteenth century. Furthermore, there is no reason why sociologists should simply declare themselves radical because they have adopted the counter-assumptions of revolutionary ideologies. The perspective of this book is that the processes which were set in train by the industrial and political revolutions of the nineteenth century have now got more or less completely out of hand and that there is every prospect of the world heading for a new Dark Age. This may not as yet be obvious for the inhabitants of the affluent countries. It certainly is for the majority of the peoples of the world who live continuously on the verge of externally inspired neo-colonial civil wars.

Both the advanced industrial countries and the countries of the third world, however, appear to be exhibiting signs of structural strain and these structural strains are translated for individual people into what Mills called 'private troubles'. The whole humane purpose of sociology is to take these 'private troubles' seriously by tracing them to their roots, even if this means being criticised for not dealing with immediate problems of suffering.

Naturally, it has not been possible within a short book such as this to deal with all the problems which are indicated in the chapter headings. Indeed, we would not claim to have dealt with any of them in any kind of a comprehensive way. What we have done, however, in the tradition of Max Weber, is to give an ideal typical account of the main structural problems of the first, second, and third world which it is hoped above all might serve as an agenda for study, as a seeding bed for programmes of comparative, histori-cal, and sociological research.

Since part of the thesis of this book is that the universities of the first world are themselves breaking up as places for serious and detached academic study, it is not surprising that I have to admit that the normal programme of teaching, seminars, discussion with colleagues, and so on, has not contributed much to the ideas set forth here. To say this is not to show ingratitude to one's colleagues, it is to note a symptom of the social decay which surrounds us. Occasions for serious academic discussion and argument rarely arise in an atmosphere of negotiation and administration. I have, however, been privileged to work with a group of sociologists at Warwick with a variety of theoretical insights, taking account of which has helped to give me my own bearings.

Another part of the thesis of this book concerns the tensions imposed upon life by the fact of privatisation in the isolated conjugal family. Sociologically speaking, this is a deprivation which we all suffer. For my part, however, it has been possible to write this book only because, within the context of my own isolated conjugal family, I have been able to subject the argument to the scrutiny and criticism of Margaret Rex, who, when it comes to it, seems to me to have an intuitive understanding of the issues which I am discussing which is rare amongst academic sociologists. Through her also I have been able to locate myself socially in a working-class community which, through the courage with which it faces poverty and exploitation, succeeds in preserving some of the most fundamental values of civilisation, despite the general degradations brought about by capitalism, bureaucratisation, and massification. To my father-in-law and mother-in-law, Frank and Edith Biggs, I, therefore, owe a very special debt.

With all the obstacles to communication which do exist, I was exceptionally fortunate at the time that I wrote this book in manu-script, to find in Olive Heaton a secretary of rare competence who could read my script and guess my meanings with a sensitivity which I found quite overwhelming. Without her, the production of this book might very well have been delayed for a very long time. To this I would add that the book and indeed my academic life itself owe more than I can say to our departmental secretary Lesley Crone.

part one

The problem of social knowledge

1 Sociology, demystification and common sense

We are sociologists, most of us, because somehow and somewhere we detect that sociology has a morally significant role to play for our personal selves and the world in which we live. We know this and we keep on doing sociology because we have the sense of encountering a truer vision of reality with the aid of sociological concepts than by any other means, whether extra-scientific means or the means provided by any of the other human studies. Yet the precise way in which sociology has moral significance for us is difficult to define and most of the attempts which are made to describe it are cheapjack ones, symptoms of the pathetic inadequacy of routinised intellectual activity in our times, rather than useful attempts to make more conscious what it is that we do.

The most common views of the sociologist's role are, in fact, almost complete opposites of one another. The first is that science can save us and that it is by the application of scientific rather than other forms of thinking to human affairs that happiness, world-mastery and liberation will be achieved. The second is that sociology which abstains from value-judgment and which seeks value-freedom is lost, so that a sociologist must be seen as having the capacity and the duty to declare not merely what must be but what should be, even though, by a strangely circular argument, it is supposed that the sociologist's value-judgments should have the authority of science.

The first view is the view of that version of the European Enlightenment from which sociology pre-eminently sprang, namely the French version represented, above all, in the positivism of Comte. Now, in fact, it is hard for the modern student to read Comte at all because our age so completely lacks sympathy with his. Not merely do we question the ecstatic acceptance of the achievements of technology which he shared with Saint Simon, but we cannot accept

3

that a science of human affairs can tell us what we should do, wherein personal happiness lies or how we should organise our society politically. Yet scientism of a Comtean kind is a suppressed assumption of the vast bulk of contemporary sociology. Either it seeks simply to describe the facts of a social situation as though they were simply external things to be manipulated, rather than the product of human choice and striving, or they suggest that all human affairs are in some way subject to the operation of social laws. Moreover, even where sociologists are themselves too sophisticated to accept these positions, they are conscious that this is the expectation which the world has of them, and that fulfilment of this expectation is a condition of their being permitted to practise their discipline with public support.

Though one might feel, therefore, that positivism in the Comtean tradition barely requires any further refutation, it is unfortunately the case that this particular battle has still to be fought. We must therefore insist that, while sociology is concerned to explore the constraints laid on our behaviour by other persons, by norms, and by 'legitimate' and 'illegitimate' power, we are not simply concerned as sociologists to expose empirical regularities nor scientific and theoretical necessities in social life. We are faced with a much more complex subject matter which involves a dialectical interplay between human striving and social constraint. We need to do justice, that is to say, both to phenomenal and noumenal man.

Twentieth-century barbarism involving the destruction of human life on an unprecedented scale in world wars and colonial wars, the practice of genocide and torture, the crude recurrence of financial and political corruption in public life, and the irresponsible destruction and consumption of natural resources to a point at which the survival of mankind for more than a few more generations cannot be guaranteed, has clearly demonstrated that the promise of a scientifically managed social order was not to be fulfilled. Not surprisingly, therefore the cry has been raised that, far from sociology abstaining from value-judgments in order that it should gain the benefit of insight into scientific necessity, it must at all costs make these value-judgments, because value-freedom means simply that the sociologist would be consigned to a mere technician's role, working at the behest of politicians not subject to any moral restraint. Curiously, the view that sociology must in a rather simplistic sense be value-free, has been attributed by Gouldner in his famous 'Anti-Minotaur' essay (1973, p. 3) to Max Weber, whose own position was very much more complex than this (cf. Tenbruck, 1959 and Dawe in Sahay, 1971), but that need not concern us here. What is at stake is the assertion that sociologists should make value-judgments and not simply confirm the facts in a value-neutral way.

There is indeed a sense in which such a view is permissible and useful. This is the sense in which it is advanced by Myrdal in his famous appendix on 'Facts and Valuations in Sociology' (1944 and 1958) which is a logical extension of Weber's own position (1949, p. 81). According to this view, sociology always looks at facts from a particular point of view or rather looks at the question of the necessity of an event with an implicit question, 'necessary from what point of view?' But all that this does is to separate out the question of value-judgment from the question of scientific understanding, analysis and prediction, and the grounds for value-judgment are not seen as having some kind of scientific validity. What has surely to be resisted is that the sociologist or any natural or social scientist has some special claim to be able to impose his value-judgments on his analysis. This is a claim which has as little validity as its opposite, namely that a scientist should derive his value-judgments from the facts. In both cases the door is opened to political advocacy and propaganda, which sociology can and should avoid. In the one case, political judgments or even prejudices may be given a kind of spurious scientific validity. In the other, they claim no validity at all, other than that of direct moral intuition.

A more beguiling, and in some ways more dangerous, version of this doctrine is that which advocates policy-oriented research. According to this view sociologists should not live in an ivory tower making discoveries for their own benefit; they should earn their keep by addressing themselves to practical problems. Unfortunately this view gives no answer at all to the question of why particular situations are problematic, or from what point of view. Still worse, the point of view may be concealed and the pretence maintained that the problem is one to which all men of goodwill would wish to address themselves. Thus, in recent British studies of race relations, when colonial migration made race relations an explosive political issue, many sociologists addressed themselves to the issues which appeared problematic from the point of view of the government but claimed to be speaking from some shared abstract moral point of view. The work *Colour and Citizenship* (Rose, 1969), which some claimed to be a British version of Myrdal's classic *An American Dilemma*, was a remarkable example of writing in this vein. Clearly, what a sociologist would have to do in this instance would be to discover and expose the policy aims of the government and other participant actors and to evaluate situations from the point of view of those various policy aims. In such a procedure, the actual policy aims might be found to be at variance with the most frequently confessed aims or, even more likely, the actions of government might be found to be at odds with its professed aims (Rex, 1973b). In this case, all too often the policy-oriented researcher might

5

unwittingly be involved in a double-deceit. First, he might, by pretending that the governmental authorities had the highest ideal aims, simply be involved in doing public relations work on their behalf. Second, given the former pretence, he might feel impelled to attribute blame or causal significance to other less powerful individuals, whose choices were actually made in contexts set by the powerful. The assumptions of policy-oriented research may thus be stated somewhat as follows: the governing authorities are basically benevolent. Assuming this, we will approach problem areas to see what obstacles stand in the way of their achieving their goals.

It should also be added that these defects may be found in radical research as well as in that which has powerful and respectable sponsors. Unfortunately, however, one response of sociologists to policy-oriented research has been to set against it radical research on behalf of the powerless, e.g. the working class, the blacks, and the students. We can only say of this that it has the most mischievous consequences. It should surely be understood by now that there is a great variety of goals amongst those who claim to speak for the working class, the blacks, and the students, and any intelligent member of the radical movements which have these social bases would do well to look as open-mindedly and critically at these goals as we have suggested a sociologist should do in looking at the goals of government. This by no means suggests that the use of sociology should lead the radical to abstain from action. It does suggest that he should act with care and precision and not engage in utopian fantasies about what his action is likely to achieve, because it is taken collectively on behalf of 'the forces of progress'.

Karl Mannheim (1954) saw these problems well enough, but he tended to the extreme view that there really was no way out for social science other than to rely upon the political intuition of a free-floating intelligentsia. We would not take that view. We argue here that a truly reflexive sociology is possible, and that a critical sociologist can evolve a method for describing social structures and analysing their function for various social participants, including the uncritical sociologists who describe them from undisclosed policy points of view. We may, of course, be fully reflexive and recognise that our own critical position is not free of taint, but we can and shall argue that a truly critical sociology, which looks at facts about social relations and structures *and* at policy goals which sustain them, has *relatively speaking* a greater validity than other theories, because it puts more of its propositions to some kind of empirical test.

Disenchantment with positivist science which claimed to talk about neutral facts 'out there' in the external world has led some sociologists in recent times to go back to Thomas's injunction to see social facts in terms of the participant actors' definition of the situation (Thomas and Znaniecki, 1958), but this has led to the unjustifiable assumption that what are called 'members' meanings', descriptions and definitions have as great a validity as any meaning, description or definition which a sociologist might give (see Garfinkel, 1967). In our view, a sociologist who hypothesises that a certain social structure or pattern of social relations is affecting human behaviour may point to a number of areas in which falsifiers of his propositions might be sought, and it is this capacity which gives him the right to claim that his descriptions have greater validity than those either of 'members' actually participating in the social relations described or of other participants for whom such social relations are part of the environment which he seeks to describe. In other words, we accept that there is some validity in the Marxist notion of false consciousness, even though we may disagree with the way in which the Marxist arrives at his conclusion about falsity (see Rex, 1973a, p. 220).

It is understandable that members' meanings should have been rediscovered and celebrated in recent years. It is because the questions 'who is wicked?', 'who is criminal?', 'who is mad?', have too often been settled in terms of meaning systems imposed by the powers-that-be, and sociologists, questioning these meanings, have gone on radically to show that even taken-for-granted answers to questions like 'who is a woman?' can be argued about (Garfinkel, 1967). But the opposition here is assumed to be between sociologists working for the powers-that-be against 'ordinary people' in 'everyday life'. In fact, what is not recognised is that the members' meanings which we confront may be manufactured by the powerful and that the sociologists' new look at the situation in terms of artificially constructed and controlled concepts might be more rightly understood as emancipating than these members' meanings can possibly be. This brings us to our central thesis about sociology and demystification and de-ideologising.

Our thesis is this. (1) Men today live in a world in which survival depends upon understanding the social structures within which they live or might have to live out their lives. In particular it implies understanding what it means to live (a) in a basically capitalist society in which profit-seeking corporations have a high measure of freedom in decision-making within an arena partially controlled by moral and political forces, (b) in a centrally planned society of a communist type where the most important tensions are to be found in the political structure, and (c) in formerly colonial societies which start from a base-line of relatively unfree labour institutions and alien political domination, and which are seeking, subject to severe

7

institutional and non-institutional restraints, to overcome the poverty of at least some of their members. (We do not claim these as adequate descriptive sentences to indicate the structural problems of the three worlds. We may offer rather more satisfactory and detailed descriptions in later chapters. What we are seeking to do at this moment is to indicate the broad nature of what sociology can do.)

(2) These structural facts about the politics of the modern world are the major structural facts within which we live our private lives. The tendency in dealing with private misfortune is for applied social science disciplines to arise which refer these misfortunes to personality factors or to their immediate social contexts. We would not wish to deny the importance of such disciplines, but we do wish to emphasise the importance to private troubles of the great public issues.

(3) It is necessary to describe the major social structures of the three worlds and to understand their internal workings as though they were stable, but concentration for analytic purposes on structures is by no means inconsistent with a study of change and revolution. It is necessary, therefore, for us, as sociologists, to study revolutionary forces within the established social structures of the first and second world and, even when they have not succeeded, to consider the degree to which the claim to have upheld a legitimate order by the powers-that-be is being successfully maintained. It is equally necessary to show the way in which the three worlds impinge on each other and the way in which the third world seeks its emancipation from the other two. In short, on the dynamic side, the sociologist must study the potentiality for class war in the first world, the struggle against bureaucracy in the second, the process of denial of moral legitimacy as it occurs in both of these and, last but not least, the revolution of the poor and wretched of the earth.

(4) Of course the justification of our assertion that there are problems with which sociologists should or can be concerned depends upon arguing our way through many epistemological difficulties. This, however, we shall do. What we have to note here is that the members' meanings of those who act as ideologists for the powers-that-be are on the whole designed to present the world to us in a particular light. Sociologists, on the other hand, have trivialised the world. What we are pleading for and campaigning for here is that sociologists should take on these ideologists in intellectual argument about the important issues and, by exposing their ideological distortions, reveal some of the loci of power and the sources of pain and suffering which they conceal. We do not, however, seek to replace one ideology by another. Rather, by removing the comforting myths which conceal reality, we seek to show the world to be an

uncomfortable place which can only become comfortable through the control, by ordinary men and women, of the agencies which now control them.

(5) To counter the ideologists it will often be necessary to take what will be called by many a nihilist view (Deakin *et al.*, 1970). We should be prepared to describe structures of social relations without assuming that they must be preserved or that they must be changed. Chaos, anomie, and social breakdown must be entertained as likely possibilities, along with order and revolution. It is consistent with this that at times we may ask questions about what is necessary from the point of view of this or that collectivity, but we do not take the point of view of *any* group as valid in its own right. Our nihilism is essential to the demystification of the world. It thus goes without saying that it is a nihilism with a profound moral purpose. By destroying, even for a moment, the sacredness of the world view of priests and lay ideologists it opens up the possibility of true moral judgment which is not itself a sociological matter.

(6) The justification of this position depends upon our being able to show that a truly nihilistic sociology is possible. On this we would say:

(a) that, of course, the possibility is only a relative one since statements about social structure and social relations are inevitably 'indexical' in Garfinkel's use of the term (or, to use a more usual language, closely related to, and discovered in the context of, everyday speech) but that none the less it is possible to derive a common language about social relations which can be agreed not only among sociologists but amongst laymen in many different worlds. This is what Simmel and Weber sought to do and it is what we shall be doing here;

(b) that, while it is not possible on some levels entirely to eliminate value-judgments which will be written into language itself and hence into cognition, it is none the less not the case that once we have agreed on what is the given subject matter of sociological study, we cannot proceed to further phases of analysis in a thoroughly objective way;

(c) that it is possible for sociologists not to be confined to a second-hand view of the social world as perceived only in and through actors' definitions of the situation or members' meanings. They can, with the aid of a sociological language, look at social relations 'from the outside', as all actors themselves sometimes do, but in a controlled and disciplined way, so that there are set procedures for resolving disagreements about what is the case (see Rex 1973a, p. 220).

These are points which we will seek to prove in subsequent chapters, but we shall seek to prove them in simple and straightforward language, because the business of arguing about them has become inhibited by the technical jargon which sociologists, and particularly philosophically-oriented and epistemologically sophisticated sociologists, have introduced into their subject. Indeed it is not too much to say that the layman who seeks to understand and command the modern world is subject to a double process of mystification. The first is the mystification of the world through ideological meanings. The second is the mystification which arises in sociology itself when, after arousing a hope of a demystified reality, it then (a) makes the task seem enormously difficult, if not logically impossible, (b) uses such language in doing this that, even if it does claim to point the way to successful understanding, provides tools of a kind which only a highly sophisticated craftsman could use. In the light of this élitism it is little wonder that many intelligent men and women, in their political and private lives, are inclined to put more faith in 'praxis' or in brute common sense than in the stumbling uncertainties of sociology.

What we are proposing is a double task and a double revolution in sociology. First we have to eliminate the unnecessary difficulties which the arcane languages of the most recent sociologies have placed in the way of anyone seeking to achieve a real understanding of the world. Second, we have to recall sociology to an interest in the central structural problems which face us in the social world which we inhabit. This book should be, above all, a testament of faith that this is possible and that sociology is available as an instrument of social and self-understanding, as well as of emancipation to anyone who wishes to use it.

Before proceeding to the main body of our work, it will perhaps be useful to illustrate what we mean when we say that sociology has doubly mystified rather than demystifying the world. We shall do this by referring to a number of recent authors. We do so, not because we wish to deride their work, but precisely because they are talking about some of the most important problems of all. The lay reader will see from this precisely how sociology has become knotted up in its own language. The writers to whom we will refer in particular are: Talcott Parsons, Alfred Schutz, George Herbert Mead, Harold Garfinkel, Claude Lévi-Strauss, Louis Althusser and Jurgen Habermas.

The general climate in which Parsons worked was atheoretical in the extreme. Indeed it is still the case that American sociology has an almost schizoid character. The vast bulk of writing, especially in the journals, consists of what amounts to exercises in social statistics, in which the variables studied are, in all likelihood, not sociological at all, while here and there questions of theory are discussed without reference to empirical research. But what Parsons was seeking to do was, first to ask questions about social action, social relations and social systems, and second to consider the way in which all social action could be illuminated by showing its role from the point of view of the social system, that is to say how it was ever possible for social order rather than a war of all against all to exist. There is no doubt that this is an important problem, even for those who do not share Parsons's concern with 'order. One of the questions which we would undoubtedly wish to ask is that concerning the social mechanisms whereby human beings are prevented from clashing with one another, both because even an understanding of conflict presupposes this, and because no conflict theorist ever goes to the extreme of holding that all social relations must be conflictual. Yet somewhere along the way Parsons loses us, both in his substantive concerns, and in his use of language.

What seems to be the case is that Parsons originally sought, as Max Weber did, to understand social structure in terms of action. Moreover, he wished to offer a theory which did justice to 'voluntarism', i.e. to man's capacity to choose his own course of action (Parsons, 1965). Yet Parsons sought to solve this problem by bringing it within a mechanistic scientific framework. In his crucial introduction to Weber's work (Weber, 1947) he argues both that sociology should concern itself with the functional integration of social systems and that the study of action implies the acceptance of a psychological dimension in sociological theory. Thus, instead of the notion of social structures which oppress and inhibit human action being seen as themselves the product of human volition and action, action itself becomes the product of 'patterns of value-orientation' which are needs for the properly socialised individual and have the fortunate property of integrating the collectivity.

In fact, incidentally, Parsons (1951) gives us a valuable tool for the classification of kinds of social relations, according to whether they involve emotions or not, according to whether they are specialised or not, whether they involve one individual seeing another as a member of a category or as himself, and whether one individual responds to the other variably in terms of his achievements or in a fixed way. This would, by itself, be a valuable contribution to the basic language of sociology and would spell out some of the meanings implicit in Tönnies' pioneering work (1955). Moreover, having set these possibilities out, Parsons is able to pose important problems about the way in which individuals switch from one type of behaviour to another and the way in which order depends upon segregating different patterns of social relations from each other. Within the overall mechanistic system, in fact, we have the notion of alternative patterns. If the model is conceived as being like a toy railway it is not of the simplest kind where the trains simply go

11

round and round, but a system with points and signals so that individual trains may be diverted from one track to another.

All this is of considerable interest but it is hardly helped by Parsons's terminology. The way of classifying social relations comes under the heading of the 'Pattern-Alternatives of Value-Orientation as Definitions of Relational Role-Expectation Patterns'. This, of course, is by no means clear, but it apparently refers to the more complex part (Section F) of Parsons's table of the elements of social action, for he does say 'we are here dealing with the foci for the patterning of social relations'. But before he comes to this he has already said 'we are concerned with the patterning of the collectivity-integrative sub-type of the moral type of evaluative action-orienta-tion (E-3-b in the outline') (1951, p. 59). It really is hard to know what it is exactly that we are supposed to be talking about!

The pity of this is that Parsons has two great merits. First, he understands the primacy in sociology of the study of social relations understood in terms of the action frame of reference. Second, he boldly applies his theories to the comparison of major socio-political structures, commenting on such questions as the possibility of a classless society, the disappearance of religion, of the family and the state under communism. Unfortunately, however, anyone who is interested in understanding these problems is likely to have two doubts about the Parsonian system. One is whether so sophisticated a system of conceptualisation may not require so much time for its own mastery that it will not permit any real effort to understand the empirical world. The other is whether, in the cloudy ambiguity of some of the concepts, there are not possible areas of dispute in which the opaqueness of the theory permits some sleight of hand in the development of the argument. Maybe spending time on the Parsonian system is a worthwhile exercise for pure academics. It is a cumbersome tool in understanding the social structures of the modern world. One is reminded, above all, of the intellectual parallel with Hegel.

Parsons's theories have been criticised as being over-preoccupied with the problem of order. Thus one would expect, on the one hand criticism from the point of view of conflict theory, and on the other from those who are less concerned with the system producing action-orientation patterns built into participant actors' heads than with these actors' ways of defining the situation. We should, therefore, ask whether conflict theory, and particularly sociological Marxism, has more to offer on the one hand, and on the other, whether much can be learned from those who emphasise the actors' own subjective definitions of the situation.

So far as conflict theory is concerned, the problem which much of it poses, if we are looking for an alternative to Parsons, is whether it is really an alternative at all. This is particularly true of Coser's discussion (1956) of the social functions of conflict, which is readily containable within a slightly modified Parsonian system. It is much less true, however, of Dahrendorf, who originally criticised Parsons in America (1968b) and later produced an English version (1959) of his work on class conflict. Whatever criticisms we might otherwise make of it, Dahrendorf's work does at least meet our demands for a relevant sociology, in three respects. First, it is clearly written and is about social relations understood in terms of social action. Second, because of this, it retains a clear conception of the possibility of conflict in social affairs. Third, it is concerned with the crucial issues in the study of political and social structure. For this reason we shall find ourselves, in due course, discussing many of the issues Dahrendorf raises, and precisely on the level on which he raises them.

Marxism, apart from the work of Dahrendorf, finds expression, as sociology rather than as economics, in the work of the Frankfurt refugees and in their American successors, such as C. Wright Mills. As will be seen from the chapters which follow, our own approach, though it will be more theoretical and analytic, has much in common with that of Mills, but the work of a writer like Marcuse (1954) represents another arcane tradition which must be mystifying to the layman and which has its problematics in the work of Hegel rather than in the empirical world.

Far more influential in America than the theory of social conflict, however, is the work of the phenomenological school, and it is here that one finds the development of mystifying obscurity on a scale which, in the last analysis, bids fair to outdo Parsons. We shall say something here of the significance in this respect of both the 'pheno-menology of everyday life' school which derived primarily from the teaching of Alfred Schutz, and the school of symbolic interactionism which derives, above all, from the work of George Herbert Mead.

Schutz's heritage is a double one. On the one hand he wrote a book which he conceived of as a kind of footnote to Weber. On the other he sought, separately from this, to develop philosophy in the direction of the phenomenology of everyday life. No one would wish to deny Schutz's intellectual stature. What is at issue here, however, is whether the refinements and complexities which he introduces in his sociological and philosophical writings should be treated as the whole of sociology or as a prolegomenon to it. Our complaint is that the tradition which has arisen out of Schutz has tended to do the former.

Schutz's work on Weber was designed to show the complexity of the epistemological problems facing the sociologist and partici-pant actors in imputing motives to other actors. Weber had been aware of these problems and, in trying to say what he meant by

13

action and social relations, had taken over much of the language of Dilthey and other contemporaries. In doing so, however, he none the less deliberately chose not to allow the philosophical problems inherent in that language to prevent him going on to develop concepts useful in the comparative and historical study of social structures. To some extent he swept them under the carpet. There is no reason why his scholarly successors should not sweep them out again, but when this leads, as it does amongst some of our latter-day phenomenologists, to a denial of, or loss of interest in, Weber's actual accomplishment it can only be deplored.

The basic problem for Weber was to develop concepts of social action and social relations which were close enough to the concepts used by participant actors in their subjective understanding of their situation to be useful in explaining their behaviour. He was insistent, however, that it was not his aim to substitute the concepts used by actors themselves for constructed sociological concepts. Schutz, *in his comments on Weber* (1967) saw this well enough, but in his philosophical writings (1964), about the nature of social reality, *when he did not claim to be doing sociology* but rather discussing what must be assumed in constructing the notion of a world of everyday life, he was no longer discussing the conceptualisation of sociologists. Those who subsequently misunderstood this part of Schutz's work as being sociology therefore tended radically to devalue any serious attempt to transcend the possibly false consciousness of participant actors by a radical attempt to reinterpret the world in terms of sociological concepts.

Still worse than this, from the point of view of sociology, was the retention of overtones of the transcendental phenomenology of Husserl in the work of Schutz. Schutz encouraged his students to 'bracket away' the world created by scientific concepts and to look at the everyday-life world. Husserl, however, had urged the bracketing away of both of these in order to ground philosophy in the direct intuition of fundamental essences and structures. Thus one finds, all too often, that phenomenology opens up the way for the substitution of intuition for observation so that, developed in this direction, it leads to a radical devaluation, not of theory but of empirical research of a disciplined kind.

We shall have occasion to make our own position clear on some of these issues in later chapters, and it might well be that some of those who belong to the phenomenological school will call our work 'positivistic'. To this we may at least reply that our sociological perspective might be attacked from the opposite side as being anything but positivistic. But more important than this, we wish only to claim here that our epistemological doubts should not be kept so continuously before us that they prevent us doing sociology.

Schutz is much concerned with the philosophical questions underlying the work of Max Weber, particularly what is meant by meaningful action and what is involved in an actor attributing meaning both to his own action and that of others. It is important that the significance of this set of problems should be understood, provided that having understood it we go on to study social structures. Therefore it is important that what is being said should be very clear. In Schutz's work on Weber it is tolerably so, and what he says does have implications for sociological conceptualisation and social analysis, even though he sometimes becomes preoccupied with purely philosophic questions. Thus we may learn something of importance for research in his discussion of typification (Weber's ideal types) and his interesting distinction between relations with consociates and with contemporaries, predecessors and successors. We may also learn from him to distinguish between action which is meaningful and that which is purposeful. All of these notions are useful in helping us to clarify the significance of sociological ideal types. It may be less important for us to know about the notion of the *durée* (pure immediate experience) which by the time it is known is already in the past tense, to make too much of the distinction between 'because motives' and 'in order to motives', or to realise that the goal states which we fantasise in purposive action are fantasies in the future-perfect tense.

The merit of Schutz, however, is that he did at least start from sociological questions. This is not necessarily the case with the founding father of the sociological school known as symbolic interactionism, George Herbert Mead (1934). Mead was a philosopher and a psychologist. As a philosopher he was interested in the emergence of the self, and amongst philosophers he was distinguished as having argued for a social interactionist account of the origin of the self. As a psychologist he was interested in the continuities and discontinuities between the behaviour of animals and the behaviour of man, and saw the uniqueness of human behaviour as lying in its symbolic nature. But what is the significance of this contribution for sociology?

The first problem which strikes the reader of Mead is that his work gives us less guidance on how to do research on human social interaction than does even Alfred Schutz. Notions like 'taking the role of the other', 'making a gesture to one's self', or 'the generalised other', are not as clear as equivalent notions in Schutz, and it is arguable that the notion of a twofold self as including a bundle of impulses called the 'I' and an incorporation of the generalised other called the 'me' is less clear and less fruitful than Freud's theory of personality.

In fact the most researchable part of Mead's work is arguably in

15

the field of psychology rather than sociology. It concerns precisely the relationship between the 'I' and the 'me' and the varying degrees of sincerity which are involved in the 'I's' submission to the 'me'. But a theory of personality and role-playing of this kind is not of itself sociological. It tells us nothing about social structure, for social structure implies action and men in symbolic interactionist theory do not act, they simply devise strategies for preserving their selfhood in the face of society. This is particularly true of the men who occur as actors (in an almost literal sense) in the work of Erving Goffman (1969; see also Dawe, 1973).

Since, however, the concept of self depends upon *symbolic* interaction, another line of development in modern sociology has been that which emphasises the extent to which the meaning of human action depends upon the labels which are attached to it and it is argued that there can be disagreements about labels. The tragic consequence of this line of thought, however, is that it leads to the illusion that the world consists of nothing more than labels which can be changed at will. It is understandable that such a doctrine should be popular amongst radicals at a time when the labels and meanings imposed by the powers-that-be are in disrepute. But this hardly makes for an adequate sociology by itself. In fact the whole doctrine could only make sense within the sociology of deviance which must (or at least should) assume that there is something to deviate from. Sadly, however, deviance theory has proceeded largely without trying to establish this linkage between sociological theory as such and the theory of deviance (see Lemert, 1951, 1967; Howard Becker, Jnr, 1963; Rex, 1973a, p. 225).

The perspectives of phenomenology and symbolic interactionism have now been succeeded by a very particular doctrine and cult called ethnomethodology which, it should be noticed, is not claimed by its founder, Harold Garfinkel (1967), to be sociology though this claim is made by others, especially Aaron Cicourel (1963, 1968, 1973). What ethnomethodology seeks to do is to gather together every conceivable epistemological doubt about sociology and to try to offer an alternative way of explaining meaningful human action and interaction to that offered by orthodox sociologists. In particular it emphasises natural language – the language of everyday social interaction – and argues that social interaction can only be understood if we turn our attention to the important topic of how such meanings are taken for granted and sometimes have to be re-negotiated.

The main points which we would wish to make here about the anxieties of ethnomethodology are that, though they are understandable and though it is sometimes useful to look at conflicts of meanings and labels, the degree of the difficulty which they present

16

to sociologists is greatly exaggerated and reaches its absurd logical conclusion when Garfinkel invites his students to doubt and question the taken-for-granted meanings of the family breakfast table. In fact, while we may admit that sociology could do well to be cautious about the common-sense meanings which it assumes, it can also be over-cautious and, because it pretends to have no meaningful communication with the world, cease to be able to talk about that world altogether.

It is perhaps also important to add that ethnomethodology has suffered peculiarly from the unique language of its founder, which has unfortunately been copied by his disciples. Thus, for example, on the first page of Garfinkel's chapter 'What is Ethnomethodology?' we find the following (1967, p. 1):

> [The] central recommendation [of these studies] is that the activities whereby members produce and manage settings are identical with members' procedures for making those settings 'accountable'. The 'reflexive' and 'incarnate' character of accounting practices and accounts makes up the crux of that recommendation. When I speak of accountable my interests are directed to such matters as the following. I mean observable-and-reportable, *i.e.* available to members as situated practices of looking and telling. I mean too that such practices consist of an endless, ongoing, contingent accomplishment; that they are carried on under the auspices of, and are made to happen as events in, the same ordinary affairs that in organising they describe; that the practices are done by parties to those settings whose skill with, knowledge of, and entitlement to the detailed work of that accomplishment – whose competence – they obstinately depend upon, recognise, use and take for granted; and *that* they take their competence for granted, itself furnishes parties with a setting's distinguishing and particular features, and of course it furnishes them as well with resources, troubles, projects and the rest.

This is strange language indeed, and perhaps serves to make one ethnomethodological point, namely the infinite variability of human language and meaning systems. But the mischief in it lies in its turning away from any study of social structures, which are the starting point from which making things accountable must begin. We accept that meanings and social relations are continuously re-made, but they are not re-made only by linguistic changes and in any case sometimes for long periods they don't change at all. One only has to ask a slave or a prisoner whether, in his experience, 'the activities whereby members produce and manage settings of

17

organised everyday affairs' are 'identical with members' procedures for making those settings accountable'. He would say that this was a funny way of talking and show us his manacles or window-bars.

Quite different preoccupations are to be found in European sociology. We shall look at three of them. The first of these is the doctrine of 'structuralism' which starts with the work of the social anthropologist, Claude Lévi-Strauss, but which has far-reaching influence as the highest form of scientific intellectualism in the human studies. The second is the anti-humanist Marxism of Louis Althusser and his pupils, which dominates French Marxism as well as the neo-Marxism of many young students in Britain and elsewhere. The third is the continuing Hegelianised Marxism of Frankfurt.

The social anthropology of Lévi-Strauss starts from the recognition that functional explanations are inadequate as a means of dealing with a number of empirical problems. Radcliffe-Brown (1968), for example, had claimed that the explanation of recurrent social activity must lie in the contribution which it made to the maintenance of the social structure, the latter term being taken to refer to an ongoing network of social relations. Thus, forms of kinship could be explained by the actual duties required of and performed by relatives for one another. Similarly, myths, rituals and symbols could be explained by showing that they helped to reinforce attachments to socially significant objects (1964). If however, one looks even at Radcliffe-Brown's own work, it is clear that, so far as kinship is concerned, Radcliffe-Brown's own explanations (1956) often do not refer to actual duties and obligations, but rather take note of the fact that the rules of kinship operate according to such structural principles as the 'unity of the lineage group' and, in the case of myth and ritual, his explanations of the function of symbols are peculiarly far-fetched.

What Lévi-Strauss (1963, 1967, 1968) seems to have recognised is that, first in kinship, then in myth, and finally in nearly all human activity, there were discernible structural principles, out of which cultural and social forms were built. One did not need further explanation of the forms of cultural and social life other than that they were analysable in terms of structural principles, combined usually in terms of a number of binary oppositions which could be combined, re-combined, inverted and developed in a variety of ways and in quite disparate areas of activity, rather as a musical theme might be developed.

The recognition of such structures is undeniably important and it would not be claimed here that the problems with which structuralism deals can, as yet, yield to any other form of explanation. But to say this is not to say that such explanations are not theoretically possible, particularly if some of the self-imposed limitations of functionalism are abandoned, especially its denial of history and its insistence on functional integration. Moreover, the great merit of such explanations as the functionalist offered is that they made sense of behaviour in terms of models of purposively oriented action. Explanations of this type are compelling in that when we place the activity within an understandable framework of meaning our curiosity comes to rest. We feel that we now understand. The structuralist alternative is to invite us to accept that explanation has been accomplished because the structures which are discerned in social and cultural life have a logical form and are paralleled by structures discernible elsewhere, e.g. in language as it is analysed by the science of linguistics. But beyond this Lévi-Strauss claims, though he does not prove, that the structures which emerge in social life have a psychological basis in the mind, and even a physical basis in the human brain.

The message of structuralism, then, seems to be this. The forms of social life which perplex and puzzle and sometimes oppress us can be understood *scientifically*. There can be no real voluntarism in human affairs, and the wisest path for the politician would seem to be to co-operate with the inevitable, even though in concession to what he calls one of his mistresses, namely Marxism, Lévi-Strauss may see the onward march of the structural and historical forms as dialectical. Such a position may give satisfaction to the scientist. It hardly does much for the ordinary man who wishes to understand and master and control his world.

Marxism in contemporary Europe is torn between two poles, represented by the early humanistic Marx of the period before 1845, and the increasingly scientific Marx in the years after this. After the publication of the 1844 manuscripts (Marx, 1959) the tendency of Marxian scholarship was to emphasise man's capacity to change the social relations which oppressed him. This had a particularly wide appeal in the years of intellectual and political liberation after Stalinism had been overthrown in the communist countries and in the international communist movement. But this utopian phase in Marxist thinking is much discounted by Marxists, particularly in France, and more particularly in the work of Louis Althusser and his followers.

Althusser emphasises that, after 1845, there was a radical epistemological break in Marxist thinking and that, after that point, he no longer looked at society from the point of view of individual action. The 'sensuous human activity' to which Marx refers in the *Theses on Feuerbach* (Marx and Engels, 1962) is seen as being held in balance with the 'ensemble of social relations' and 'the earthly family' of the productive system, and all this is a transitional phase. Thereafter what Marx was interested in was, according to Althusser (1969),

19

the working of social and economic formations which had their own laws of structure and development.

At first sight this looks like a retreat from a sociology of social action and social relations into systems theory and there is indeed a parallel between the development which Althusser imputes to Marx between 1840 and 1850 and that undergone by Parsons between 1940 and 1950. Althusser, however, being located in France, is more concerned to relate his own work to that of the structuralist school and sees the various practices which make up his socio-economic formations as structural elements.

One would fear that such a theory might combine all the worst elements in scientism and in the monolithic integration of systems theory. What becomes important for Althusser, however, are the ways in which the relation between the various practices is not entirely predictable in terms of scientific laws. These practices have a degree of independence of one another even though the economic factor asserts itself in the last instance and what precipitates change is a process called over-determination, in which the 'contradictions' of one practice become overlaid on another until the whole system breaks, rather than simply through the basic contradiction asserting itself and ramifying throughout the system.

An uncharitable view of the Althusserian philosophy is that it is an intellectual justification of political opportunism, for there is virtually no political decision which could not be justified in terms of it. On the other hand, we should note that this philosophic system has gained widespread recognition amongst the political young of the late 1960s and early 1970s because it seems to explain events by referring them to a body of systematic theory, in this case so it seems to us, the distillation of the more simplistic aspects of the Marxian heritage which were bequeathed to the movement by Engels.

Against this background the work of the Hegelian Marxist school at Frankfurt has far more appeal to political activists and humanists. The school never abandoned the Hegelian belief in progress towards a moral, cultural and political goal, but by the time its members had gone through the fire of Nazi persecution they had lost their conviction about the goal of the historical process. They could not be content with Dilthey's alternative world views (1957; Lichtheim, 1970) nor with Max Weber's more radical relativism, and still continued to look for a sociology with a moral purpose. The more important recent attempt to do this is to be found in the difficult and obscure work of Jurgen Habermas.

In his famous inaugural lecture, Habermas (1972) refers to three kinds of science. The first is analytic and empirical and has as its goal the control of the world of things. The second is hermeneutic and has as its goal the increase of inter-human understanding. The third, however is critical and emancipatory and it is this which is central to social and political life. We cannot enter here into the complex internal debate about the 'critical theory of society' among such participants as Marcuse, Horkheimer and Adorno. Neither can we pursue the question of its relation to the phenomenological and positivist movements. What is of interest is Habermas's attempt to locate a sphere of human and social study which is genuinely critical and emancipatory.

The best way of explaining Habermas's position is to say that, for him, the paradigm of a critical emancipatory science is to be found in psycho-analysis. The psycho-analyst neither seeks merely to discover the laws of the patient's behaviour nor to understand how he sees his world. Rather he offers an explanation to the patient which purports to be a true explanation of the patient's conduct and, if it is true, it is accepted by the patient himself and liberates him from his fantasies and from the compulsions of his behaviour. It is suggested that there might be a social equivalent of this, through which the social scientist, confronted with men whose view of the world is distorted by ideology, is able to offer an explanation which enables them to understand their true conditions and, by understanding, to find their way to freedom. Now, from the perspective adopted here, one is inclined to say of Habermas's work that 'we have been writing prose all our life, though we had not thought to give it that label'. His implied condemnation of purely analytic-empirical and hermeneutic science certainly has justification so far as large areas of sociological study are concerned, but can it really be said to have validity as a criticism of the work of Weber and Simmel? They are of course, in our sense, 'moral nihilists' or 'relativists' and show neither the Enlightenment-based hopes of critical theory nor the commitment of the Frankfurt school to revolution. But does Habermas really propose revolution? Would Marx not say of him that he proposed only a thought-revolution? Is it not possible that the situation of social science is akin to that which would exist in psycho-analysis if the patient recognised the truth of his analyst's explanation but continued to suffer? The demystification of the world might only be expected to expose its painful reality not to change it. That, from the point of view of the sociological perspective adopted here, is as far as we are prepared to go. Of course we may, in our role as human beings who are also political animals, go on to liberate ourselves, but that is another matter.

This extended excursus into the recent history of sociology was made, it will be remembered in order to undo the double mystification of social reality, of which we accused the sociologists. We do not wish simply to be philistine about this. We recognise the specialist tasks which each of the schools referred to has undertaken, and we recognise the value of localised intellectual traditions in which one man stands, intellectually speaking, on the shoulders of another, but, with this said, it is also true that there is a tremendous exclusivity about sociological schools and movements and cults, and this has disastrous consequences.

All sociology and philosophy is to some extent relative to its times, even though it is also in part of universal significance, and the consequence of this important proposition is that it is not necessarily the most illuminating way of approaching our social and cultural reality of the world of the late twentieth century, bound and hobbled by the insights of American functional-integrationist, phenomenological or symbolic interactionist perspectives. If we have to 'do a Garfinkel' on our social institutions, then let us do so by finding our own Garfinkel. Neither can we accept that there is some universal concept of science or Marxism or progress whose past insights should bind us. Let us by all means learn from French positivism, from Hegel and Marx, but let us have the originality and creativity to write as though Hegel, Marx and Durkheim or Lévi-Strauss, Althusser or Habermas had never existed. Otherwise we might all simply wear uniforms or join churches.

Our perspective is unashamedly a moral one. Like Habermas we want men to understand their world in order that they may be liberated from oppression but, lacking a moral perspective other than that which says that men should be able to act in freedom, we also call for an exposure and rejection of the values that are built into the pseudo-scientific world of the ideologists. For this reason we called ourselves nihilists. Finally, however, we do believe that there is an epistemological problem involved in knowing the world, and that we should prove what we know. In this sense our work will be 'empiricist' and even 'positivist', for we do not propose to proceed by residual proof simply to that which cannot be doubted, nor to simply declare that somehow truth is gained through uninstructed practice or experience. The nature of our world has to be discovered by empirical and historical study and, if we are to change the world, we would dare to say that wisdom dictates that we should first seek to understand it.

Let us now try to put together a sociology which will help intelligent men and women to understand the political world of our own times, using the insights of the past, but being prepared to see for ourselves and to take from our predecessors those aspects of their understanding which really do illuminate *our* problems. We are not concerned simply to locate ourselves academically, even though what we will do will be the best which we can to enrich the academic heritage.

2 The givens of sociological analysis

In attempting to gain recognition as a science, sociology has had to assume the appearance of a science at every stage, from that of observation through to the validation of theoretical 'laws'. This has involved the pretence that there really is no difference between the methodological problems facing the sociologist and those facing the natural scientist. A particularly ludicrous statement of this position constitutes the organising forms of Durkheim's best known, and certainly his worst and most scientistic, work *The Rules of Sociological Method*. There (1962, p. 25) he actually suggests that 'value', a concept in economics, can be treated like any other 'thing' in the universe and subjected to a series of scientific procedures, by which he means that we should

indicate first of all by what characteristic we might
recognise the thing so designated, then classify its
varieties, investigate by methodological inductions what
the causes of its variations are and finally compare
these results in order to abstract a general formula.

But positivism was to go still further than this. In the wake of the logical positivist movement for a single and unified science, George Lundberg wrote (1939, p. 38):

I use the word 'physical' in quotation marks in order to
emphasize that I do not recognise the word as denoting, for
scientific purposes, any unique character of the phenomena
to which the word is usually used to refer, as contrasted
with the phenomena designated 'social', 'cultural', etc.
Since all phenomena are 'physical' from my point of view,
I retain the word only to designate a conventional

23

distinction which must be defined, if at all, only in
terms of the degree of universality and uniformity of
responses of human beings to some phenomena as contrasted
with others.

Now it is obvious, as soon as we try to do any work in the social
and cultural sciences, that this will not work. Suppose, for example,
that I ask a research assistant to undertake the most elementary
task of going into a room to tell me what is in it. In what sense
could he go in equipped with a list of the characteristics of possible
things which he might find there? What is a 'thing', anyway? And,
if he took his line from Lundberg, would he not
(a) present us with a considerable problem in that his responses
might not be 'uniform' with other human beings, including myself,
(b) perhaps find himself unable to say anything at all because,
in so far as he tried to produce unquestionable responses, he would
be confined to making reports about coloured shapes.

The difficulties which emerge when the problem is stated this way
have led many sociologists to deny that it is possible to make
observations after the manner of the physical sciences at all. Hence
some hold that the study of social reality involves a direct perception
of forms or essences, some that we can only understand the social
and cultural world through some technique of getting inside the
meaning systems of everyday life and language, some that the
making of value-judgments is essential to the perception of social
forms, and finally, there are those who argue that social knowledge
is gained through practice.

The position which we would take on this matter is as follows:
(a) the observation and recording of social facts will, in practice,
involve the *uncritical* acceptance of language and meanings used in
everyday life, and must do so if we are to make any serious progress
with the study of major social structures,
(b) that, with this said, there are clearly moments at which the
meaning and the 'thingness' of an object are in doubt and in which
procedures of argument and analysis might be devised to settle the
meaning in a particular case, and
(c) that because of the position (a) taken above, there is a great
deal to be said for a specialisation within sociology of those who
make it their task to look critically at the meanings which are otherwise uncritically assumed.

The real problem in sociology in recent years is that, because of
doubts about the possibilities of the observation of social facts in
a direct manner, some sociologists, particularly those influenced by
ethnomethodology and by structuralism, have ceased to do anything
but (c). While in later chapters we shall work very largely within

24

the terms set by (a), what we propose to do here is to consider some of the problems involved in (b) and (c).

One point, perhaps, needs to be re-emphasised here. This is that we cannot speak, in any simple sense, of the 'data' of sociology. Neither coloured shapes, behaviour, the movement of pointers on dials, statistics recording the frequency of behavioural attributes, nor responses to questionnaires, are of themselves of any sociological significance unless they are interpreted in terms of some meaning system. Because of this we find it convenient to use the term 'the givens of sociological analysis'. While the literal meaning of the term is the same as data, it may perhaps be regarded as free of the overtones of sensationalist epistemology which attach to the term 'data'.

The great danger, as we see it, which follows for sociology in the wake of the recognition of the distinctiveness of the subject matter of the socio-cultural studies, is a retreat into some kind of irrationality. Curiously, some anti-positivist authors tend to do positivism the credit of assuming that only its methods are precisely definable and that if they do not work we can work in an entirely undisciplined way, and, particularly at the level of observation, say what we like. One aspect of this is that it is assumed that the problem of meaning is a single and simple one and that it can be resolved at a stroke by saying 'members' meanings', 'deep structures', 'value-judgment' or 'praxis'. We believe that the problem is many-sided and calls for quite specific procedures to deal with each problem.

As we see it, the question of what is there in the room involves, over and above the question of what coloured shapes there are, the question of what names or labels are to be attached to objects and from what sets of names and labels these are to be drawn; second, the question of what relation these objects have to human actions and potential human actions; and, third, what relationship they have to systems of social relations. The third of these questions depends upon answers to the second, and the second on answers to the first, but we should never forget that, as *sociologists*, the answer which we want above all is the third one, for we want to be able to look at cultural objects as our givens and learn from them something about a structure of social relations, a form of social interaction, perhaps a kind of chess game in which these objects are the pieces.

Some of these questions are philosophic questions and some are not solely sociological questions. Thus there has developed a shadowy kind of discipline on the margins of sociology, which could best be called the philosophy of the cultural sciences. It is represented by the work of the later Wittgenstein, by phenomenological philosophy in the European tradition and by the American phenomenological tradition which ends with ethnomethodology (see Wittgenstein,

1968; Winch, 1963; Spiegelberg, 1965 – for a comprehensive account of the phenomenological tradition; Roche, 1973). The debates within these traditions are highly technical and obscure and they deserve respect in and for themselves, but to some extent they must also be criticised because they fail to do justice to the *sociological* dimensions of the problem they are discussing. Thus, while we, as sociologists, might feel ourselves to be out of our depths in a profound philosophical debate, we do none the less claim that we are looking for resolutions of our problems which explain the real accomplishments, and possible future accomplishments, of sociology. Peter Winch, for example, seems to have written an important philosophical work, but those who feel that he has shown that Weber's sociology was impossible might do well to reflect on the scale of Weber's theoretical and comparative historical work (1968a, ch. 2 onwards) which followed the early chapters which cause Winch's anxiety. There is little point in proving that Weber's work was impossible. What we should do is to see whether we can give a better account of the epistemological problems which he solved in practice than he was able to do in his arguments with Dilthey and others (Weber, 1947, 1968a, ch. 1).

The first problem, then, is the question of the stock of labels which we have available to us. What happens when we go into the room to observe it is that we 'thingify' the room by the attachment of labels to our sensations. Thus, as I look around me now, I respond immediately by saying that I can see books, shelves, paper, a table, a telephone, spectacles, and a cup. How is it that I am able to do this, and what would be involved in my getting anyone else who acted really stupidly to agree that these terms should be used?

For immediate purposes, the most important point which we would make at this moment is that we use labels drawn from classificatory systems. The terms 'book' and 'paper' refer to the world of communication. Other terms which belong there are 'letter', 'newspaper', 'pen' and 'television programme'. When I say 'book' I make it clear that I am referring to an actually accomplished object offered for communication, unlike 'pen' and 'paper' which are the means of communication only. I also distinguish it from 'letters', 'newspapers' and 'television programmes' even though these are also accomplished objects offered in communication. On the other hand I might also see the book as made of cardboard and paper and, in labelling it as a book, distinguish it from a variety of other objects, which are made ultimately from wood. So one could go on indefinitely, but the main point should be clear. It is that those who use such terms, including a sociological observer, restrict the range of empirical possibilities in multiple ways by the mere use of the terms. On the whole, moreover, the use of such a term in sociology would never be questioned. But there is a case for the systematic analysis of the taken-for-granted meanings of everyday language, and this should be the task of the expert in linguistics.

To say this is not to overlook the fact that the processes which are important in the making of meaning may not also have importance in the ordering of social relations. Thus it is argued by the structuralist school that the formal properties of language on the most abstract level are also expressed in non-linguistic forms of symbolic behaviour, that is in cultural symbols. Thus the same structures which are apparent in language are also apparent in myth (or more generally in culture), and in kinship (or more generally in social organisations). On the other hand, it is argued by Garfinkel that if we probe the taken-for-granted meanings of everyday language we find the real basis of social order. There is truth in both of these contentions, but this by no means justifies us in building the whole of sociology upon them. Rather we should say that the use of this, rather than that, abstract form in the elaboration of a cultural pattern, or the agreement on an arbitrary and ultimate restriction of the permitted range of possible meanings, is a constraint to which all social life must be subject.

The problems which arise here are not, however, the same as those which arise from the fact that the use of labels or words to attach to things might not be merely cognitive, but also evaluative and social. The choice of ranges of meaning is subject to normative control, it is true, and thus involves social agreement, but over and above this, language has an evaluative dimension by means of which objects are seen as having, not merely a particular place in a total empirical order, but as being good or bad, beautiful or ugly, authentic or inauthentic, and so on. This means that the use of language implies the shared acceptance, by its users, of a particular normative order and, since the evaluative and cognitive elements in language are difficult to separate from one another, there is a sense in which all users of the same language are caught up in a normative order. Moreover, beyond this again, the naming of objects might imply a reference to action, to social relations and roles, so that to use the language already implies being committed to a certain conception of normal action and of social order. This, however, takes us beyond the simple question of labels to a discussion of the second and third aspects of the meaningfulness of social and cultural objects which we have mentioned above. Before we consider this, however, we must also consider the question of change and conflict in language use.

We have clearly avoided a number of problems in this discussion by confining ourselves to the discussion of the simple utilitarian objects which furnish a room. But we should probably not get very far in our description before our use of terms was called into question. One observer might say 'there are six books on the table'. The other might then reply 'I would say there are only four books and two journals', and, to cut a potentially difficult argument short, they might then agree on the rule: 'a thing counts as a book when it contains chapters or articles and does not have a common name with other like publications, from which it is distinguished only by a number'. Thus it is worthwhile to remember that meanings are not merely given in systems, but are continually negotiated and renegotiated. Moreover, there is always a possibility that two observers may think they are using the same term when in fact they are not. Each may connect it with other terms in his own way. In such cases a point of misunderstanding may later arise in which some negotiation and arbitrary agreement will eventually be necessary.

Most social and cultural terms are usually used on the basis of classificatory decisions made by those in an institutional position to declare who falls and does not fall under such labels as normal, mad, subnormal, a suicide, and so on, and ethnomethodological and, more generally, phenomenological methods have been frequently used to expose the relativity of these usages. In a time of social change and upheaval, it is probably particularly likely that such analyses will be undertaken, for the academic's desire to probe and analyse will only reflect a more widespread social malaise and conflict over meanings. What these studies show, however, is that the preliminary phases of social investigation cannot be undertaken with only a brief check on the meaning system being used, for that system may itself be being negotiated. Here, therefore, one is forced to describe the actual social process of negotiation and decision making in order to discover the fluctuating basis of even the cognitive order.

It is important that we should admit all of this, without going on to the exaggerated position of holding that all meanings are in continual flux and that the only thing which one can do in describing social and cultural objects is to describe the transactions and negotiations which go on between individuals, for it is a fact of social life that, for most of the time, most meanings are agreed and, even negotiations such as we have been discussing, assume a great deal that is taken-for-granted. It is this taken-for-grantedness which makes social relations either of a stable and orderly, or of a conflictual, kind possible, and when we go on to discuss not simply the problem of everyday meaning, but of social and cultural facts, it will be necessary to argue that the world need not be thought of as eternally in flux, but that even revolution is only possible because there do exist social structures, the nature of which is agreed on the cognitive level between all parties. To put this sharply, if what one is doing is looking at a tiny and highly unstable piece of the total social order, such as the decision-making procedure in a suicide prevention centre or a psychiatric classification ward, then one will of course notice instability and arbitrariness. If what one is looking at is a capitalist corporation, the Communist Party of the Soviet Union, or a mining compound in South Africa, one need not spend too much time on doubting what and who falls into what category. Thus, because our concern here is a committedly non-trivial one, concerned with macro-structures, our tendency will be to relegate the question of uncertain and to-be-negotiated meanings to the interstices of social life.

It may be asked, of course, whether this is legitimate, since, having located a fundamental cause of instability in social action, we can hardly ignore the possibility that it is here that social changes begin. This plausible view, however, grossly inflates the importance of cognitive and evaluative models of the world as though that were the only factor in social life. Over and above conflicts of meaning there are also conflicts of interest, and it is these, fought out between individuals and groups with shared systems of meaning of a cognitive and even an evaluative kind, which lead to actual revolutionary change. Indeed, one interesting feature of Marxist social thought is that, as class-struggle becomes more acute, a shared and 'true' consciousness of the situation emerges. It is precisely in times of stability that confusions of meaning exist or, rather that, when confusions of meaning exist, revolutionary action is not possible.

We must now move on, however, to our second and third points, which concern the relation of labels and the object world to human action and social relations. We do this very conscious of the fact that it was not meaning as such, but action, action meaningfully oriented to another, and social relations depending upon the mutual orientation of a plurality of actors, which, for Weber at least, con-stituted the core of sociology. We would want to admit here that action assumes a meaningful world and that this meaning can be analysed in part without reference to action in terms of classifications, codes and agreements, but it is also the case that our attempts to talk about the meaning of the object world continually flounder because we can not really begin to understand what books or tele-phones are, except as means to repeated courses of action.

The problem of meaning, in fact, is, as Alfred Schutz (1967) recognised, a twofold one. On the one hand, any experience which is attended to thereby becomes meaningful. On the other, we often speak of action as meaningful when it is regarded as purposive. What we wish to do here is to give some recognition to both types of meaning and to their importance for sociology. Weber, we believe, laid himself open to much criticism by trying to classify all human behaviour which was not goal-oriented as meaningless.

In order to understand the full complexity of this problem, we may perhaps look forward to the basic model of social action which underlies our analysis in the whole of the first part of this book. This presupposes, in the first place, an actor who makes what Parsons has called an initial cognitive mapping of the world (Parsons and Shils, 1962). At this point the actor labels the objects which he sees and, in so doing, commits himself to various codes of meaning of the kind we have outlined. Second, he imagines a state of affairs which, for one reason or another, he wishes to bring about. This again presupposes the understanding of meaning. Finally, he envisages the use of some objects as 'means' and the acceptance of others as 'conditions', subject to certain 'norms', to organise a project which will bring the desired state into being. Here again, he must take for granted certain uniformities of nature and social life which seem to him to be written into the situation, for without this the very notion of means and conditions would be meaningless.

All of what we have said emphasises, as Weber failed to do, that meaning is assumed prior to action (although one can detect, as a kind of archaeological layer in the language which he uses when he speaks of an actor attaching a subjective meaning to his conduct, an intellectual heritage in which such matters were brought out into the open). But there is also another simple use of the term meaning, and that is simply 'related as a means to an end'. This is the way in which Weber uses the term and, for many practical purposes, it is all that is necessary, if we take for granted the meaning of the actor's world as something shared and unchallenged between the sociologist and participants in the world. It is this fact which will enable us to put much of this discussion behind us when we go on to construct models of social relations.

But, if Weber may be criticised for ignoring the aspect of meaning which arises independently of action, those who criticise him sometimes forget that the labelling of the object world often involves connections between terms which depend upon the notion of purpose. So much is this the case that an argument can be put for a pragmatic theory of meaning, a theory that there can be no meaning apart from the concept of action. But what is important here is that, however moderately the theory is expounded, it must still be the case that, embodied in the conception of codes of meaning is the notion of patterns of action and of actors or potential actors. When, therefore, one speaks of an actor confronting a world which is meaningful, in the sense of being described in terms of a language-code, one speaks of an actor confronting other actors, even though they may be no more immediately present to the actor than was Man Friday when Robinson Crusoe first saw his footsteps. Thus it seems as though there is an endless circle and an infinite regress.

Action is only possible in a meaningful world, but a meaningful world embodies the notion of action, which again presupposes meaning, and so on.

There are, however, two ways in which we may break out of this regress. One is to seek for an ultimate code which no longer depends upon action, but depends simply upon the classification of the attributes of things in genera, species and so on. The other is to simply take a common-sense language, as shared by observer and actor, and to go on to posit action within it. These are probably only ideals to which we can best hope to approximate, but it may be expected that the former alternative will be adopted by those who are interested in the structural study of culture, and the latter by those who are interested in major social structures. The final ideal for the sociologist would be a state of affairs in which he could turn to the findings of the linguist or the 'culturologist' and build these findings into his model of the action, which is embodied in the meanings of the world, and the total picture of a meaningful world into his model of the social actor. But this is only the beginning of our complexity. Let us now consider such objects as a schoolteacher's cane, slave-manacles, or a sherry glass. These are not merely parts of the object world, nor even only meaningful objects. They are, surely, social objects. And to understand their meaning we have first to understand what is meant by social relations.

The position which will be taken here is that the apprehension of the social element in the object world is dependent upon the apprehension of objects as involved in action. The alternative would be to say that we simply read social connections into the meanings of words; that, implied in the use of the term cane was the notion of authority, implicit in the term slave-manacles was the notion of unfree labour, and implicit in the term sherry glass was the notion of formal sociability. Such an alternative would be accepted up to a point, since it would put the explication of social meanings on a par with the explication of the sets of meanings implicit in any other area of systematic investigation. But it does less than justice to our understanding of social meanings, for it is the case that we grasp these, not merely externally as things, but as things inwardly understood, and this understanding rests upon the fact that we read them from the subjective point of view of a participant actor. Thus when we say that we apprehend authority, unfree labour, or formal sociability, we mean that we interpret the object which we actually observe in terms of a construct of some kind which posits a schoolboy and schoolmaster, slave and slave-master, or a group of friends acting meaningfully and taking account of the behaviour of others. How we arrive at this construct is a question which we shall have to discuss in another chapter.

31

We are now at a point at which it becomes possible to see what the peculiar problem of the 'givens' of sociological analysis is. Clearly the sociologist does not have any simple or hard data, or, rather, hard data only became significant for him in so far as they are meaningful. But on the other hand, it must be emphasised that not all structures which have the characteristic of dealing with a world of meaning are primarily sociological. True, any study which takes shared meanings for granted has a sociological dimension, but the whole of sociology is not contained in this sharing of meanings and it is itself a process which needs to be explained in terms of a more general and systematic theory of social interaction and social relations. What the sociologist has to deal with is the element in a meaningful world which refers to action, to interaction and relations, and clearly this is a special part of the total world of meaning, and one which has its own peculiarly complex ontological status.

When we speak of meaningful objects in the simplest sense we imply that actors whom we observe attach labels to things, and we can, by listening to and observing the way in which this labelling is done, learn much about the relations between one label and another and the implicit as well as the explicit meaning of the labels. But, in so far as we confine ourselves to the world of physical objects, it is possible to define our labels by operational or ostensive definitions, that is to say, by saying under what circumstances we use a particular label or by pointing to a thing. When, however, we pass to the imputations of motivation and action plans and to the taking account of the behaviour of another to which social labels refer, we are not talking directly about things, but rather about the theoretical interpretations which people give to things. We say 'this makes sense in terms of an actor with this stock of knowledge, in such and such conditions, subject to such and such norms, seeking such and such a goal'. In other words, our basic terms and labels in sociology, even though they appear to refer to things, actually refer to interpretive theories. This then leads on to the questions of how we arrive at such theories, whose theories they are, whether they are valid or not, and whether it matters whether they are valid or not.

In our next two chapters we shall be concerned with two kinds of data which are available to sociologists, and the use which can be made of them. The first of these consists of actors' or participants' or 'members'' theories about motivation and social relations. The second consists of hard data, particularly of a quantitative kind. Of particular importance in that discussion will be the question of whether members' or participant actors' theorising is the only kind which has any validity. Before coming to this, it is necessary to clear up some further points. These concern whether it is possible, and how it is possible, for anyone, whether actor or sociologist, to apprehend patterns-of-action-orientation* and social relations.

One answer to this question, which is sometimes attributed to Simmel (see Martindale, 1961), is that we organise our experience of social life in terms of social forms and categories in a way analogous to the way in which we organise our experience of nature. Thus, what is really necessary for sociology is an *a priori* science of the social forms akin to Kantian metaphysics, which deals with the forms in terms of which natural science apprehends natural phenomena. Of this we would wish to say that it is an attractive possibility and certainly a valuable corrective to vulgar empiricism. There is quite clearly a job to be done in sociology, through the subject turning in on itself and analysing its own language. But Simmel's own diffuse writings hardly suggest the tight and logically necessary kind of concepts which an *a priori* science would require. Still less do the diffuse social usages of everyday life. For our part we will interpret Simmel's own procedure and that of Max Weber, who, in all essentials, carried through Simmel's programme in a somewhat different manner. We shall seek to show that sociologists do not simply have a language of social forms, given, as it were, in their heads. Rather they have to make one which is agreed between them and which makes sense of the language of everyday social usage.

If we cannot accept Simmel's Kantian perspective on the apprehension of social facts, still less can we accept the notion of sympathetic introspection which appears, in the last analysis, to be the basis of Dilthey's work, or the notion of a pure apprehension of social essences which remain when scientific and common-sense views have been bracketed away. Dilthey's notions that somehow an observing participant actor or an observing historian understands expressions because these expressions produce in him reverberations and echoes of the meanings which the observed actor experiences inwardly, seems to give too little account of possible error. On the other hand, pure phenomenology, when it has bracketed away all the possible means of understanding the world as social, seems to be left with nothing but an isolated and individual ego. It is little wonder that Schutz (1964, vol. 1), in seeking to account for the nature of social reality, had to invent a phenomenology of everyday life.

If the above alternatives are rejected we must maintain that, both for the actor in everyday life and for the sociologist, the actual logic

---

* We use the term taken from Parsons here. It is unfortunately a jargon term, but it now has wide currency and has the advantage of distinguishing the meaningful elements in the planning of action and motivation from such psychological and biological elements as instincts, drives, etc. which may be subsumed under the term motivation.

of the way in which he arrives at any proposition about action or social life must be an initial act of observation, albeit of observation of the world of things and behaviour, which is constituted as meaningful by the use of language, and, after this act of observation, by offering an explanatory hypothesis, which is then tested as experience, or in some way argued for. If such procedures be still dubbed positivist, so be it. For those who do not see the world as simply divided into two great warring intellectual camps, it will still be the case that it is a very particular kind of positivism. For our part, we do not believe that the recognition of the peculiar nature of the givens of sociological analysis implies a rejection of the entire logic of empirical science and we would not want to give positivism the credit for being the sole defender of this logic*.

In undertaking to help the reader to demystify the second mystification of the social world by the philosophies of social science, we may by now seem to have become so involved in their arguments as to be caught up also in their mystifications. It will be well, therefore, to end this chapter by asking again what it is which we want to study, and reviewing the way in which we can 'observe' the object of our study in the empirical world.

For a working definition of the subject matter of sociology, we would say that it is concerned with structures of social relations. Within so broad a definition we make full allowance for the notion of change and conflict and also, no less, for misunderstanding and failures of communication. In full, therefore, we should define sociology as concerned with structures of social relations, whether these be changing and conflictual or stable and harmonious, and whether they are based upon shared and agreed meanings or upon confusions and misunderstandings. Within this, because we believe in a non-trivial sociology, we want to be able to describe the macro socio-political structures of the modern world, and the way in which more intimate and personal structures are articulated with them.

The problem which such an assignment poses for science is that there is no simple set of entities directly observable in the empirical world to which it refers. But within the world, as organised by language, we do find, over and above the meanings which derive from other scientific and non-scientific codes, implicit assumptions built into the language, which refer to action and to the taking account of the behaviour of one actor by another. It is these implicit social

---

* Readers of Filmer *et al.*, *New Directions in Sociological Theory* (1972) will see that I have been lumped together there by M. Phillipson, with Percy Cohen as an expounder of positivism in British sociology. In fact, any intelligent reading of my first book, *Key Problems of Sociological Theory* (1961) will see that there is a vast difference between it and that of Percy Cohen (1968). For those outside the ethnomethodological movement the book has appeared, paradoxically, as belonging within the camp of phenomenology.

meanings, or these theories, in terms of which the behaviour of things and people are commonly interpreted, which give the first and most elementary givens for the sociologist. He might also have to take account of the fact that such social meanings are inconsistently used and to propose a new language for talking about them.

Sociology could, however, because of the complexity of these problems, be diverted from its purpose in two ways. On the one hand it might become caught up in the general problems of meaning and the imputation of motivation. On the other it might never rise to the point at which it actually discusses the truth or falsity of its propositions. These are two tendencies which, together with triviali-sation, we need above all to avoid. So far as the first is concerned, it is simply necessary to remind those quasi-sociologists who spend their whole time discussing the philosophy of social action, as well as those empirical researchers who study meanings and rule-following and classification, that, so far as describing and analysing social reality is concerned, they have left their task half done. The in-scrutibility, the tragedy, or the pathos of human action might have been demonstrated, but the actual vexatious fact (Dahrendorf's term, see his essay 'Homo Sociologicus', 1968a), of the existence of extra-individual (i.e. social restraints on human behaviour) remains unstudied.

On the question of proving our propositions, we would make this assertion: when there is inconsistency of social usage the sociologist might offer new concepts, clearly explicated, which actually explain a world of objects and behaviour in a way in which untested common-sense concepts do not. This does not mean, of course, that he offers empirical laws of human behaviour purporting to show that mere recurrence is a proof of meaning, which is the essence of Winch's assertion about Weber. What it does mean is that, if we construct a concept like 'romantic love relationship' 'working class' or 'mar-ket', we can make clear what is involved in that construct and, in a pure empirical case, show whether all the expected consequences or a high percentage of the consequences, of that kind of structure being operative, do exist in the world of behaviour and things and labels. To sustain what we are saying on this point, however, we have to deal with the problems:

(a) of the relation between, and relative validity of, sociologists' theoretical constructs and the social constructs of participant actors, including here a discussion of the vexed question of false consciousness,

(b) of the difficulties of testing basic concepts in pure cases, of the role of ideal types and of the uses of quantification in sociology. These are some of the most important questions to be discussed in the next two chapters.

3   Actors' theories and sociologists' constructs

Quite obviously, the starting point of our attempt to lay the foundations of a systematic sociology and to apply it to the historical social structures of the late twentieth century is to be found in the work of Max Weber. Unfortunately the questions of epistemology and method which lie at the basis of his work were not fully resolved in the introductory paragraphs of his famous work *Wirtschaft und Gesellschaft* (English translation: *Economy and Society*, 1968a) and the ambiguities of the positions which he took up there have given rise to conflicting developments, which may, crudely speaking, be called positivist and phenomenological.

In fact, the eleven paragraphs of Section 1 of Chapter 1 of Weber's work discuss a number of separate, but not easily separable questions. They include a discussion of meaning, both in the broad sense of the meaning of propositions and in the sense of the meaning of action. They separate the question of rational from empathetic understanding. They distinguish sharply between all analyses of courses of action and organic, systems-based and functional approaches. They consider the relation between causal and quantitative approaches on the one hand, explanations in terms of meaning on the other. Finally they consider the relationship between meanings actually intended by an actor, average meanings, and pure types of meaning. The question of the relationship between quantitative and meaningful approaches will be considered in the next chapter, and that of functional and systems-based approaches in chapter 7. Here we propose to deal with the question of theoretical and participant actors' constructs of meaningful action.

Now what Weber says on this point is by no means clear. Thus he tells us that 'for a science which is concerned with the subjective meaning of action, explanation requires a grasp of the complex of meaning in which an actual course of understandable action thus interpreted belongs' (1968a, p. 9) and later he tells us that a motive 'is a complex of subjective meaning, which seems *to the actor himself* or the observer an adequate ground for the conduct in question' (p. 11).

These references seem to suggest that Weber's interpretive sociology implies at least some grasp of the actually intended meaning to a participant actor, if not explaining the action by reference to the actor's own account of it. But he does follow the first of those two quotations (paragraph 5, Section 1) with the sentence: 'In all such cases, even where the processes are largely affectual, the subjective meaning of action, including that also of the relevant meaning complexes, will be called the intended meaning' and then goes on in the next paragraph to distinguish three contexts of understanding as follows (p. 9):

> In all these cases understanding involves the
> interpretive grasp of the meaning in one of the
> following contexts: (a) as in the historical
> approach, the actually intended meaning for
> concrete individual action, or (b) as in the
> cases of sociological mass phenomena, the average
> of, or an approximation to, the actually intended
> meaning, or (c) the meaning appropriate to a
> scientifically formulated pure type (an ideal type)
> of a common phenomenon. The concepts and laws of
> pure economic theory are examples of this kind of
> ideal type. They state what course a given type
> of human action would take if it were strictly
> rational, unaffected by errors or emotional factors
> and if, furthermore, it were completely and
> unequivocally directed to a single end, the
> maximisation of economic advantage.

Weber then refers us to his remarks on this point in his essay on objectivity (1949).

There are three points to be noted about this paragraph. One is that Weber does include 'average meanings', whatever these may be, and 'ideal type' meanings, together with the 'actually intended meaning for concrete individual action' under the general rubric of intended meaning. Yet he does seem to be surprisingly equivocal about this. The constructs of economics are given recognition here, as ideal types, and their peculiar quality is said to reside in the fact that they posit purely rational human action. But if this is the case, does not their value lie in the fact that they can be used along with other ideal types to explain a concrete course of action in all its fullness and complexity? Yet, in his earlier essay, Weber seems to reject the notion that we can have, in the human studies, law-like statements from which, when they are taken together, reality as a whole can be deduced. He seems, therefore, to be confining ideal types to purely rational courses of action.

What then of non-rational action? In paragraph 5 Weber clearly includes this under 'intended meanings'. Consider for example this (1968a, p. 9):

> we understand the motive of a person aiming a gun
> if we know that he has been commanded to shoot as a
> member of a firing squad, that he is fighting against
> an enemy, or he is doing it for revenge. The last is
> affectually determined and thus in a certain sense
> irrational. Finally we have a motivational
> understanding of the outburst of anger if we know
> that it has been provoked by jealousy, injured pride,
> or an insult. The last examples are all affectually
> determined and hence derived from irrational motives.
> In all the above cases the particular act has been
> placed in an understandable sequence of motivation
> . . . even where the processes are largely affectual,
> the subjective meaning of the action, including also
> that of the relevant meaning complexes, will be
> called the intended meaning.

It looks therefore as though non-rational courses of action are included under the general heading of intended meaning, but not under the heading of meanings grasped in the context of an ideal type. Now Weber may or may not have meant this. It has, however, led to a widespread interpretation of his position as one in which the concept of ideal type is limited to the case of rational action only. Against this, however, we should note that, as soon as he attempts to formulate the types of social action on an abstract and formal level, Weber includes, not merely two types of rational action, but also affectual and traditional action, so the concept apparently has wide application.

The more important question, however, is what the relationship of ideal types of meaningful action is to concrete historical meaningful action. It seems that Weber sees the special role of sociology as going beyond the individual instance to an abstract ideal type. Thus he says (p. 19):

> The empirical material which underlies the concepts
> of sociology consists to a very large extent, though
> by no means exclusively, of the same concrete

processes of action which are dealt with by
historians. An important consideration in the
formulation of sociological concepts and generalisations
is the contribution that sociology can make towards
the causal explanation of some historically and
culturally important phenomena. As in the case of
every generalising science, the abstract character
of the concepts of sociology is responsible for the
fact that, compared with actual historical reality,
they are relatively lacking in fullness of concrete
content.

It may be noted here that sociology is described as a *generalising science*, a point of some difficulty, and one which seems to be at odds with the earlier essay on objectivity (1949),* but for the moment what concerns us most is the notion that it is of the essence of sociological concepts that they are 'lacking in fullness of concrete content'. This seems to suggest that, the question of generalisation apart, sociological concepts refer, not to actually intended meanings, but to ideal types.

There is, however, another point about these ideal types. In what sense can they be said to actually explain the recognised subjective motivation of the individual? Weber tells us that (p. 21):

The theoretical concepts of sociology are ideal
types, not only from the objective point of view,
but also in their application to subjective processes.
In the great majority of cases actual action goes on
in a state of inarticulate half consciousness or
actual unconsciousness of its subjective meaning.
The actor is more likely to 'be aware' of it in a
vague sense than he is to know what he is doing or
be explicitly self-conscious about it. In most
cases, his action is governed by impulse or habit.
Only occasionally and in the uniform action of large
numbers, often only in the case of a few individuals,
is the subjective meaning of action, whether rational
or irrational, brought clearly into consciousness.
The ideal type of meaningful action, when the meaning
is fully conscious and explicit, is a marginal case.
Every sociological or historical investigation, in
applying its analysis to the empirical facts, must
take this fact into account. But the difficulty
need not prevent the sociologist from systematizing

* At this point, however, it should be noted that Weber was talking about economic history rather than sociology.

his concepts by the classification of possible types
of subjective meaning. That is, he may reason as if
action actually proceeded on the basis of self-
conscious meaning.

Thus ideal types are seen here as explaining actual conduct, even
though the purposive sequence of action, of which they give an
account, are not known to the actual historical actor. This may be
acceptable, and indeed it is a position which we *will* accept. but it
should be noted that it does not completely tally, either with the
notion that ideal types of meaningful action are 'lacking in fullness
of historical content,' or that ideal types, in Weber's earlier generalised usage of the term, in his Essay on Objectivity, are regarded as
'artificial accentuations' of reality and hence never by themselves
capable of explaining concrete action, whether the actor experiences
them or not.

In fact, as we have pointed out elsewhere (1971), Weber's concept
of ideal types appears to have varied considerably, for he had three
quite distinct conceptions of them: (a) artificial accentuations which
might act as yardsticks, (b) abstract aspects of action, e.g. as in the
concept of economic man, which could be put together to produce
(c) a concrete ideal type which could explain actual action. What
we would wish to claim is that there is a place for all these kinds of
construct in sociology. We may take an extreme type, or indeed an
arbitrary type, in order to measure and compare the variation of
historical cases from this standard. We may posit hypothetical pure
circumstances and make statements about action which have attached
to them an implicit *ceteris paribus* clause. Finally we may have an
ideal type which does explain historical action even in a unique
instance.

We shall have to return, in the next chapter, to the question of
ideal types as yardsticks. For the moment we should notice that
Weber does hold that they can be used to predict and explain concrete human action, both in idealised circumstances, which could,
in theory, be produced in a sociological experiment, and in actual
historical cases. Is it this which leads him to the crucial statement
(p. 10) that: 'verification of subjective interpretation by comparison
with the concrete course of events is, as in the case of all hypotheses,
indispensable?'

We would agree with this and also with Weber's general position,
that explanations adequate on the level of meaning remain only
plausible stories unless they are 'verified' by comparison with the
concrete course of events, though much difficulty has arisen through
Weber's repeated representation of this process of verification as
one which refers to the statistical probability of the recurrence of

an event. We will, in fact, agree with Winch that explanations adequate on the level of meaning cannot be verified in this way.

What we mean by the verification of an ideal type of meaningful action is this. We posit that, in controlled or fully ascertainable circumstances, a particular explanation is applicable. This particular explanation may include other such notions as goals, means, norms, conditions and other elements. We then argue that, if our claim as to the applicability of this ideal type is valid, certain empirical events will occur. If they do occur we may then say that our ideal type is verified (or, more modestly, following Popper, that it has not been falsified). For example, if we posit that, to use Weber's example, a man chopping wood is doing so in order to earn money, it should be perfectly possible to check on as yet unascertained facts as to whether in fact he has been observed to receive payment for his work. If we found that he worked just as hard whether paid or not, or if we could simply find no evidence of his being paid, we should say that he was not working for money and that this ideal type was not applicable.

It is very important to notice here that 'verification' can be accomplished in a single instance. It does not need repeated instances and the assessment of probability. Any ideal type of action as complex as working for money or for pleasure, or for the glory of God, should have multiple empirical referents in a particular case, and it is the occurrence or non-occurrence of these in that case which justifies us in saying that an application adequate on the level of meaning is more than a plausible story. Winch is quite correct when he points out that mere recurrence (e.g. our woodcutter, repeatedly chopping wood) adds nothing to explanation on the level of meaning, but, showing that many or all of the empirical consequences of the ideal type of meaningful action do in fact occur, does do so. It is the method whereby, in sociology as well as in everyday life, we sort out valid accounts of action from mere plausible stories.

Winch, however, would not have even this. Meaningful action, for him, involves following a rule, and this can have nothing to do with cause, or generalisation, or quantity. In our view, this way of representing meaningful action quite unnecessarily draws attention away from the common elements involved in the logic of imputing motives and testing our expectations and the logic of causation generally. It is necessary to be quite clear about this.

The question of causation can be discussed on varying levels of generality. Obviously it is true, on one level and for particular purposes, to use the same terms to refer to the way in which motion is imparted by one billiards ball to another and to the purposive activity of human beings. But, when we seek to analyse the notion of cause, not on a metaphysical level, but in relation to its actual use in science and everyday life, the really important elements are of a more generalised and abstract kind. They involve the notion (a) of the observation of a plurality of events in more or less regular conjunction, and (b) the fact that this constant conjunction is one which we would expect to follow from propositions on a more general level which we believe to be true. In the case of physical events the constant conjunctions which we observe are thought of as following from general theoretical laws with the aid of definitions which make deductions from these theoretical laws to empirical propositions possible. In the case of human behaviour, once we accept that a certain general proposition about the meaning of action is true, in this case it is possible to show that the observed conjunctions follow given definitions which relate our statement on the 'theoretical' level about meaningful action to statements about observed behaviour. The main difficulties are these: (a) scientific explanation in the natural sciences approaches constant conjunctions described in empirical propositions with the aid of well-established laws tested in experimental circumstances, while the human studies have to find explanations *ad hoc* and, if they appear to be plausible explanations, to test their validity by trying to falsify them by confronting them with as yet unknown aspects of the situation, (b) the definitions which relate statements about motivation to behaviour, or statements about behaviour may be of a complex kind, because the actual behaviour which is covered by the general statement about motivation may be of a symbolic kind, or of a variety of different kinds, which may all equally be claimed to fit the explanatory statement. An extreme instance would be the case of the Freudian interpretation of dreams. The theory leads us to believe that certain kinds of dreams and fantasies will occur, but we have also to have a set of rules which justify us in saying 'this was a dream of the kind expected'.

Despite all these practical difficulties, however, the logic of scientific explanation and the logic of what was called in Germany 'verstehen' are essentially the same, and we would argue that, although the philosophical questions associated with meaningful actions and following a rule, are interesting in themselves, they do not undermine Weber's general contention that explanations adequate on the level of meaning may be 'verified', or at least tested, by comparison with the actual course of events.

Thus far, however, we have been assuming that statements about patterns of meaningful action-orientation are simply theoretical constructs which have potential empirical falsifiers, like any theoretical law. We should, therefore, ask whether it matters that these statements are formulated in terms of subjectively-understood goal-seeking. There seem to be two reasons why it is important. One is that such statements are inherently satisfying because we know by introspection what it would be like to take meaningful action of this kind. The other is that, instead of having to invent a complex set of definitions relating theoretical laws to empirical statements, we can take over a lot of hints from common sense. These are great advantages, but they also tempt the sociologist to read his explanations into the observed world, rather than genuinely seeking to test his explanatory propositions. For this reason, it is necessary, on the first point, never to rest content with an explanation just because it is inherently plausible, but always to subject it to test; and on the second, to spell out all the meanings, definitions, and so on, which common sense takes for granted, so that there are not a lot of unexplored implications in what we say.

It is now perhaps desirable to indicate the modified version of Weber, which we find is still acceptable as a basis for all serious sociology. In the first place, we agree with him that sociological concepts form a special subset of concepts which are formulated in terms of subjectively-understood meaning. This differentiates it from all forms of sociology which merely discuss the attributes of groups as though groups were things (i.e. inherently non-understandable). Second, we believe that sociological concepts of meaningful action are ideal types, rather than referring to the actually intended meaning for the concrete historical actor, or the meaning for an average actor. Third, within this, we hold that the term ideal types may refer to three types of concept: (a) one which does not describe historical reality, but actually artificially accentuates certain elements within that reality in order to provide a yardstick against which actual cases may be measured, (b) abstract ideal types which are 'lacking in fullness of historical content', but which in theory if not in practice are capable of comparison with concrete courses of events, (c) concrete ideal types which refer to actual historical events and which are directly capable of 'verification' or 'falsification'. In this last case, which is the important one, we hypothesise that a certain pattern of action-orientation underlies an observed behavioural event, and then test our hypothesis by making a prediction that other, as yet unascertained, features of the situation would follow if our hypothesis were valid, and then checking as to whether or not they do occur.

There are, however, still two points to be made about sociological concepts. One is that, although the meaningfully adequate explanation which the type offers is in no way strengthened by repeated recurrences, but is validated in a particular instance, one's research problem may sometimes be that of formulating, on a theoretical level, a type which, while not fully confirmed in any one case, is sufficiently confirmed in many cases for us to say that it is a type of general application, or of application to more than one case. A type used in this way would be neither an average type, nor simply a yardstick agreement by which existing cases might be measured. Weber does not mention this possibility, but it is an important one and one which underlies many of the structural ideal types which he uses and into which a great deal of historical experience has been distilled.

Finally, we should notice that in our discussion above we have, for the most part, been discussing the most elementary sociological concepts of all. Indeed, we might be inclined to call them sub-sociological. They refer simply to patterns of action-orientation. But when we are dealing with major sociological and historical problems, what we shall be using are concepts of social relations. These suggest, not merely that a series of observable events are connected in terms of one individual's subjectively formulated action plans, but by these action plans, as they are affected by that individual taking account of the behaviour of another. In this case the number of potential verifiers or falsifiers of the proposition 'here we have a social relation of type r' is much greater than is the case when our hypotheses refer only to individual actors and their actions.

We have yet, however, to address ourselves to the central question which is posed by the title of this chapter. This is that of the relationship between meaning understood in the context of a pure or ideal type, and meaning for a concrete individual historical actor. The problem here is that, while many positivists and behaviourists claim that it is quite impossible to know an observed actor's own 'actually intended meaning', ethnomethodologists claim that actors' accounts are 'indexical', that is to say that they fall under a category of 'expressions whose sense cannot be decided by an auditor without his necessarily knowing something about the biography and purposes of the user of the expression, the circumstances of its utterance, the previous course of the conversation, or the particular relationship of actual or potential interaction that exists between expressor and auditor' (Garfinkel, 1967, p. 4). Moreover, the ethnomethodologists go on to say that, in any attempt to explain events in terms of non-indexical theories, 'in every actual case without exception conditions will be cited that a competent investigator will be required to recognise, such that in that particular case the terms of the demonstration can be relaxed and never the less the demonstration be counted an adequate one' (p. 6), and that the 'first problematic phenomenon is recommended to consist of the reflexivity of the practices and attainments of the sciences in and of the organised activities of everyday life which is an essential reflexivity' (p. 7). What this seems to mean in plain English is that members' accounts, of their own activities are always located in a particular context, that attempts to offer alternative scientists' accounts of a non-located kind must involve a relaxation of the rules to say that each case is in some sense, a special case and that even the scientists' accounts must be understood reflexively, that is to say, in terms of the scientists' purposes and so on.

By and large, it should be admitted, Max Weber comes down on the positivist side of this argument, whenever he talks of the explanation of behaviour in terms of ideal types of action, for he does believe that such explanations have an explanatory power, regardless of the concrete meaning which the actor attaches to his action in a particular case. But there are two points on which Weber is not clear. The first is what the basis is for assuming that the sociologists' explanation has explanatory power and a privileged status compared with other accounts. The second is whether, in fact, it is to some extent parasitic on members' theories and therefore takes into itself much of the open-endedness and lack of clarity of participants' theories or members' meanings.

It should be pointed out at this stage of the argument that the problem we are now discussing is *the* most vital problem, given the purpose of this book as a whole, for, if we take members' meanings to be ideological and mystifying, we *must* be able to show that, in some degree at least, sociologists' theories have a greater claim to acceptance.

Unfortunately, it must be admitted that Weber does not establish his case very well. He vacillates between a concept of ideal types relatively empty of content and therefore free of the particularity which surrounds members' theories and a notion of meanings which are adequate from the point of view of the actor. Thus he seems to come down in favour of the former notion when he says (1968a, p. 22):

he may reason as if the action actually proceeded
on the basis of clearly self-conscious meaning. The
resulting deviation from the concrete facts must
continually be kept in mind whenever it is a question
of this level of concreteness . . . . It is often necessary
to choose between terms which are clear and unclear.
Those which are clear will, to be sure, have the
abstractness of ideal types, but they are nonetheless
preferable for scientific purposes.

On the other hand he also speaks of (p. 9):

explanation which requires a grasp of the complex of
meanings in which an actual course of understandable
action, thus interpreted, belongs,

and later of (p. 11):

45

the interpretation of a coherent course of conduct
being 'subjectively adequate' in so far as, according
to our habitual modes of thought and feeling, its
component parts taken in their mutual relation are
recognised to constitute a typical complex of meaning.

Weber really is very difficult to understand and to pin down on
these points. He appears to confuse the notion of complexes of
meaning divorced from action, and meaning in the sense of being
relevant to the attainment of a goal, as well as the logical question
of the explanatory power of ideal types with the psychological
question of whether the actor is really conscious of the meaning of
his action or not. We must therefore try to resolve some of the issues
for ourselves.

It will be recalled that we said, when discussing the relation
between explanations which were adequate on the level of meaning,
and explanations which were causally or scientifically adequate, that
the validity of sociologists' ideal typical explanations could be tested
by comparison with the actual course of events and, in the broadest
terms, the logic of proof here was no different from that in other
scientific explanations. Indeed, if what we mean when we say that
A caused B was that B followed A and that it followed necessarily
or could be expected to follow, given our established beliefs in
general propositions, we could also speak of 'causal explanation'.
There are, however, two important potential differences which we
should note.

The first of these difficulties concerns the philosophic problems
involved in the distinction between purposive action and causal
sequences. The second concerns the definitions which enable us to
argue that one meaning implies another and that we can deduce
empirical statements from theoretical statements. In both cases it is
necessary to argue that sociological explanations must, in practice,
take a lot for granted.

It is absolutely true that the sociologist cannot answer such questions as what it means to have an end or to employ means to attain
that end. But, taking a common-sense view of purposive action, we
can say, that given the best scientific or common-sense knowledge
of causal sequences by an actor, given certain factual conditions in
which he has to operate, and given certain norms governing his
action, if we know his goals we may expect him to act in certain
ways. The philosophic problems of purposive action do not, in
fact, prevent us from making such deductions, because the common-
sense conception of purpose is shared by the sociologists.

The second difficulty concerns the assumption of common-sense
meanings. It must be admitted that in constructing ideal types of

meaningful action we usually take over, without acknowledging that we do so, the common-sense meanings assumed by the actor in his language and his view of the world. Special problems arise when that language, either on the verbal or on the more general cultural-symbolic level, is not understood. In this case we have to 'learn the language' before we can begin to establish our explanatory ideal types.

Does this then mean that ideal types are in fact indistinguishable from the actor's own accounts? By no means. For, whereas the actor's use of meanings is open-ended, situation-bound, and often inconsistent, the sociologist who uses these meanings in order to provide definitions and rules of transformation in his ideal typical theory when he uses it for explanatory purposes can, if he wishes, always subject the interpretations and meanings which he takes over from the actor to some kind of test, and he is likely to do so when he finds himself in dispute with his fellow sociologists. He may then argue with them about the internal consistency of the concepts being used and about whether or not the descriptions of the social and cultural world used by the actor are justifiable or not. It should be noted here that, although the ethnomethodologists and other phenomenologically-oriented sociologists believe that the 'integrity of the phenomenon' should be preserved and that meddling with or seeking to alter 'members' theories' is undesirable, they do none the less probe the members' meanings which they encounter. How else is one to interpret Garfinkel's attempts to get at the taken-for-granted element in actors' speech?

The particular problem which the phenomenologists and ethno-methodologists have difficulty in dealing with is that of 'false consciousness'. It may well be, of course, that for certain purposes some sociologists may wish to establish the actual facts of the actor's own consciousness in an uncritical and descriptive way. But surely for most purposes we may wish to enquire whether the actual meaning of the actor's action is not different from his own account of it? For example, is it not common in such spheres as race relations research, to seek for an explanation in terms of an ideal type of action which systematically explains both the action and the theories in terms of which the actor rationalises what he does? The notion of a set of sociological concepts, a sociological language and socio-logical theories enables us to do this. At the very least, surely, the sociologist can claim that he can give a different and competing account of the actor's actions from the actor's own.

There is this much in common, therefore, between our rendering of Weber's position on the value of ideal types and the critique of phenomenology offered by Lucien Goldmann when he says (1969, p. 32):

> The weakness of phenomenology seems to us to lie
> precisely in the fact that it limits itself to a
> comprehensive description of the facts of
> consciousness . . . . The real structure of historical
> facts permits, however, beyond the conscious meaning
> of those facts in the thought and intention of the
> actors, the postulations of an objective meaning
> which often differs from the conscious meaning in
> an important way.

The difference between our own view and that of the Marxists on this point lies really in the fact that we lack their metaphysical certainty about truth and objectivity. All that we have claimed is that sociology can give a different and competing account of the meaning of action, not that it can give a true and objective account. None the less, this does not mean that the sociologist's account is yet another account, no better than that of any ideologist or of the actor himself. We had best explain what we mean here, by the use of a concrete example.

It is common amongst white South Africans to claim that a whole series of restrictions on contact between black and white are consequential upon the need to prevent exposing themselves to the germs and diseases carried by the black population. A sociologist, however, might seek to explain the overall pattern of motivation by the fact that whites are seeking to avoid contact with blacks except in circumstances where the blacks are clearly subordinate. Thus, the fact that the whites employ black maids to bath and otherwise tend their infant children, seems to argue against the members' theories and meanings and those of the actors.

An extreme view which is sometimes put in order to debunk sociological, as distinct from members', theories is that the question of what tests are to be used to decide between valid and invalid explanations rests only upon agreement between the sociologists and that, therefore, the sociologist makes an 'act of faith' or is accused of subscribing to a religious or political theory of truth. There is some truth in this contention, but there are also ways of putting the matter which seem deliberately to distort what the sociologist does. If his procedures do depend upon agreement between his own sub-community of like-minded sociologists, and this is called a 'political theory of truth', it is still none the less important to bear in mind that we are not saying, for example, that what is true or not true is decided for political purposes by a political party.

It is important, moreover, to make a fundamental distinction between the sort of political theory of truth used by ideologists and that used by sociologists. The ideologists' 'political theory of truth' rests upon tacit agreement on undisclosed and perhaps deliberately concealed value-judgments. No doubt, we must admit that some value-judgments of this kind also creep into the paradigms of science, as Kuhn (1962) has suggested, but the difference surely lies in the fact that such value-judgments in science are kept to a minimum and, at least potentially, may come up for review and certainly, so far as this book is concerned, our confession of moral nihilism denotes our intention to root out such value-judgments as ruthlessly as we can and to try, so far as we can, to subject ourselves to a set of values which is based upon a desire to achieve agreement among a group of observers, whose first commitment is to find ways of testing propositions which satisfy all of them, regardless of whether these tests bring into the open and into question the value-judgments of the politicians, and thus ideologists. Ultimately the question here is one of moral integrity.

When all this has been said, it is important to notice that, in saying that the ideal types of sociologists are distinct from actor's theories, we may still admit that the latter have some role in the process of formulating the former. Weber, for example, did not start developing ideal types of action *ab initio*. He started with the formulation of an ideal type of the capitalist spirit *derived from history* and derived from the writings of a concrete historical individual, Benjamin Franklin (Weber, 1962). The difference between his use of this type and its use by some exponents of a looser version of *verstehen* is that he sought to limit the open-endedness of the concept by emptying it of some of its meaning, and making its remaining meanings internally consistent and capable of comparison, both with other actors' meanings and theories and the social world which appears as external to those particular actors.

One can, in fact, represent a very large part of the task of the sociologist as that of cleaning up and systematising the language of common sense and everyday life. What Weber did, going beyond the terms of his Protestant ethic study, was to try to clarify and systematise a number of other social languages as he found them in actual historical contexts, thus leading to such concepts as patrimonial administration under traditional authority in China. Then, when this had been done, he was able to show the way in which meanings and structures which they sustained in different historical circumstances were comparable, and finally, having developed, not simply a number of totally discrete ideal types, but ones which were strictly comparable (e.g. feudal, patrimonial and bureaucratic administration) he sought to reduce all of these to their elements and this involved an analysis of the basic forms of social relations and, even more fundamentally, of social action.

The surprising thing perhaps in this process is not the gap between ideal types and actual historical social languages. Rather it is the fact that social languages in different historical contexts have, at least at an underlying abstract level which is partially understood by the participant actors, a great many concepts in common with one another. Moreover their languages are often not simply about motivational and cultural matters but about the world of social relations in which an individual lives and which appears to him as an environment. Nevertheless, when one looks at social terms used in everyday historical languages, one finds that these are particularly open-ended and loaded with concealed value assumptions. Thus it becomes very important for the sociologist to look for that which is common in structural terms in a variety of different situations and also to try by starting from the simplest terms about which agreement can fairly readily be reached to the more complex structures. Thus, for example, we may recognise a common pattern of feudalism as underlying political administration, the organisation of academic research, and the world of violent crime, and, by abstracting from the particular contexts, indicate the common structural features. Then, working from the other end, we might start by talking about relations of authority and chains of administration command, and arrive at an even clearer and more satisfactory concept, which articulates with sociological concepts in other areas.

We do not believe, however, that the kind of sociological theory which will emerge from this exercise will be a general theory of a systemic type. It will rather be a systematically developed set of ideal types, in terms of which the recurrent bits of historical social structures may be analysed. In this sense it will be much closer to the language of everyday life than most sociological theory. Unfortunately phenomenological sociologists and ethnomethodologists have too often sought to dissociate their work from all structural sociology, representing all that is not cast in terms of members' meanings or the actor's definition of the situation, as though it must either be positivist, in the sense of quantitative sociology which takes no account of meaning, or structural-functionalist, and as such separated from an interest in the meaning of social action. We believe that there is a kind of structural sociology of a Weberian kind which is based upon a dialogue of languages and which leads to a systematic sociological typology. It is in fact the closest of all sociologies to the work of the latter-day phenomenologists. But, unlike these, it still continues to interest itself in actual historical structures as they appear to the sociologist and not merely the structures which actors believe to exist, or believe that they make, in the process of thinking them to exist.

In the next chapter we will be concerned to show how easily sociology may be led away from an adequate type of conceptualisation by the attractions of quantification, although we will also show that properly interpreted quantified data has its place in sociology. Here we have been concerned to show that the insights which can be gained from the action frame of reference need not involve a total loss of objectivity, nor lead to a trivialisation of our concerns. We wish to rescue and retain the notion of structures of social relations amongst actors as the central one for all sociology, and particularly for a politically relevant sociology. But such structures are not of themselves given in observation and research. What are given are actors' theories and members' meanings on the one hand, and quantified data on the other. It is a mistake to elevate either sort of data to a central place in sociology. That central place belongs to the systematic typology, in terms of which we interpret our experience as controlled by social structures.

4 Ideal types, structure and quantitative aspects of sociology

One of the most centrally significant cultural facts which the sociologist has to face in our times is the replacement of sociology by social statistics. Professional success in academic life, as well as recognition as a sociologist in the larger world, has come to depend upon the possession of the necessary expertise to demonstrate more or less complex statistical relationships. Today, so-called sociological journals are largely devoted to articles of this kind, and any article which fails to approximate to the standards of statistical expertise required is regarded by the editors, and by the academics who have displaced sociologists in the majority of schools, as sub-professional. The fact that most of the articles prove nothing sociologically significant about more than a sample of the population of the world, which is random in more senses than one, and that they are essentially non-cumulative in the results they produce, is thought to be of little account.

As we have already said, we regard sociology as being concerned with structures of social relations and such social relations may be further defined in terms of actors communicating expectations to one another more or less successfully, and other actors responding to these expectations in terms of compliance or conflict. It should be clear, if this is what sociology is about, that it cannot be explained in terms of what Lazarsfeld calls 'variate language' (McKinney and Tiryakian, 1970, pp. 301–18). Such language might be used in a preliminary stage of investigation before sociological analysis begins, or it might be used if ideal typical models, in the action frame of reference, were impossible, and the sociologist was not able to get beyond analysis in terms of essentially non-human elements and their attributes, thought of as 'social forces' (see e.g. Lundberg, 1939). More usually, however, sociological analysis proper would only begin after a relationship between variables had been disclosed.

Weber, it must be admitted, confused the issues here by trying to combine a subjective analysis of social relations and structures with a probabilistic one in terms of variables. It is not merely that he made the mistake, as Winch has suggested, of believing that statements of meaning could be confirmed by causal statements. He clearly does say that comparison of an ideal type with the actual course of events involves an assessment of probability of recurrence and not merely the complex verification in a particular instance to which we have referred. Thus he defines an explanation which is causally adequate as follows: 'The interpretation of a sequence of events will . . . be called *causally* adequate in so far as, according to established generalisations from experience, there is a probability that it will always actually occur in the same way'. Moreover, when he seeks to explain the difference between ideal types of meaning and actual intended meaning, he immediately sees ideal types as referring to generally recurrent phenomena. Thus, not merely does he say that an actor may be unconscious of a pattern of motivation and meaning which actually explains his behaviour, he also sees an ideal type of individual meaningful action as serving to explain recurrent behaviour (1968a, p. 10):

> Verification (by comparison with the concrete course of
> events) is feasible with relative accuracy only in the
> few very special cases susceptible of psychological
> experimentation. In very different degrees of
> approximation such verification is also feasible in the
> limited number of cases of mass phenomena which can be
> statistically described and unambiguously interpreted.

Most important of all, however, is Weber's double definition of a social relationship. On the one hand there is the expected reference in his subjective structural sociology to mutual orientation: 'The term social relationship will be used to denote the behaviour of a plurality of actors in so far as, in its meaningful context, the action of each takes account of that of the others, and is oriented in these terms'. But this is surprisingly and irrelevantly supplemented by a reference to probability (p. 26): 'The social relationship thus [*sic*] consists entirely and exclusively in the existence of a probability that this will be a meaningful course of social action'.

These two definitions are in no way necessarily connected with one another. In the first, the relationship is defined in terms of expectations and response, which do not refer, of necessity, to probabilities of action. In the second, one has the probability of the coexistence of two types of action without these being dependent upon any one's expectations, indeed without their being meaningfully interpreted at all.

Now of course Weber would wish to hold these two types of explanation together. He sees statistical proof as important only in so far as it enables us to sort out true explanations, adequate on the level of meaning, from mere plausible stories. On the other hand, he will never rest content with a mere statement of blind statistical probability, since it is precisely the merit of sociology that it can go beyond this to explain the statistical relationship in terms of subjective meaning. Thus: 'If adequacy in respect to meaning is lacking, then no matter how high the degree of uniformity and how precisely its probability can be determined numerically, it is still an incomprehensible statistical probability'. But these modest assertions are not by themselves capable of containing the use to which Weber puts the notion of probability. He seems to be offering us, not one sociological methodology, but two. In the definition of a social relationship, indeed his position is positively schizoid. It is not surprising, therefore, that Lazarsfeld and Oberschall (1965) have sought to claim Weber for statistical positivism. That *they* are able to tell a plausible story while simply leaving out or dismissing the whole notion of subjectively defined social interaction and relationships is an indication of the degree to which it is possible to dissociate one side of Weber's work from the other.

If this is true of Weber, who after all is the outstanding sociologist whose ideas communicate with the phenomenological tradition, it is of course far more true of sociology in the positivist tradition in its classical sociological form in France and in the more recent unified science movement. Thus for Durkheim, science requires that sociology deal with 'things' which are not only external from the point of view of an individual actor but have no reference to human action at all. If his first definition of social facts as external to the individual and exercising constraint over him appears to refer to the subjective point of view of an actor, it is one which he seeks to escape from by redefining them simply from the point of view of an observer as being 'general in a given society and having an existence independent of their particular manifestations'.

Modern positivism in its heyday was represented by the work of George Lundberg. Strangely, this type of positivism was not at first atheoretical, for it sought to explain all social and other phenomena in terms of theoretical concepts derived from physics. The physicalist theory, however, was based on the notion of forces, all of which were subject to measurement, and this eventually gave way to a general kind of quasi-operationalism which defined, say, intelligence, as that which intelligence tests measure. Beyond Lundberg, the simple technical needs of market research opened the way to social surveys, cross-tabulations, and the quest for statistically significant relationships. In Lazarsfeld and Rosenberg's *Language of Social Research* (1962), for example, a discussion of the properties of social groups follows a discussion of the findings of market research, and groups in the sense of a plurality of persons orienting their conduct to one another, gives way to groups treated as things with measurable dimensions and attributes.

In Great Britain, the country in which empiricist traditions were stronger than anywhere else, it was exceptionally difficult for sociology to establish itself because of a tradition which could best be described as based upon the book-keeping of social reform. Thus, in 1961, it was necessary, in pleading for sociological theory, to draw attention to the fact that there was theory buried in the very categories which the social book-keepers used and to try to go on from this slight empiricist foothold to argue for theory of a more systematic kind.

It was, of course, always the case, and still is, that statistics, quantitative methods and mathematical methods had their place in the total process of social research and sociological analysis. In fact, the sad thing about the philistinism of the statisticians was that it led eventually to their contribution being undervalued and for the anti-positivist movement to take its stand on an anti-quantitative platform. For our part, we would suggest that now that sociology is more widely seen as being dependent upon theory, the time has come to discuss the functions which quantification can perform.

There are certain sorts of quantification, of course, which have only limited usefulness. These include measured properties which have no clear relationship to social structures, measurement of attitudes towards a variety of questions and objects, official statistics based upon highly dubious categories and tabulations claiming to be about 'social structures' which are not explicable as structures of social relations. While we should not neglect any sources of data which might be intelligently used for sociological purposes, even if they fall under these headings, the mere fact that they do refer to quantified data has given them a prestigious status in social science far beyond their merits.

Taking first measurable properties, we find here that, not merely does research focus on some types which are more measurable than others, but that, within the actual topic, those aspects of the phenomenon which are measured are not necessarily those which are of any theoretical importance. Thus 'intelligence' is something which lends itself to measurement in psychology, but when we ask what intelligence is we are told that it is what intelligence tests measure, and if we then say that we would like to know what the theoretical relationships to other empirical phenomena are, we are apt to be sneered at as believing in 'essences'. In fact it is a legitimate question to ask what the theoretical significance is for psychology in its wider aspects of what is measured in intelligence tests, and has nothing to do with essences. What theory does is to establish the relationship between one area of research and another, and to suggest relevant questions which can be used in the construction of measuring instruments. In the absence of theory, what is often done, in drawing up measuring instruments, is to appeal to public opinion and to ask panels of judges which questions or statements reflect a given quality in the highest degree. If this is not done, questions might be included on a quite arbitrary basis. In the first case, the absence of genuine constructed theory leads to an appeal to actors' theories. In the second, theory is dispensed with altogether.

The sort of empiricism and quantification which we have been discussing is peculiarly rife in psychology, but there are many attempts to use measurement scales in a similar way in sociology. Thus sociologists might seek to measure integration or anomie or alienation and, quite apart from the fact that these terms are in any case misused because they are not simple empirical concepts but have their primary significance in philosophical anthropology, one finds that the full range of significance of the concept is held to be exhausted by what is contained in the test.

A particularly efflorescent area of development of quantitative scales is to be found in the testing of attitudes, which for many laymen is of the essence of sociology. It is true, in fact, that the more sophisticated attitude studies may have such significance since, particularly if they are precisely socially located, they may go part of the way to telling us something about expectations and responses in social relations. In the main, however, attitudes are conceived of as tendencies to act or as expressing positive attitudes of liking, or negative attitudes of disliking, given physical and social objects. They are not thought of in relation to action and still less to anything so sophisticated as taking account of the behaviour of another in planning one's own action. Rather they are simply attributes of individuals, rather like height or skin colour. Thus one has a world of objects which affect one another because they have attributes rather than a world of acting and interacting individuals.

Particularly ludicrous are those attitude studies which, in addition to the defects mentioned above, have built into them an evaluative element. A good example of this was provided by the study of attitudes carried out in connection with the survey of race relations in Great Britain, and published in *Colour and Citizenship* (Rose *et al.*, 1969). According to this study, the people of Britain were classified as tolerant to intolerant on a five point scale, and a person who expressed approval of only one hostile statement about immigrants was classified as tolerant-inclined. Clearly it was possible to re-word such data and show that the population of Britain was far less tolerant than was made out. But, in fact, the whole of this debate was naïve. As was argued in *Race, Community and Conflict* (Rex and Moore, 1967), the real import of 'attitudes' is the role which they play in action. Thus the study carried out in Birmingham argued (p. 2):

> It may be that amongst the people of Birmingham whom
> we studied some discriminatory behaviour was due to
> innate and universal tendencies. And it may be that
> some of it was the product of personality disturbance.
> But it is also the case that a great deal of it was
> sufficiently explained once we knew something of
> Birmingham social structures and conflicts, and the
> constellation of interests and roles which was built
> into Birmingham society.

Here we see quite clearly, not merely a difference between psychology and sociology, but also between an atheoretical pseudo-objective empiricism and theoretically guided social science.

It has long been a scandal in criminology that criminal statistics tell us nothing of any use in the understanding of the causes of crime. If sexual offences of a particular kind go up in a police area, the statistics might signify nothing more than the fact that a new Chief Constable has taken over. But if this is so obviously true in the case of criminal statistics, it is also true in a great many other areas. Children may be classified in terms of intelligence or attainment, but who does the measurement, and how? What significance should we attach to the fact that a certain percentage of the population earn more than £2,000 per annum and the remainder less? What is meant by class in studies of social mobility? Are we sure, for that matter, what is meant even by elementary demographic categories? These questions have been sharply and correctly posed by writers like Cicourel (1963, 1968), and they are all too inadequately dealt with by sociologists who say that we must make the most of what statistics we have and that having some precise answers is better than having none, even if we are unsure of what they mean. Little wonder that ethnomethodologists have ceased to look at hard data at all, and tend to confine their research to a study of the actual processes of classification, without considering the evidence provided by their results.

It is interesting that tables of social statistics were commonly referred to in Britain for many years as accounts of 'social structures' (Carr-Saunders and Jones, 1927; Marsh, 1965). The same kind of usage still continues when complexes of variables may be said to refer to social structures, and here, indeed, various patterns of interrelation between the variables may be said to define social groups. To all intents and purposes, then, our explication of the meaning of the term group in terms of the mutual orientation of action, is irrelevant. So also is sociology as a subject, for the whole world is thought of as consisting of particular complexes of variables. As against the official statistics approach to social structure, and that which looks at groups in terms of variable elements, we would want to insist on the reference of the term to structures of social relations. There is a world of which we can achieve a high degree of theoretical understanding rather than one in which the best that we can do is to read off a series of largely accidental empirical facts.

While deploring much of what is done under the headings above, however, we would wish to point out that even quantitative data of these kinds can have its sociological uses. While the prostitution of social science techniques leads to the measurement of that which is easy to measure no matter how theoretically irrelevant, it is still true that measurement is the most exact form of observation, and that *sociologically* significant aspects of human behaviour should be observed precisely and, if possible, in quantitative terms. Attitude studies can be placed in social contexts understood theoretically in terms of meaningful action and interrelations, and we can surely hope, within institutional studies, to look at the expectations which one individual has of another in quantitative terms.

So far as official statistics are concerned, the surprising thing is that what began as a critique of the statistics leads eventually to a turning of attention in research to other matters altogether. Yet what might have happened is that, having discovered the real practical contexts in which classifications were made, we might have produced totally new tables with new headings, or sometimes simply the old tables with new headings. True, if we pursue the subtleties of the classification processes to the ultimate, every act of classification may be different, and the tables which conflate different decisions under the same heading may be actively misleading, but there can be some generalisation about acts of classification as about anything else, and it seems more than likely that, when the present falling apart of sociological research ceases, sociologists might begin to discover some statistical facts and produce some statistical tables which take account of the subtle insights of the ethnomethodologists.

Finally, when we turn to social structures defined only in terms of variables and not in terms of social relations, expectations and so on, we may still accept them as a second best where nothing is known about the orientation to action and interaction of the participants, or as a first stage of sociological study which presents us with material which has to be explained in terms of general socio-logical models. The problems here are exactly the same as those involved in Durkheim's use of statistics, which will be discussed below.

With all of this said, however, we have still to look at those cases in which quantification is used in conjunction with genuine socio-logical concepts.

In the first place, statistical facts about recurrent human behaviour present us with data to be analysed, as do isolated pieces of evidence. We have said, it is true, that the testing of whether or not a particular pattern of action-orientation, or a social relation construct, has relevance to observed behaviour, can be accomplished even without looking at other cases. When, however, we are confronted with a recurrent relationship between one index of human behaviour and another, this is something which cries out for meaningful explanation. For example, if we are confronted with a proved statistical relationship between being the child of a broken marriage and committing juvenile delinquency, we should go on to hypothesise something about the orientation to life of the young boy or girl from a broken home and the commission of delinquent acts. This would be a complex hypothesis and its validity could be shown by observing whether or not expected forms of behaviour, other than delinquency, did in fact occur .Thus we go from facts to a hypothesis adequate on the level of meaning. We then test the hypothesis independently of the behaviour originally under consideration, and conclude that it can be used as a valid explanation. In some cases, of course, we might do better than this, in that we can turn to an accepted and established body of theory for explanations. It is, how-ever, the case in sociology that we are able to offer and test meaning-ful explanations *ad hoc*. This means that we are rarely in a situation where we cannot and do not seek to understand statistical relation-ships on the level of meaning. On the other hand, statistical investi-gations do, on occasion, throw up surprising relationships which upset our 'plausible stories' about the meaning of human conduct, and demand that we renew our initiative on the level of understand-ing and theory.

This discussion leads us, naturally enough, to a consideration of the work of Durkheim. We have already seen that he seemed to turn away from the study of meaningful structures of social relations to the empirical study of recurrent phenomena entirely externally. If we follow through his argument in *The Rules of Sociological Method* (1962), moreover, it is clear that, in part, he wants to scientise sociology by quantifying it. Thus we are told, at the end of the book, that the most appropriate of Mill's methods for use in sociology is the 'method of concomitant variations'.

But *The Rules of Sociological Method* is a crass book, probably designed to gain recognition for sociology among scientists. As Ernest Wallwork (1973) has recently pointed out, however, it is an unrepresentative book, and all Durkheim's early work, particularly while he was in Bordeaux, was concerned with externality as seen from the subjective point of view of the actor. In fact he starts with the problem of describing 'the facts of the moral life' and particularly the tension between a Kantian notion of duty and the notion of social sentiments as a cause and a basis of morality, and he takes this preoccupation into his study of law (1964a), education (1956), and religion (1964b). Even in *The Rules of Sociological Method* this is his starting point, and the problematic thing for Durkheim is not how non-quantitative facts like duties or cultural constraints can be used by the sociologist, but how quantitative facts can. There is thus an interesting argument lying behind his transition from his first to his second definition of social facts.

This argument starts by conceding that the basic social facts are things like obligations, duties and so on, which represent the demands of other persons or cultural constraints such as the language or the currency which provide the means and the conditions of our interaction with others. But then Durkheim becomes concerned with social facts which are not fixed, such as the pressures of the crowd on the individual, which seem to exercise a vague power over him, which it is difficult to capture in a meaningful ideal type, and finally there are those aspects of human behaviour which statistics show to be subject to 'external' influences, but which may not be experienced in this way by the actor. The notion of 'having an existence independent of its individual manifestation', in Durkheim's definition, is a survival of his earlier notion of externality experienced subjectively, and it seems essential to him. But when the actor himself fails to recognise this independently existing external fact, what does the sociologist do? Durkheim's answer is that the sociologist must give a concrete representation to the 'collective current' which is undoubtedly there.

Obviously Durkheim's commitment to positive science was enormously strong, and many of these concepts (not least that of the collective current) are positivist concepts designed to avoid using subjective action language by introducing metaphors (in the case of collective currents an electrical one, which is used again in *The Elementary Forms of Religious Life*).

It is very important, however, to see the way in which Durkheim handled statistics and what he used them for. In his classic, statistically-based, study of *Suicide* (1963), he by no means confined himself to claiming that differential suicide rates were to be explained in terms of collective currents. He deliberately broke down his statistics so that they could be looked at comparatively in terms of different subjectively-formulated models of social action and social relationships. Sometimes this is done at a diffuse and generalised level, as when he tries to contrast the kinds of solidarity involved in altruistic and egoistic suicide. But, throughout the book, there are brilliantly perceptive suggestions as to why a Protestant should be driven to suicide more frequently than a Roman Catholic, and why officers should commit more suicide than enlisted men, and so on. In each case the starting point of this analysis was the subjective standpoint of a particular type of actor. The curious thing is that Durkheim never spelled out the methods whereby these constructs were developed, tested and applied. He thus seems to have done his sociology intuitively and confined his discussion of methods largely to the pre-sociological stage in which data were collected to be presented for sociological interpretation.

One should not, however, underrate the importance of Durkheim's statistical studies for sociology. As we have suggested, the two basic sources of data for sociologists are actors' theories or meaningful interpretations of their social world, and various forms of hard data. But, whereas it is relatively easy to see how sociological constructs apply to the former, it is by no means so easy to see how they apply to the latter. Durkheim, with his curious notion of collective currents, opened the sociological door to this sort of data, and, having done so, went on to give a magnificent demonstration of how such data might be interpreted.

A good example of the value of confronting sociology with statistical relationships to be interpreted is provided by the following. In a book of readings on marriage and the family (Judson et al., 1957), Margaret Mead argues that the American family ideally postpones the birth of the first child until two years of marriage have elapsed. She adduces, in evidence for this, an account of the orientation to life of the young couple in subjective terms, and her story is a plausible one. The next reading in the same book, however, records the statistical fact that, in the average case, the first child is born within eleven months of marriage. Even if we allow for the fact that biological accidents occur, there is a gap here, and Margaret Mead's plausible stories have to give way to new hypotheses. What this shows, above all, is that received notions and plausible stories about what is expected are sometimes belied by the facts. Similarly, Durkheim suggested to us that there were a range of unknown social pressures at work and that the first stage along the route to building theories about them was to find out what the facts were.

Weber, who manifestly started from the other end of the research and theorising process to Durkheim, none the less recognised that his action explanations applied to statistically recurrent events as much as to single instances (even though, it may be worth repeating, he was wrong in thinking that meaningful explanations could be, or had to be, verified by statistical recurrences). He did, also, specifically indicate certain classes of statistics which he regarded as capable of sociological interpretation, and certain others which were not (1968a, p. 12).

> There are, (he writes) statistics of processes devoid
> of subjective meaning, such as death rates, phenomena
> of fatigue, the production rate of machines, the amount
> of rainfall, in the same sense as there are statistics
> of meaningful phenomena. Examples are such cases as
> crime rates, occupational distributions, price
> statistics, and statistics of crop acreage. Naturally
> there are many cases where both components are involved,
> as in crop statistics.

We have not yet, however, considered the most essential element in Weber's method, the use of ideal types and its relation to quantitative data. To do this, we must go back to the notion of ideal types applying to concrete individual instances, ideal types applying to a sample of cases and thus involving some type of generalisation, ideal types which refer to abstract aspects of human action, like those of the economist, and ideal types involving the artificial accentuation of certain elements of reality, which may be used as 'yardsticks'.

Now in the first and simplest case, as we saw, the ideal type might come to mind as a plausible hypothesis to explain a puzzling phenomenon, then be tested against evidence of the actual course of events in areas where the facts had not been previously known, and then used as a valid explanation. The application of such a hypothesis and explanation to a sample of cases, however, is more difficult. The cases are not all completely the same, and one cannot expect them all to confirm the predictions of our hypothesis in all of, say, ten respects. In this case, we must either construct an average and test our hypothesis against that, or we must try to construct as internally coherent and meaningfully consistent an ideal type (or perhaps coherent and consistent *types*) as possible, and measure the deviation of particular cases from this (or these).

Now at first sight, averages are not easy to construct, when we are concerned with types of action-orientation or social relations. As Weber puts it (1968a, pp. 20–1):

> It is important to realize that in the sociological field,
> as elsewhere, averages, and hence average types, can be
> formulated with a relative degree of precision only when

they are concerned with differences in degree in respect
of action which remains qualitatively the same. Such
cases do occur but in the majority of cases of action
important to history or sociology the motives which
determine it are qualitatively heterogeneous.

So when we are concerned to establish some such construct as
a sect or a manor, it is not easy to reduce the constituent elements
of action and relations to quantitative variables which vary from
case to case, but in any case if it were possible to do so for, say, ten
variables, which permutation of values for these variables would
constitute the average? This is also a problem in Durkheim, who
talks as though average types are used in the biological sciences in
the description of species for classification. But nowhere does he tell
us how one would construct an average frog or its sociological
equivalent.

Yet we should not entirely dismiss the notion of quantification
within ideal types. If one takes the case of bureaucracy, for example,
this refers to a structure of social relations among whose elements
are 'the recording of official acts in the files' and the 'separation of
domestic and business affairs'. If one sought, as Weber did not, to
discover an average bureaucracy, these could be treated as dimensions or variables, and quantitative averages obtained. Extending the
notion, if all the structural elements could be quantified in this
way, we could speak of an average bureaucracy. In fact, however,
where this has been tried, what is sometimes called 'operationalising
Weber' has usually distorted the variable elements in his ideal-
typical structures and even then what has been aimed at is not
an average case but a series of structural profiles (Pugh et al., 1963,
1968; Hinings et al., 1967).

We have suggested that, in the absence of adequate ideal types
of structures of social relations, it might sometimes be useful, as a
preliminary stage, or as a second best, merely to record the relationships between a series of indices, regardless of their meaning from a
subjective point of view. This is a style of sociological work which is
much in favour in the comparative study of national socio-economic
systems (see Lipset, 1963 and articles by W. Moore and M. Levy in
McKinney and Tiryakian, 1970). We would suggest, however, that
whenever such studies are undertaken they should be followed by
meaningful structural interpretation, or better still they should be
approached with a stock of structural questions to put to the statistics. Apparently, however, work of this kind continues because the
revolution in data-processing has elevated the accomplishment of
rough computer work to a central place in social research. Moreover,
if one looks at gross statistics it is possible to arrive fairly uncritically

at conclusions about such matters as the convergence of different socio-economic systems, which would not stand up to a more meaningful structural analysis.

It should be noted that our relatively negative attitude to the use of statistical averages is not tied, as it is in Weber's argument, to the notion that ideal types refer to abstract elements of action only. He himself follows the quotation above by saying: 'The ideal types of social action which for instance are used in economic theory are . . . unrealistic or abstract in that they always ask what course of action would take place if it were purely rational and oriented to economic ends alone' (p. 21).

Apparently he believes that while such abstractions may be treated as measurable variables concrete cases may not, but this really leads him to his most characteristic point. The abstract ideal type is not thought of, as it could be, as one which, if taken along with other complementary types, might enable us to produce a composite concrete type capable of explaining the particular instance. Rather it is confused with the notion of the ideal type as an extreme case which may be used as a yardstick.

Despite the confusion, however, the notion of the ideal type as a yardstick is an important and useful one. Actually there is no reason why it should be a limiting or extreme case. Weber believed that this was so because in thickening out his ideal types in a meaningful way he naturally tried to make them coherent and pressed his meaningful starting point to its logical conclusion. But once one has the elements, which compose the situation contained with the type clear, it is possible to use it as the standard against which actual empirical cases may be compared, whether qualitatively or quantitatively. Moreover, when several related ideal types, such as Weber's types of administration, are used together they can be even more revealing. Very often one can say of a deviant bureaucracy, not merely that it deviates, but that it deviates in a known direction.

The yardstick ideal type may also be regarded as one which refers to a structure which exists, other things being equal, in ideal circumstances. In that case it becomes more than a yardstick, and it would be more like the pure case in the natural sciences. Unfortunately, we can only rarely do what the natural scientists do, namely create ideal circumstances and see whether all the elements which we claim to exist actually do so. Possibly this will be done in the future with more sophisticated computer simulation. In the meanwhile, however, the pure case which we use as a yardstick may not be established itself by some sort of experimental test. It tends to be accepted simply because it is logically and meaningfully coherent.

What we do need to notice here, however, is that whether they are relatively arbitrary constructs, or constructs of how social structures would be in ideal circumstances, the elaboration of such structures does enable sociologists to do useful comparative and historical work. Some at least of the comparisons will be quantitative, and here again we are able to point out that the use of ideal types of a Weberian kind by no means precludes the possibility that measurement has a role to play in sociology. The only point which we would wish to resist is that which claims that precision of measurement in human behaviour by itself constitutes sociology, whether it refers to ideal types of social structure or not.

We can now see, having reviewed the questions, how the uses to which the two main forms of sociological data, namely actors' theories and hard quantitative data, may be put in sociology. Quite clearly, both have an important part to play. If the practical procedures and theories which are involved in selecting candidates for employment are a relevant form of data in a study of selection, so also are such factors as the occupational background of candidates' parents, their income bracket and their education. But what makes both sorts of data live sociologically are the ideal types of social structure in terms of which we interpret them and which constitute the true focus of the sociologists' attention. Anyone who fails to concern himself with the construction of these will fail to do sociology and will be ill-equipped to help us in our task of demystifying the modern social and political world.

part two

Basic problems of theory building

5 Social structures, the building blocks of history

It is surprising how little systematic sociological theory is studied at the present time. In so far as it is it tends to be identified with the structural-functionalism of Talcott Parsons, and Weber's monumental and unsurpassed attempt to systematise the concepts which he had felt bound to use in doing comparative history tends to be either forgotten or raided for theories which can be applied to small-scale situations. Our belief is that a non-trivial sociology, concerned with the peculiar world-historical problems of our time, has to build on something very like a Weberian foundation, even though, from its basic concepts onwards, it must be sensitive to aspects of modern social structure which Weber left out (even though it is surprising how few of these there are and how frequently we recognise our own condition and our own problems in what he has to say about another civilisation).

Given the dominance of Parsons, however, it is perhaps as well that we should look at the points at which the Parsonian and the Weberian types of sociology diverge. In the first place, we should look at the concept of a completely institutionalised social relation in Parsons's *The Social System* (1951) both because, like the work of Simmel and Weber, the focus *is* on social relations, and because this is the starting point on which Parsons builds his system of sociological theory or, substantively, his system of society. In the second place we should seek to understand this statement in depth and relate it directly to Weber by looking at Parsons's introduction to, and critique of, the first four chapters of Weber's *Wirtschaft und Gesellschaft* (1949, Introduction).

In *The Social System* Parsons writes (pp. 36–9):

> The problem of order and thus the nature of integration
> of stable systems of social interaction, that is of social

structure, thus focusses on the integration of the motivation of actors with the normative cultural standards which integrate the action system, in our context, interpersonally. These standards are . . . patterns of value-orientation and as such are a particularly crucial part of the cultural tradition of the social system.

The orientation of one actor to the contingent action of another inherently involves evaluative orientation because the element of contingency implies the relevance of a system of alternatives. Stability of interaction in turn depends on the condition that particular acts of evaluation on both sides should be oriented to common standards since only in terms of such standards as 'order' are either the communication or the motivational contexts possible. . . .

There is a two-fold structure of 'binding in'. In the first place by virtue of internalization of the standard, conformity with it tends to be of personal, expressive and/or instrumental significance to ego. In the second place, the structuring of reactions of alter to ego's action as sanctions is a function of conformity with the standard.

The institutionalization of a set of role expectations and of corresponding sanctions is clearly a matter of degree. This degree is a function of two sets of variables; on the one hand those affecting the actual sharedness of value-orientation patterns, on the other those determining the motivational orientation or commitment to the fulfilment of the relevant expectations . . . a variety of factors can influence this degree of institutionalization through lack of these channels. The polar antithesis of full institutionalization is however, anomie, the absence of structured complementarity of the interaction process or, what is the same thing, the complete breakdown of normative order in both senses. This is a limiting concept which is never descriptive of a concrete social system. Just as there are degrees of institutionalization so there are degrees of anomie.

Now Parsons clearly does not take social order or the structural complementarity of role-expectations for granted. He always assumes that social interaction is 'doubly contingent' and that a problem of order is posed by the existence of alternatives which are available to the actors. He therefore posits a situation in which 'ego' and 'alter' have a need-disposition to conform to a common standard and also want each other's approval for fulfilling expectations. But seeing that a variety of factors might affect this institutionalisation, Parsons (a) recognises a range of possibilities ranging from complete institutionalisation to what he calls complete anomie, but (b) decides to concentrate on institutionalisation or how order is achieved. It is characteristic of Weber's sociology, on the other hand, that he seeks to deal with the full range of possibilities in interaction, regardless of whether or not these involve order. We shall follow him in this, seeking to show also that the frame of possibilities includes more than simply two ranges from institutionalisation to anomie.

Parsons had already rejected Weber's perspective on sociological theory on two counts. One was his rejection of the concept of system and of function, the other his rejection of psychology (Weber, 1949, Introduction). Weber had said that the 'organic' approach was useful only as a preliminary orientation to sociology, and that sociology was bound to go beyond talking about system properties to analysing social structures in terms of the action frame of reference. On the other hand he very much feared the psychologising of sociology, believing that his ideal types of action were socially and culturally structured and required no psychological assumptions beyond minimum ones about the tendency of human beings to seek goals and to express emotions.

As against this, Parsons believes that he has reconciled the structural-functional approach (or the organic approach) with the action frame of reference. At the level of interpersonal relations he posits acting individuals, but he also argues that their action may be so structured that both the social relation at the micro-level, and the total society at the macro-level, will form a smooth-functioning and integrated whole. This structuring takes place through the individual actors' being so worked on by the socialisation process that they develop psychological need-dispositions which direct their conduct along lines which make social order possible. Unfortunately, since Weber's career ended before Parsons's academic career began, it is impossible to be sure how he would respond on these points.

For our part we are not prepared to concede to the need for order, or to socialisation, anything like the central role which Parsons assigns them in his account of social life. Rather we wish to discuss systematically the full range of possibilities which the double contingency of social interaction opens up, recognising only that an assumption has to be made that human beings, when they are socialised, are not so constrained in their choice by psychological factors that they cannot choose to act in a variety of ways and that, in the fulfilment of their needs, with the aid of structures of social relations, the kind of structure which they use in one context might

71

affect the operation and the structure of another. The extent to which ineffective socialisation affects social structure will be implicit in later chapters,* even though we shall not, as Parsons does, find a place here for a theory of social deviance and control. More immediately, we shall turn to the question of the functional inter-relation between different social structures and institutions, as soon as we have adequately discussed the concept of structure.

Now our starting point must be, as Weber's was, the main types of social action, considered in formal terms. Here, it is widely recognised, Weber's position was far from satisfactory. Without going into the difficulties, which his fourfold classification into two types of rationality, affectual and traditional action, raise, let us simply make some suggestions ourselves. In our view, meaningful action may be of the following types: (a) technical-rational, in which the goal is clear and the means chosen to achieve it are simply those which, in the light of scientific or common-sense knowledge, are the most effective ones, (b) economic-rational, in which *ends* are weighed against each other in terms of some common standard, like utility or cost, (c) normative, in which the choice of means is governed by some rule other than a purely scientific one, often taking the form of a taboo on certain courses of action, but also possibly encouraging certain sorts of action as good or ideal, even though they are not necessarily efficient as means, (d) expressive, in which an inward state gains expression through a symbol (in so far as representing this as goal-oriented action of looking for an appropriate symbol is regarded as inadequate), (e) traditional, which differs from normative action (c), in that (c) has a more systematic justification, (f), emotional, which probably approximates to (d) above, but is an unsystematised version of (d) as (e) is of (c).

It is important to notice that ideal types of action and of social relations are by no means confined to those which are built upon rationality. Indeed we might point out that it is curious that Weber is accused of a rationalistic bias when his two rational types of action included only *Zweckrationalität*, which involved an essentially evaluative act of weighing means or ends against each other, and *Wertrationalität*, which was specifically a non-utilitarian form of action. We would, in fact, agree that the purist case of rationality, what we have called technical rationality, provides us with the simplest case for analysing social structures, but in all the cases mentioned the action may, in Weber's words 'take account of the behaviour of others and be thereby oriented in its course'. That is

---

* Chapters 9 and 12. We do not deny the importance of a theory of socialisation here. We simply assume, for the most part, that individuals have been social-ised so that they are capable of exercising choice.

to say, all of these types are sociologically relevant, and our use of the action frame of reference in no way implies a rationalistic bias.

Actually, it is worth while remarking in parenthesis that Weber's critics, who have usually begun by taking exception to his designation of the modern capitalistic and bureaucratic world as rational, have not always made it clear what they mean by the rationalistic bias. In fact we would suggest that Weber is positively confusing in that he speaks of rationalisation in relation to any form of systematisation (this is the meaning of rational implicit in the notion *wertrationäl*) but also uses it to refer to economic action and to non-traditional scientific action. This involves, if anything, a too wide usage of the term rational, and this even apart from another distinction he makes between formal and substantive rationality. But his critics accuse him of too narrow a usage. What Weber does is to reveal the full range of types of *meaningful* action. His critics seem to want him to talk about a wider range of action types. It is hard to understand this because nothing at all of significance can be said of meaningless action.

It should be noted that these types of action, like Weber's, constitute part of an alternative answer to the problem of order, for it is assumed here that not all action is simply selfishly purposive, but at the same time it must be noted that, even if we start with action which is normative or expressive, it may be carried out in a world in which other actors neither share the same standard nor have a need-disposition to conform. In these circumstances order may be achieved through the use of other sanctions.

Any of these forms of action may take account of the behaviour of others, either by noting it and responding to it as an empirical fact or as indicating expectations which must be responded to. The simplest case is that in which the individual actor (ego) feels that he has no control over the behaviour of the others and simply assumes that behaviour as a condition of his own, though he may, by deploying sanctions of one kind or another, seek to alter its course. Much economic behaviour is of this kind. But the most important problems begin when, from the point of view of ego, demands are made on his own behaviour by others. Then a number of possibilities exist.

The major possibilities are these. First, alter may or may not understand ego's expectations, In the extreme case he might find ego's expectations utterly incomprehensible, or at the other extreme he may fully understand them. Obviously, however, most actual social relations fall somewhere between these two extremes, being based upon only partial understanding. Second, however, alter may or may not accept the demands as legitimate. If he rejects them

73

entirely and seeks to block ego's attempts to achieve his goals, we may speak of conflict. But here again there is a full range of possibilities, ranging from complete compliance to complete conflict.

Thus we notice at once that, if we do not assume that the problem of order must be solved, there is not simply one kind of relationship to be explained but a variety of different ones, so that we might say that any particular relationship lay at some point within a triangle, whose corners would be (a) complete communication and complete compliance, (b) incomplete communication and (c) incomplete compliance, although this is a simplistic attempt at diagrammatic representation which does not fully account for the range of possibilities.

Weber, at this point, raises the question of order in his own way, by pointing out that social action and social relations might be simply a matter of usage, a kind of group habit, of custom, if the group habit is of long-standing, or of self-interest which, far from meaning a war of all against all, is the basis on which much of the world's action and interaction depends. As he says of this last category (1968a, p. 30):

> Many of the especially notable uniformities in the course of
> social actions are not determined by orientation to any sort of
> norm which is held to be valid, nor do they rest on custom,
> but entirely on the fact that the corresponding type of social
> action is, in the nature of the case, best adapted to the
> normal interests of actors as they themselves are aware
> of them.

None of these represent strong answers to the problem of order, and the much more important concept is that of a 'legitimate order'. According to Weber's definition, 'action', especially social action which involves a social relationship, may be guided by the belief in the existence of a legitimate order. As an example of this Weber says (p. 31):

> when a civil servant appears in his office daily at a
> fixed time he does not only act on the basis of custom
> or self-interest which he could disregard if he wanted
> to; as a rule his action is determined by the validity
> of an order (viz. civil service rules) which he fulfils
> partly because disobedience would be disadvantageous to
> him, but also because its violation would be abhorrent
> to his sense of duty (of course in varying degrees).

More generally (ibid.):

> Only then will the content of a social relationship be
> called an order if the conduct is approximately, or on

the average, oriented towards determinable maxims.
Only then will an order be called 'valid' if the
orientation towards these maxims occurs amongst other
reasons, also because it is in some appreciable way
regarded by the actor as in some way obligatory or
exemplary for him.

Interestingly, the points which Weber makes cover exactly the
same ground as does Parsons's discussion of institutionalised
role-expectations and relations. But how much more equivocal
is Weber's acceptance of the inevitability of either the maxims or
the sense of duty. These are not Parsons's shared value standards
or need-dispositions to conform. Order may be the case or it may
not. If it does exist it may arise out of usage, custom, or self-interest.
Finally, somewhat half-heartedly, the parties to a network of social
relations may, amongst other reasons, accept that there are 'maxims'
governing their behaviour.

None the less we now have another possibility in social relations
over and above those which depend upon the communication-
misunderstanding variable, and the conflict-compliance variable.
This is the extent to which the parties to a relationship conceive of
themselves as being subject to a legitimate order. So we may say
that any social relation has to be placed somewhere along each
of the lines in Figure 1.

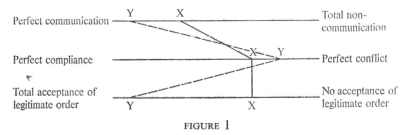

FIGURE 1

The profile shown by the unbroken line refers to a situation in
which alter 'gets the message' reasonably clearly but not completely but, with the understanding of the situation which he has,
sharply rejects ego's expectations and regards them as nearly completely illegitimate. There may, of course, be many such profiles.
The profile Y represented by a broken line, however, presents some
difficulties, because here alter is represented as accepting that there
is a legitimate order which should govern his conduct, and he also
fully understands what is expected of him, yet he acts in conflict
with these expectations and the legitimate order. This is a case of
true deviance which Weber does not discuss, but which must some-

75

times occur. We have argued elsewhere (1973a) that it is important to distinguish this case from all cases of misunderstanding, conflict and non-acceptance of a legitimate order, and that unfortunately they remain hopelessly confused in the theory of deviance.

The next sections of Weber's own work focus on the extension of the concept of legitimacy in ways which prepare the ground for his discussion of leadership, but he then returns to a discussion of what Parsons might call non-institutionalised social relations and to a classification of types of social relation.

Since we have indicated four ways in which actual social relations might depart from the ideal of 'complete institutionalisation' it is important to point out that each of these leads, not merely to a structural concept, but to a dynamic structural concept. In the simplest case of conflict we obviously have the basis of formal conflict theory, for it is to be assumed that when alter fails to fulfil ego's expectations both will deploy sanctions and that, failing the physical destruction of one by another, or an abandonment or destruction of the relationship, they will eventually reach a point at which the cost of continued conflict becomes too high and they will accept each other's terms, with or without discovering any kind of belief in a legitimate order.

So far as the problem of communication is concerned, an original state of 'anomie' in Parsons's sense would, sooner or later, lead to a clash and to some attempt to re-negotiate meanings, until at least a working basis is found. Lack of belief in a shared moral order might lead either in the direction of permitting the development of an open power struggle or might, in certain circumstances, lead to the gradual implicit acceptance of one. Finally, deviance will lead to the initiation of processes of social control.

It should be noted, then, that social order at the level of social relations is highly unstable, and this fact may lead to a continuous process of restructuring. This is why Simmel (1969) preferred to speak of 'sociation' rather than social relations. Moreover, it is likely that even the processes of restructuring may be less stable than some of the participants claim them to be. A real conflict of interest may be defined by one of the parties as anomie or misunderstanding, and new definitions successfully imposed for a while. The legitimate order which emerges from the power struggle may be a fragile one which lasts only so long as there is a balance of power, and collapses when that balance is destroyed. Finally, what exactly is deviance may be a matter for dispute, and the processes of social control may therefore be of a complex kind, and often confused with problems of conflict, anomie on the communication level, and doubts about the legitimacy of an order.

At this point of outlining a theory of social structure we can only indicate some of the broad lines of potential change in social relations. But in any case such theories are probably not best understood in the abstract. Conflict theory, as it is sometimes called, when it operates on this level, very often only succeeds in confusing the issues and, when it is tied to conflict resolution, may quite deliberately be concerned to do so in order to preserve peace or to preserve the *status quo*. This is particularly true of some attempts to apply conflict theory to international and industrial relations. Far from it being the case that an interest in conflict always implies a radical approach to sociology, this might be a happy hunting ground for the more sophisticated conservative. On the other hand, the distinctions which we have drawn here will serve to undermine that type of theory.

Sociology can, in fact, get quite far in its analysis in any case if it confines itself to a study of dyadic relationships. It is useful to recognise the distinction between different kinds of relationship as Tönnies (1955) and Weber (1968a, p. 41) both did and this is an area where Parsons's pattern variables are really extraordinarily valuable as an aid to a morphology of social relations. Quite apart from their alleged position as patterns of evaluative action orientation for the system as a whole, the recognition that, in his dealings with alter, ego might regard the relationship as an affective or an affectively neutral one, that it might be of specific or diffuse importance, that alter may be seen as a member of a category or an individual, that alter may be responded to variably in terms of his achievement or in a stable and standardised way, and that ego might act for himself or on behalf of a collectivity, helps us to discriminate one kind of social structure very sharply from another, and the thirty-two possible combinations of the five pairs provide an excellent framework of classification. In this matter Parsons has greatly added to the analytic insight implicit in Tönnies's work and Weber's section on communal and associative relations.

The dynamic theory of social relations which we have outlined, moreover, provides us with a sociological theory capable of wide-ranging application. It is by no means the case that 'methodological individualism' of Weber's kind confines us to a study of sociation between individuals. Implicit in the notion of the ideal type is the notion that an individual course of action may be imputed to a collectivity so that the sort of theory which we have outlined has application to marriage, to education, to industrial relations, to revolution and to international relations, and would enable us to make analyses of these situations of considerable value, even if we had no larger concepts of multi-person structures.

Nevertheless, the development of sociological theory on a more complex level does require this notion of multi-person structures, and thus implies a theory of groups, or quasi-groups like classes and nations and of market relations, which are the major social structures on a formal level which shape our modern world. With their aid we shall be able to look at such questions as the structure of formal organisations in business and politics, the relations between corporations in a capitalist society, collective bargaining processes, class struggle and revolution, as well as some of the major forms of domination. It is precisely these concepts which we need in our analysis of the first, second and third worlds.

It is at the point of the analysis of group structure that Simmel's work becomes so disappointing and its inherent tendency towards trivialisation is exposed. For instead of going on from his analysis of the dyad to an analysis of the group, he turns to trivial studies of the effect of the presence of a third party or, more generally, the effect of numbers on social life. Too often this part of his work turns out to be of purely psychological significance. It was left, therefore, to Weber to carry out his programme, and it is interesting to notice how, from the moment at which he discusses open and closed social relationships, Weber goes beyond Simmel in a systematic way, although including some of his insights, e.g. about superordination and subordination within a larger structural context.

Weber's group theory, formulated with his own special historical and empirical problems in mind, includes the following elements:

(a) Whether a social relationship is open or closed or not – an essential and important element in determining whether certain advantages can be monopolised. Under the heading of closed relationships, Weber includes kinship, emotional and erotic relationships, organisations, such as religious ones with shared beliefs, and organisations monopolising political advantages. On the other hand, audiences are examples of open relationships and so are some kinds of political and religious organisations looking for support.

(b) The imputation of responsibility and representation. The first of these implies that in certain of their actions all who are members must recognise that their actions are imputed to the members as a whole, and that they will also be regarded as being involved in the action of others. Representation implies that certain members are deputed to act on behalf of the whole.

(c) Leadership and administration. Groups may exist without leaders, but some groups will have them. Weber confines the term organisation to a group which has a 'chief' or other 'person in authority'. Such an individual has a representative role, but also has to take executive action in cases where the exact action is not specified in the order of the group, and also has to ensure that that order is enforced. Under this heading too, one gets references to the basis of authority, including the authority of the chief over members, of the chief over his staff, and the staff over members. The foreshadowing of the possible bases for obedience in any of these pairings is to be found in an earlier section. Later we see that Weber operates with the notion of traditional, rational-legal, and charismatic authority, and patrimonial or feudal, bureaucratic or charismatic administration (this last through a band of disciples).

(d) More specifically, Weber considers the question of the degree of independence of the group from other groups, the question of how far it requires action of its members or merely regulates their action, the distinction between organisations which engaged in continuous rationally planned activity (enterprises) or not, and whether they have an administrative staff as in formal organisations. Finally there is a consideration of power and domination and an interesting note on the state 'which exercizes a monopoly of the legitimate use of physical force in the enforcement of its order' and a church, which exercises a monopoly of 'hierocratic coercion'.

As one reads these sections of Weber's work, one is struck by the fact that most of the structural types which he appears to arrive at solely by definition and deduction are, in fact, types which have been important to him in his study of law and economic history. To take but one example, he is much concerned with the relationships between guilds, castes and modern economic organisations. He is also concerned to comment on related work by his contemporaries, especially Tönnies and Simmel. Because his historical knowledge is so wide and because the issues raised by his contemporaries are so important, these sections of Weber's work are, and will remain, a storehouse of sociological concepts of an unsurpassed kind.

None the less, it is important, if we are seeking to understand the modern world, that we should go through these topics again with our own purposes in mind, emphasising different elements in the structures which Weber does describe, and bringing in at this point other structures which he either discusses later or leaves out of his work.

The first interesting question is that of the structure of groups, and here we may take Weber's point that their first defining feature is that of responsibility and representation. It should be made clear that groups may exist without leadership. In any case, however, a set of problems arises in group structure akin to that which we noted in talking of structures of social relations. If all the members of a group have common expectations of a member this may be called his role. But the situation where this is the case has been shown by very nearly every analysis of the problem, but most especially Merton's (1957b, p. 113 ff.) to be atypical. Most usually, what an individual is expected to do in a particular case is a matter of conflict as between different 'expectations'. Moreover, the whole set of contingencies which we outlined as making for instability in social relations apply here.

While it is possible for a group to exist in which all are equally responsible for each other's action and required conduct is so stereotyped that decision making, where necessary, can be left to each member as part of his role, groups do in fact commonly have to cope with two other contingencies. One is that, on occasions, a particular individual must speak for them in the outside world. The other is that, in order to deal with new contingencies which have not been provided for, either there must be continuous discussion to reach agreement, or someone must be given executive responsibility. Herein lie the germs of leadership.

Two separate types of question arise with respect to leadership. One is the historical and psychological question of how individuals came to be leaders. The other is that of the basis of their authority. On the first question an important contribution was made by Parsons and Bales (1956), who argued that in any group two kinds of leader emerged. One naturally offered technical advice, while the other was the most-chosen, the most-admired or the most-loved one. These they referred to as instrumental leaders and sociometric stars. But this point refers only to incipient leadership in relatively transitory task-oriented groups. When it comes to the grounds for accepting that the authority of the leader is legitimate, no one has suggested a better classification than Weber's threefold one of traditionally, rationally-legal and charismatically based authority.

When we speak of authority, however, we are including, along with the notion of executive powers, the notion of powers of enforcement. This is an additional and analytically distinct element of leadership. It becomes the more necessary the more far-reaching and removed from common sense executive decisions are. When they are of this kind the rank and file cannot be expected to see their significance directly, but have simply to make a commitment to the leader, and that commitment will be justified in something like one of the ways in which Weber suggests.

Cross-cutting these distinctions is that between communities and associations, which is merely the projection on to the group level of Weber's distinction between communal and associative relations. Clearly communities depend more upon immediate ties of affection, mutual responsibility and upon traditional or charismatic bases for accepting representativeness and leadership, while associations depend more upon expediency as a basis for co-operation, division of labour in the exercise of responsibility, and representative and rational-legal authority coupled with the use of an administrative staff. The most extreme form of association is that which organises its administrative staff both in terms of an efficient division of labour and in terms of a hierarchy, through which the work of underlings is supervised by their superiors, so that from an executive point of view, and from the point of view of the enforcement of an order, the will of the leader is efficiently carried out by many agents and his own capacities much enhanced. This will be true whatever the purpose of the organisation, whether it be a church, a capitalist enterprise, a political party, or a government department. A community, on the other hand, has no purpose in this sense and can dispense with bureaucracy. One of the problems of an association which depends upon bureaucracy lies in finding and motivating both bureaucrats and ultimate actors or workers. We shall see later that this is the central problem of both capitalist and communist societies.

It should be noted that, at this point, we are concerned with the forms of social structure regardless of their purpose. This differentiates what we are doing very clearly from the work of, say, Malinowski in his *A Scientific Theory of Culture* where the focus is on the relationship between needs and functions, and all 'institutions' are simply said to have a 'personnel' and 'norms'. Our focus here is on the differentiation of types of personnel in different social structures, rather than purposes. The relationship between this work and that of Radcliffe-Brown and Parsons, however, is more complex because, for them, the needs which institutions fulfil are concerned with the maintenance of structural forms, so that Simmel's distinction between form and purpose disappears. For the moment, however, we will follow Weber and Simmel in following through separately the study of relations and structure and returning later to the question of functional interrelationships between one structure and another.

Finally, however, we should note that an analysis of relations and groups does not exhaust the systematic listing of structural elements which sociology requires. The most important other interpersonal structures are what we will call quasi-groups, like classes and nations and markets, the latter being probably the most important formal structures in the 'first' world.

Weber perhaps would place classes and nations under the heading of open relationships (with certain reservations). He also discusses later the questions of whether classes and status groups are communities. Neither of these starting points, however, seems adequate to do justice to the curious kind of entity which something like the British working class or the Irish nation is. On the one hand such an entity is marked by a very strong sense of group identity. On the other, it has a curiously unbounded character.

Some would argue that the very notion of a class is something of a myth, or the intellectual product of a failed prophecy, and that, at best, it exists only in the minds of those who believe in it. But if we look carefully at the problem we will see that there is more to the structure of class than this. In the first place it is true that some workers join trade unions, and that even those who do not have their working lives partially regulated by trade unions. It is also true that unions unite to form a formal organisation which purports to speak, and to some extent is recognised as speaking, for at least a considerable body of wage workers. Second, union activity becomes linked with political organisations and in some countries union interests become a prime determinant of the behaviour of political parties, so that we can speak at least of that somewhat changing population, who officer, support, work for, vote for, and more generally support the trade unions and associated parties, as a working class. There is, however, more to it than this. The class has a culture which unites its members, even though this culture also has regional connections and, as has recently been argued by Bernstein (1971, 1973) and others, it has its own way of using language so that, although it is not divided from other classes by the use of an actual different set of terms to describe the world, it is partially bounded by its language code. All of these factors help to explain, though they do not explain fully, the 'we-feeling' which finally makes it possible for the working class to exist as a sociological entity. Thus we have a strange kind of quasi-group in which one cannot speak of members, but which none the less people may say they belong to. There are card-carrying members of trade unions. There are no card-carrying members of the working class.

The concept of a class as we have used it here is, of course, an ideal type. So are similar concepts of social strata. In practice, class loyalty and stratum loyalty compete with, and are undermined by, other loyalties such as those to the family and its private property, and to the nation, and the notion that the working man has no nation is far from reflecting twentieth century historical reality. None the less, because there is a tendency in industrial society for groupings of this kind to form, sociology can usefully deploy such ideal types in its analysis.

The nation, of course, often appears as a compulsory association, with membership officially noted and recognised. But this is only if the nation has a state. In fact, many nations do not have states, and exist in the mind in the same way in which a class does. In these cases, however, the lines of demarcation may be clearer, in that those who are members of the nation often have their own religion, culture and language to distinguish them. None the less, the boundaries of the nation are not clear. It has a core of organisations as the working class does, but whether or not to identify with his nation is a decision which a man must make, and members come and go.

Core members, on the other hand, keep alive the notion of the nation by metaphors, especially those which liken it to a family. There can be little doubt that national and ethnic groupings of this type are sociologically important. Marxists are particularly aware of this, because the emergence of working class consciousness is so often impeded by national consciousness.

Quite different in its inception, from the set of groupings we have been discussing, is the interpersonal structure called a market. At first this looks like a complex structure of conflict relations. There are buyers and sellers who have conflicting interests, in that each seeks as much as possible for as little as possible. There are competing buyers and competing sellers, all of whom seek to get custom at each other's expense. Bargaining conflicts are then resolved by the use of sanctions, the specific market sanction being to seek another exchange partner. Eventually conflicts are settled in terms of agreed prices for commodities.

Market structures, however, are inherently unstable. Both buyers and sellers predictably react to the use of the sanction of going to other exchange partners, by organising those exchange partners into a monopoly. When a stage is reached in any market in which there is monopoly on both sides, new sanctions may be used and these will be along an increasing scale of power and violence. In industrial relations, the first stage is the resort to the lock-out and the strike but, both before and after strikes occur, representatives of both monopolies might agree on dispute resolution procedures. When these break down, more violent methods might be used, and one side might seek to eliminate the other, either literally by killing its members, or by possessing the property which gives it its negotiating position. In industrial relations, the workers might seek to take over the means of production, while the masters might seek to end free labour and to own or command the labour of the workers.

This ends our abstract discussion of social forms on the level of relations, groups and multi-person structures. We must now adopt a slightly more empirical perspective and look at some of the structures which are actually important in modern social systems, relating this discussion back analytically to what has been said in this chapter.

6 Some major problems of social structure

Sociology began its life as a distinct discipline with the quite clear goal of understanding the modern social and industrial order. The immediately preceding social orders in Europe were either residually feudal, and understood themselves in terms of a notion of Natural Law which governed nature and was obligatory for men, or despotically governed nation states in which the social order was dictated by the monarch. But in the nineteenth century political, social and intellectual emancipation from the law of God and the law of the King seemed possible, and in each of the major European countries men rejoiced in their new freedom and speculated on the possible kinds of social structure, government and belief systems which might characterise the new world. In the most general terms we may say that, in Britain, the emphasis was upon economic freedom, in France on the liberation of science and technology, and in Germany on the increasing command of the human spirit or mind over the material world.

The processes, both social and intellectual, which were initiated then, have not yet reached their fulfilment, and the task of understanding the new society is far from complete. Before we begin to look at it, however, it is perhaps of some importance to foreshadow the note of pessimism which will emerge more strongly in the last pages of this book. We shall strike this note, not merely because of the manifest fact that the hopes of the Enlightenment have now faded in the face of threats of economic catastrophe, nuclear destruction, ecological disaster, and a loss of moral purpose amongst the population at large, but for the fundamental intellectual reason that a critical look at the theories of the Enlightenment suggests that there was no basis, except in foolhardiness, for believing that what was happening with the industrial and political revolutions of the eighteenth and nineteenth centuries would lead to a better, more free, and more satisfying way of life for men. In fact it might well have been possible, without adopting the reactionary position of a de Maistre, to see the new social world as fraught with danger and potential disaster. No one at the time really saw it that way. It seems to be the task of sociology in the present day, when nearly every hope about social structure which the Enlightenment raised has been disappointed, to understand our predicament and to begin to look at what is before us. It is at least worth considering whether what faces us is not an industrial utopia but a new Dark Age. If to say this is to go beyond the bounds of description or analytical sociology, at least it may serve as a corrective to the naive optimism of the Enlightenment.

Generally speaking, the further back one goes in the history of sociological thought, the more unrealistic do views of the emergent social structure, which sociologists offer us, become. It is worthwhile reviewing them briefly:

Comte and Saint-Simon

The most crucial structural change underlying the work of the founding fathers of French positivism is the decline in the importance of the clergy, religion, and an economy based upon landed property, and the relative growth in importance of the scientific intellectual, of science and technology, and of a manufacturing economy. Saint-Simon celebrates the rise in political importance of the new industrial classes, and envisages the possibility that the new intelligentsia will not merely promote industrial efficiency, but actually show, by scientific means, what social structure is most likely to facilitate it. Yet there is little here by way of analysis of the characteristic structures of social relations or of the interests which might give them their dynamic. Comte repeats much the same thing in his version of the Positive Philosophy (1858), although he does begin, in his 'Social Statics' (ibid., vol. 2, ch. 6), to give an outline of the enduring elements of social structure. These are the family, the division of labour, and the state. Already the decline of kinship as the major structural form is acknowledged, and the human individual is seen as a complex of roles in a domestic community (to all intents and purposes the isolated conjugal family). Beyond this, the main structuring principle of the new social order is the division of labour, taken to mean both the fact of occupational specialisation and the division between property-ownership and entrepreneurship on the one hand, and propertylessness on the other. There is no recognition here of the corporation and how it is constituted and the main focus is on the actual and potential types of relationship between individual families. Clearly there *is* a gap here between the actual and potential,

D

and what Comte, following Saint-Simon, proposes is a body of sociological preachers who will moralise the system and create order instead of anarchy by the moral direction which they impose on the economy. The community as a territorial social unit largely disappears in this picture, giving way to the family, and the larger world of social relations is seen as a moralised market place. There is, as yet, no clear analysis either of the industrial town, the industrial firm, or the political structures of the new order.

Herbert Spencer

In many ways even more crass is the evolutionary account of social structures offered by Herbert Spencer in England (1967). Despite his perception, on the general philosophic level, that the evolution of the form of all things was from incoherent homogeneity to coherent heterogeneity, the ultimate social 'organism' which emerges is that which emerges in the market place. All concepts of hierarchy, whether political or economic, are assigned to a past in which men organised for war rather than for industry and when the English socialist, Hyndman, challenged him on the question of whether hierarchy and planning were not more likely in a society efficiently organised for industry, Spencer made it clear that he wanted individualism for its own sake, or because the new social order would be that which arose out of contracts between free men. Again there is no concept of the nature of the industrial organisation or of the domination of man by man through economic power. The state is a night-watchman state, and education is the education of individuals for the struggle for survival.

Hegel and Marx

The development of philosophic and social thought in Germany was more complex and always did take seriously the question of the moral direction of the social order. Moreover, on the structural level, it moved from Kant through Hegel to Marx, placing a greater and greater emphasis upon the facts of social structure as they affected the human condition. Kant posed the question of the basis of moral action in a world without either an institutionalised God or an all-powerful king, and tried none the less to preserve the notion of *moral* action governed by an *external* constraint in an individualistic world. Thus his world consists solely of individuals and a generalised conception of moral duty. Hegel went far beyond this to describe Spirit embodied in a cultural, social and political world.

In *The Philosophy of Right* (1962), Hegel drew the contrast between

86

civil society dominated by egotism and selfishness (Spencer's industrial society) and saw Spirit as transcending this state of affairs
through the state and through the universal class, the bureaucracy,
which had no selfish interests of its own. On a more abstract level
he (1964) saw the world of nature, history, and culture as one in
which Spirit was alienated from itself in created things and sought
to repossess and recontrol those things for itself through the processes
of thought and philosophy. Clearly Hegel reflected more sharply
than the writers of the French Enlightenment or the utilitarian
tradition in Britain a consciousness of a world which was getting
out of hand, but he rationalised this as being a part of the eternal
onward march of the Dialectic, and ultimately saw institutions only
in ideal terms.

The young Hegelians all stuck to the Hegelian notion of a world
which had got out of hand and their's was always a critical philosophy
in which social institutions were seen as alienating man from himself.
This was true of religion (Feuerbach, 1957), money (Hess, 1921;
Marx, 1967b) and of the state (Marx, 1967a). But Marx gave the
doctrine a new twist by analysing the interrelationships between the
whole complex of institutions, and by putting productive institutions
and the division of labour at the centre as the origin of all other forms
of alienation.

In Marx, the world of Adam Smith, of the economists, and that
which Spencer was later to project within sociology was brought
within a critical framework and, instead of something called the
division of labour being accepted as the structural framework of the
new social order, we are actually invited to look at the institutions
of production and to note the domination and exploitation of man
by man which goes on there (Marx, 1959). Even Marx, however, has
little to say about the structure of industrial organisations, because
for him the crucial structural and dynamic factor is the 'class with
radical chains' which must overcome alienation and restore man's
control of his own destiny through an act of revolution (1967a).
Potentially, of course, Marxism has much to say about industrial,
urban, and governmental structures, but it can be argued that the
idealisation of the role of the proletariat diverts attention away
from these things to the question of the re-moralisation of society
in general, and problems are wished away through the myth of the
proletariat, as much as they are by Hegel's universal class and the
positivist priesthood. By contrast, we are asking that the notion of a
re-moralised society should be based on realistic structural description and analysis.

If, however, Marxism has a utopian and revolutionary perspective, it does also have a legacy to those who genuinely wish to
understand the structural order of the new industrial world. By

contrast with Spencer, and Comte, and no less Saint-Simon, Marx sees the new *industriels* critically, and a picture is drawn of the capitalist entrepreneur launched on a process of social degradation in which he comes, not merely to exploit his fellow men, but to destroy society itself. On the other hand, when messianic hopes about the proletariat have been set on one side, and the prospect of proletarian hegemony considered more realistically, there remains in the concept of the proletariat a concept of human community, which is at least reflected in defensive social institutions, which make a human and social life possible in small islands within a sea of individualistic economic anarchy.

The second phase of sociological thinking about social structure begins at the end of the nineteenth century, when the new capitalist industrial order is undergoing a new phase of development and is bound to be concerned with controlling economic impulses and with cementing together a new social order through moral education. This contrasts with the earlier phase, when social philosophy and sociology had concerned themselves with identifying the historical agents, who by their very existence, were thought to point the way to a new moral and social order. Before we hail these new thinkers as resolving the problems raised by their predecessors, however, we should envisage the alternative possibility, namely that, in posing false solutions, they made it still more difficult to look and see what was going on in sociological and structural terms. Thus we might ask whether what they accomplished was not in fact a mystification of social reality, on a higher level than the ideologists it is true, but a mystification none the less. The key tendencies here are French positivism in its modern Durkheimian form, English Fabianism and German romanticism.

Durkheim

Durkheim is a remarkable figure by the standards of the intellectual history of any subject. There are so many possible starting points which can be imputed to him that there will undoubtedly be a flourishing secondary scholarship surrounding his work for many years to come (see Lukes, 1973; Nisbet, 1965, 1967, 1970; Wolff, 1960; Wallwork, 1973; Giddens, 1973). For our part, what we would wish to emphasise here is his concern with explaining human action as operating within a moral rather than any other sort of framework.

One thing which should never be forgotten about Durkheim was that he was concerned, at the outset of his career, with the problems of moral philosophy posed by Kant. The notion of the externality of social facts which recurs in so many different forms in his work has its origin nowhere else than in the notion of the categorical imperative. Yet Durkheim is not simply a bourgeois individualist (even though he was undeniably a bourgeois) writing of a world of moral individuals. He wished to show that the external constraining fact of morality could be embodied in social institutions and indeed that the moral was the social just as much as the social was the moral.

This seeking for an institutional basis for a moral order, however, led Durkheim into much wishful thinking. In some ways we may say he finds his messiahs in institutions rather than classes of individuals. Thus, while once again one finds the division of labour discussed without any separation of the question of ownership and non-ownership from that of occupational specialisation, one finds in Durkheim's work something more specific. The moralisation of the division of labour is to take place through 'occupational associations', but these associations are seen in such highly generalised terms that debates still go on, more than fifty years after his death, as to whether he meant guilds, industrial firms, or some other type of corporation. For someone who placed industrial organisations at the centre of things as the organisations which would replace kinship at the structural heart of society, Durkheim did precious little industrial sociology.

English Fabianism

So far as English Fabianism is concerned, it is arguable whether it was the inevitable antithesis to utilitarian and Spencerian individualism or merely its logical successor. Sidney Webb, it is true, assumed the former and spoke, in his original Fabian essay (1889), in quite terrifying terms of the way in which the individual in the future would find his happiness as a cog in a vast social machine. But, in fact, there is not even remotely a picture of this vast social machine in the work of the Webbs or their successors. The world of Fabianism is a world of individuals with problems, and it is an enlightened body of civil servants and local government officials which will solve them. But compared with Hegel's universal class, the positivist *industriels*, or Marx's proletariat, these bureaucrats remain a shadowy body. Trade unions are specifically set on one side as not providing the basis of the new governing class. Like local government bodies they are organisations to be studied and administered rather than bodies which do the administering, and, if public ownership is a central method to be used to direct the economy, it is still not clear to whom the new economic planners will be responsible. In part, one suspects that the Webbs took the British status system for granted and, in part, imagined themselves as setting up a new system of educating bureaucrats. It was therefore not surprising that, at the end of their lives, they (1941) hailed the Soviet Communist Party as the kind of Guild of Leadership suited to the business of planning *and* to carrying the masses in support of the plan. None the less, for authors who placed such faith in bureaucracy, the Webbs did little to analyse its nature.

Tönnies

The one remaining line of thought which we should mention as forming part of the second wave of sociological thinking about industrial society, was that of German romanticism as represented, above all, in the work of Ferdinand Tönnies (1955). In some ways he is a sociologist whom we tend to pass by with only a mention, but he undoubtedly raised issues which were not raised, or given the same centrality, by any other sociology. These concern the question of kinship and bureaucracy and of rural community and urban society, issues just as important as those of the division of labour and politics which preoccupied the other writers whom we have discussed so far.

Tönnies saw pre-industrial rural and domestic society as standing in sharp contrast to the world of modern industry, of the city and of economic individualism. He probably would have agreed with Parsons as to the main dimensions of the difference. His concern, however, was with the different psychology and, indeed, the different metaphysics underlying the two social orders. One rested on the real will and was found more commonly represented in the behaviour and attitudes of women. The other was based on an artificial will, and was characterised in the world of men. This latter world expressed itself in industry, but it also expressed itself in the City. *Gesellschaft* represented a new social principle requiring its own sociology distinct from that of *Gemeinschaft*.

In Tönnies, however, we notice something which affects late nineteenth century writing and is even more evident in the twentieth. This is a loss of moral perspective and a tendency to substitute typology for criticism. There is nostalgia for a lost past, it is true, but ultimately *Gesellschaft* is as good as *Gemeinschaft* and, realistically, all that one can say is that it is another type of society. There is only a pale reflection here of the moral concern with which Durkheim approached the contrast between mechanised and organic solidarity, recognising always that the latter might collapse into anomie.

Before we turn to Weber's resolution of some of these problems, it would be useful if we were to restate, and perhaps modify, our original position on the value-freedom of the sociologist, and of the possible role of the subject as part of our intellectual culture, for we seem now to be criticising the mainstream tradition of sociological theory, since the Enlightenment, for moralising too much, and some late nineteenth and early twentieth century sociology for moralising and criticising too little. We do believe, however, that these two positions are compatible and it is important to say why.

What we want to express, above all, when we speak of our own moral nihilism, is our disengagement from the value-judgments which rationalise the world as it is and represent it as a satisfactory and moral place. When we first argued this, we had in mind the distortions of the very problematics of sociology which were involved in policy-oriented research. Now, as we turn to the sociologies of the European Enlightenment and their immediate successors, what we see is an excited acceptance of all that is new, and many undiscussed assumptions about the possibility and the morality of the new order. We share the moral concern of the Enlightenment sociologists, but we cannot but be cynical about their moral enthusiasm, for we can now see, with hindsight, just how wrong they were to place their hopes where they did. Very often it is precisely those institutions and processes which they saw as liberating, which are now seen as forms of oppression. But we do not simply wish to say that sociology should lose its moral concerns. If it should be suspicious of new nostrums in the light of past disillusionment, it should none the less realise that the heady optimism of the nineteenth century led to, and was abetted by, the inadequacy of structural description which their sociology involved. What we need to do now is to study in detail and reflect on the main structures of the modern industrial order, both in themselves and in their interrelations. The first conclusion to which this must lead is that the ideological pictures of these structures, which exist both in political ideology and, in a more sophisticated form, in sociology itself, must be ruthlessly criticised. Therein lies our cynicism and moral nihilism. But, with this done, we may ask, at least tentatively, what the role of the sociologist today really is, and whether, accepting that many of the new social developments, which were once hailed with utopian enthusiasm need, in retrospect, to be seen as social disasters, to ask what, realistically, men may do to recapture control of the social world in which they live. We take our own lead here from Max Weber and, in the next few pages, we shall outline something of the peculiarity of Weber's own structural descriptions before going on to indicate briefly what we see as the principal social-structural elements of our own moral and political problems.

Max Weber

The first thing to notice about Weber, in the light of the present discussion, is that he combines in his work the notions of value-freedom and that of relevance for value. The first of these notions was one on which he insisted in dealing with his colleagues and contemporaries in the *Verein für Sozialpolitik*, the so-called Socialists of the Chair. Weber saw that they were, in fact, smuggling in value-judgments under the guise of speaking scientifically about practical problems of government (rather as the British Fabians were inclined to do in their discussions about administering people) and, finding himself in disagreement with those value-judgments, sought to reserve his own right to make different ones after the structural issues had been made clear. Interestingly enough, the occasion of his major argument about this concerned the question of public ownership in the Vienna tramways, which raised for Weber the whole question of the nature of bureaucracy and its role in economic life (see Simey, 1966).

On a more general level than this, however, Weber faced the question of whether there was some general standard, in terms of which the progress of society could be judged. Dilthey had clearly accepted a moderate form of relativism, speaking of a limited number of possible world views. Possibly Weber retained some such conception, particularly in his typology of world religions (Parsons, 1974) but he seems eventually to have accepted in practice a very radical relativism akin to what we have called moral nihilism. But he did also believe that the scientifically neutral study of social structures permitted the separation of value problems from purely empirical and causal ones, and invited the sociologist to make value-judgments and to use these to select his starting point in sociological analysis and, as we have seen in chapter 2, to illuminate social reality.

Commentators argue as to whether Weber had any kind of philosophy of history, in the sense of trying to demonstrate the direction of social history and to evaluate it. He is, in any case, accused both of hailing the rationalisation of the world through bureaucracy as being the major achievement of modern man, and of having despaired of a world in which the bureaucratic principle embraced all human life. Probably, however, these two perspectives are not incompatible. We can look on history as a process of continuous rationalisation and can note the extension of bureaucracy to more and more spheres. We can also see it as inevitable. But what we make of this in value terms is a different matter. Weber was certainly never enthusiastically excited by the idea of a bureaucratic utopia, but he saw the achievements of bureaucracy as involving gains as well as losses. Description of the bureaucratic phenomenon, however, was quite central to his work, and that description involved value decisions as to what were the problematics of this type of social structure.

There is one final point to be made about Weber's view of value-judgments. This is that he did explore value questions implicitly through one variant of his notion of ideal types. As we have seen, Weber would start from certain central elements of a structure and follow them through to their logical conclusion. One some occasions, indeed, he spoke of ideal types as 'utopias'. While he clearly did not mean that they were 'utopias' in the simple sense, one may at least wonder whether he did not ever see himself as using his types, not merely as cognitive, but as moral, yardsticks.

We really only begin to understand Weber, however, if we seek to understand what his major area of empirical concern was. This was the understanding of Western capitalist industrial society, and its relation to other forms of capitalism and of industrial society. Although, as we shall see, this involved an interest in functional questions about the relation between one institutional order and another, it also involved another curious and characteristically Weberian feature. This was the fact that the structures of capitalism were looked on as structural bits and that these bits were the building blocks of history. History might involve progress, but the bits repeated themselves in new combinations, and it was possible, therefore, to make comparative and historical analyses of social forms in precisely the sort of way which anthropological functional-ism declares impermissible.

Probably the best starting point for the student who wishes to understand Weber's method is to read his *General Economic History* (1961) and then to ask himself what Weber regarded as the main structural features of capitalism of the Western sort. First, he tells us that capitalism is *not* definable in terms of greed, because greed is universal and capitalism is not. Second, there is an elementary form of social organisation called the capitalist enterprise in which an individual or group counts his or its resources, embarks on an activity for a period, and then does a further accounting to see whether there is a profit. Since, however, this type of enterprise occurs in the ancient civilisations and in feudal times, especially in relation to riskier ventures such as war, tax-farming and voyages, it is not specific to the West. What is specific is its use to exploit market opportunities in a peaceful way, its application to central rather than marginal economic activities, and its operation on a continuous basis.

Once this much is established, the question arises of what sur-rounding circumstances are best fitted to the operation of such enterprises. On this, Weber's first point would be that the greater the possibilities of rational-calculation, the more will capitalist enterprises flourish. To this end there must be rational and pre-dictable law, a stable currency, rational rather than traditional forms of technology, a centrally and hierarchically organised division of labour so that the operations of all agents within the enterprise can be predicted, and free markets for capital, raw materials and labour.

It might well be argued that this allegedly value neutral description of the elements of capitalist social structure shows bias, particularly when we look, not so much at the elements themselves, as the imperatives which they are said to impose on the surrounding structure. Thus there seems to be no reason why continuous rational capitalism should not use non-peaceful means if it is likely to get away with it, and it is arguable whether the element of free markets is as essential to rational-calculation (if not to capitalism) as Weber makes out. There is, however, no need to take Weber's theoretical constructs as gospel on these points. What we can do is to look carefully at all the bits, see whether their description is accurate, and see whether they do fit together in the unique way which Weber suggested. What is true is that by specifying structures in so much detail, Weber does open up these questions for us. These are interesting lines of enquiry suggested, for example, by taking up the notions of rational-calculation and bureaucracy in productive enterprises independently of the question of the structure of capitalism, and of rational-calculation and bureaucracy independent of productive enterprises.

This, of course, is precisely what Weber did. The elements which occur in the structural development of capitalism are all essentially detachable bits. They may be compared with, and their understanding is enriched by, comparison with related elements in other cultures. So, for example, we may compare bureaucratic administration under rational-legal authority with patrimonial administration under traditional authority and other related forms. Or we may compare the religious doctrines more closely associated with rational-calculating capitalism with other religious doctrines. Thus the analysis of capitalist social structure leads into the analysis of the elements of other cultures.

The comparative perspective in Weber's sociology also means that new developments within a culture, society or civilisation are less likely to be wholly surprising. If we know about 'adventurer capitalism', or the latifundia of ancient Rome, or of patrimonial administrative structures, we are unlikely to be surprised by many of the developments which take place within imperial as distinct from national societies, and it is for this reason that Weber does not appear insular in the way in which almost all the other classical sociologists do, in dealing with the 'new' problem of the 'third' world. Of course his concepts need revising, as for instance through extensions of his notions of authority and administration to cover the historical uniqueness of the post-colonial single-party state. But to say this is not to say that this very distinctive style of sociology does not enjoy enormous advantages of flexibility.

Apart from deepening his insights into Western social structures, by relating them to comparable non-Western structures, however, Weber also widened his own approach by looking at a great many other structures apart from those which followed directly from his conception of the Western capitalist enterprise. Thus he is interested in the question of social class and status, in types of domination, and the city. It is true that, taken by itself, Weber's approach to problems of comparative social structure, via the rational-calculating spirit of capitalism, directed attention away from such factors as class relations, but it is quite wrong to suggest, as Dobb does (1946), perhaps writing at that time in ignorance of the major bodies of Weber's work, that whereas for Weber the definition of capitalism is in terms of the rational-calculating spirit, Marx understood capitalism's true nature by seeing it as definable in class terms. Weber was by no means the kind of sociologist who offered a monolithic one-factor explanation. He was interested in a wide variety of empirical problems such as the relation between ancient and mediaeval agriculture, the growth of guilds, the nature of Western, and other cities, and the basic forms of domination, authority, and administration.

What Weber does, in relation to Marx's sociology, is not to refute his sociological concepts but to relativise them.* Marx may be seen as having shown, on the structural level, that, although post-feudal Western societies boasted that they no longer had classes, in fact the hidden sociological secret of bourgeois society was that quasi-groups or collectivities of a new kind were bound to emerge from the basic productive relations of capitalism. In the labour market, bargaining groups arose, and the union of these, coupled with the escalation of sanctions, led to a revolutionary situation.

Now Weber would never have denied the usefulness of testing a structural hypothesis of this kind. More than this, his whole view of theory was such that, even if empirical evidence from history seemed to falsify the hypothesis, it was still important as a part of the total corpus of ideal types. If, in fact, one spelt the hypothesis out theoretically, one could see that the labour relation rested upon a more general concept of market situations and that, wherever

---

* For a very thoroughgoing analysis of the relation between Marx's and Weber's structural concepts see Giddens (1973). This text only became available to me in proof after this chapter was written, but it explores the relationship between these two analyses far more insightfully that any text known to us in English.

95

there was a market situation, the kind of possibilities envisaged by Marx in the labour market might ensue. (It is only an empiricist reading of Weber which makes him out to have ignored the possibility of classes arising in market situations acting as historical agents, and to have treated them as statistical categories distinguished by differential life chances. How could he have done this without forsaking the action frame of reference, which was central to his work?)

But once again we can see how, given the cast of Weber's mind, the Marxian analysis of class, and the wider category of class situations, leads him to even more far-reaching concepts. There are other forms of stratification, if one is to use that inadequate term as a loose label, than class, and it seemed to Weber that domination through market power was only one way in which inter-group domination might occur. Apart from 'acquisition classes' there were also status groups which had a distinctive role in society, and a distinctive way of life. Such status groups often dominated a society and imposed their way of life on it. The Chinese literati were such a ruling stratum, so also were the mediaeval nobility. No less, whatever their role in the market, the bourgeoisie attaining political ascendancy and imposing their sway on all social relations (as envisaged in *The Communist Manifesto*) was a ruling stratum of this kind.

The concept of class and stratum domination again interconnects with another question distinct from that of class in general, and that is the question of domination, authority, and administration in general. Men obeyed, Weber saw, not for one but for many reasons. He was certainly no historical idealist in this matter. One common reason for obedience was simply compliance with force. Another was a market factor, obedience because of a 'constellation of material interests'. Only after these have been mentioned does Weber go on to discuss the situation in which those who obey do so because they have a subjective belief that those who rule them have a legitimate right to do so. Therefore one has the brilliant ideal typical analysis of kinds of legitimate authority and administration, which is so spectacular in its historical sweep that it is often seen as Weber's most characteristic piece of work. Yet even here the administrative system is seen as in complex interplay with types of economic organisation. Thus, Weber's analysis of patrimonial administration is to be thought of as complementary to, rather than a denial of, the kind of analysis carried out by Wittfogel (1957) of oriental despotism.

The line of development of the conceptual approach, which we set out in the previous chapter, is very much that of Weber. Of course this does not mean taking over all of his ideal types uncritically, but we too are concerned with analysing the complex social structures of our time in a state of revolutionary change or dis-integration, and we too need to look to history to see whether the social forms which might emerge in the chaos about us are not illuminated by past experience. Moreover, the sheer moral rela-tivism of Weber, derived from his rich understanding of the variety of history, enables us to escape from perspectives which are either ideological or utopian. Evaluation of structures, perhaps even hope, will emerge later in our work. But hope is not to be cheaply won. It can only be realistic if it is held and advocated by someone who has looked at the full horror of history, of the plunder of the ancient world by the Romans, the barbarian invasions, the release from moral restraint of capitalist rapacity during the so-called Renais-sance, the assault by Europe on the human and material resources of the rest of the world, from the sixteenth century onwards, or the barbaric world wars and colonial wars, which used advanced technology to achieve more violent and more refined means of mass murder. It is only then that one can begin to ask what is humanly possible. A sociology which does less than this becomes, on a more or less complex level, merely the ideological tool of powerful ruling or revolutionary forces, needing a self-justifying myth. What we shall be doing in later chapters is to try to offer a sociology of our 'three worlds' which has a wide enough historical perspective and which therefore escapes this ideological trap.

Before we move on to make this sort of analysis, however, we must consider another dimension of theory. The style of theorising which we have so far discussed has what Parsons called a 'mosaic' quality. Bits and pieces are taken out and fitted together, but there is no apparent reason given why particular patterns form, or why one pattern leads to another. This seems, therefore, to ignore the indictment which Malinowski and Radcliffe-Brown brought against the comparative method, and it also lacks any conception of the engine of political change which is provided in Marxism, for ex-ample, by a dynamic political economy. Thus we will have to con-sider the degree to which we may expect the bits and pieces of socio-logically-oriented history to be systemically interconnected, and we shall also have to consider systemic contradictions, as distinct from conflicts between actors and groups, as a source of social change.

When this task has been accomplished, however, we would still wish to retain the perspective of *this* chapter. Indeed, we would give it priority. Of course we would not deny that each social system has, to some extent, its own systematic logic, but it *is* also true that the social forms which men use repeat themselves in history, and that it is only when we study these social forms, divorced from the purposes which they serve on a functional and systemic level, that we fully understand what is involved in 'sociation'. Simmel and Weber understood this and so also, perhaps, did Marx, in the watershed period of his theorising, when he spoke of the human essence as being found in the 'ensemble of social relations'. It may be true that there are dominant and leading institutions, whether these are the productive ones or not, and it may sometimes be convenient to refer to these as 'base' rather than 'superstructure'. But there is also a sense in which it is only when we look at pure forms of social relations apart from their purposes that we see the base on which all more idyllic social conceptions arise. It is striking how these bases of social action have repeated themselves in many different societies and different institutional contexts.

7 Structures, system and conflict

All that we have said so far about structures of social relations concentrates on the form of these structures, regardless of the purposes to which they are directed. In this we are following, in essence, the programme of Simmel and also that of Weber, in so far as he confined himself to an analysis of social forms. But it is also clear that Weber did concern himself, not merely with forms in the abstract, but with the forms of legal, political, religious, economic, and other institutional areas, and that he saw these separate areas as to some extent functionally or purposively interconnected. The question which we must now face is what advantages accrue to sociology from going beyond explanations of behaviour in terms of models of social structure of a formal kind to explanations in terms of institutional interconnections. In fact, we will concede that both types of explanation have their relevance and importance and, like Weber, we shall use both, but we shall also argue that, in the last analysis, 'functionalism' has become too much the prevalent mode of analysis in sociology and that the subject would be enriched by more attention to formal and structural studies.

In order to state the difference between formal structural sociology and functionalist analysis, it is useful to begin by looking at the conceptual framework used by Malinowski in *A Scientific Theory of Culture* (1944). This work serves as a kind of base-line against which other forms of functionalist analysis can be compared, rather than any kind of final statement of functionalist theory and methodology, but by the very simplicity of its conceptualisation it serves usefully to pinpoint theoretical problems which are concealed in later sociological statements.

The first point to notice is that Malinowski chooses the '*institution*' rather than any form of association or other structure as the 'concrete isolate of sociological analysis'. Moreover, he claims to be

99

offering, not a theory of society, but a theory of *culture*. According to the textbooks, these terms are crucially different from, though complementary to, terms like social relation, group, association, and society. An institution is sometimes defined in terms of rules independently of persons, but in order to distinguish it from more general terms, like custom, it is said to refer to rules relating to some important recurrent activity. Culture is something which can be inherited, and which exists independently of those who inherit it. It includes, apart from material artifacts, many non-material elements, including the norms which form part of institutions.*

Malinowski seems disinclined to press these distinctions in elaborating a general framework for social anthropology, and his usage of the term 'institution' is therefore somewhat idiosyncratic. None the less, what he does show is that there are connections as well as differences between institutional and structural analysis. Thus when he tells us that an institution has six distinct elements, its charter, personnel, norms, material apparatus, activities, and function, he points in part to more or less observable, in part to theoretical elements, and in part to social, and in part to cultural elements. Thus charters, personnel, norms, material apparatus, and activities can, loosely speaking, be observed. Functions cannot. On the other hand, while charters, norms, material apparatus and activities come under Tylor's definition of culture, personnel, or at least the relations between personnel, do not. Thus there is a strictly sociological element built into this concept of culture. Possibly it is there, concealed in the theoretical notion of function, but it is certainly there in the concept of personnel.

What should concern us here, however, is what is added to sociological analysis by the focus on the interconnections between social structures and their purposes or consequences and the interrelations between them. Here Malinowski is unique amongst the functionalists in claiming that the function of social institutions at the basic level is to satisfy biological needs, but he, like others, claims that some of the most important social institutions have the function of sustaining other institutions. It remained for Radcliffe-Brown and, in a different way, Parsons, to claim that the sole concern of the sociologist or social anthropologist lay in the contribution which institutions made to sustaining other institutions and structures, rather than in meeting biological needs.

One important difficulty in analysing Malinowski's theory, and

* We do not feel the need here to give final definitions of these terms. Useful attempts at defining all of them are to be found in such texts as MacIver and Page (1969) and, of course, so far as culture is concerned, there is the classic definition of Tylor (1929). What we are aiming to do is simply to distinguish two complementary modes of analysis, the structural and the functional.

indeed of all later functionalists and systems theorists, lies in his use of what is, in effect, a metaphorical language. The concept of need has a clear enough meaning in biology, and when we speak of satisfying biological needs we know what we are talking about, but what are the needs of institutions? Does the concept not to some extent imply an organic analogy? This is, of course, explicit in the work of Radcliffe-Brown, but even in Malinowski there is the notion that if certain effects within an institution's structure were not produced it would collapse and 'die'. We have sought to show elsewhere (1961) that this belief is untenable.

In fact an alternative model of 'functional' interconnection can be made in a sociology of the Weberian type, i.e. in terms of ideal types in the action frame of reference. This is clearly what Weber is doing in his original essay on objectivity. Surprisingly, very few sociologists have sought to account for functional explanations in this way since then and they have, on the whole, been accounted as critics of functionalism by the functionalists, and dismissed. Merton's (1957a) dismissal of Myrdal is an important case in point here.

Weber's functionalist approach is clear when he seeks to explain to his contributors the limits of what will be admitted to a journal concerned with economic institutions. There he speaks of economic facts, economically conditioned facts and economically relevant facts, noting that while some facts are primarily economic in their significance for the society, the economic historian or economic sociologist will also pay attention to those non-economic institutions which have an effect upon, or are affected by, the economic ones. Rejecting the notion of the materialist conception of history, in so far as it is regarded as dogma, he then goes on to say that there are a number of alternative points of view from which one can regard socio-cultural reality, and the clearest and simplest way of interpreting this is to say that a chain of interrelated socio-cultural events may be looked at from a religious, an economic, a political, or some other point of view. Since Weber dissociates himself from the notion that there are absolute value standpoints which can be used at this point, he would seem to be pointing to his own version of functionalist analysis.

What the action model suggests when it is applied to functional systems, is a model of a hypothetical actor with, say economic goals, who, in pursuing those goals, takes account of, say, religious factors, as means or conditions of his actions. Alternatively, the situation may be analysed from the other end. Moreover, there may be other starting points, and the means-ends chain may be of varying lengths. Only in the case of a complete chain, linking one action with another and regarding the final end as the means to the initial action, would

101

one have the form of closure which functionalism suggests. In most cases, one would be concerned with short-term means-ends sequences or 'functional relationships' and one would in no way exclude the possibility that some institutions and activities did not fit into means-ends schema or were dysfunctional to the particular end in view.

This way of setting up models for functional explanations suggests that Weber's 'methodological individualism' on the theoretical level is applicable, not merely to the analysis of social interaction, social relations and society, but to systems of institutions as well. Once we grasp that we are talking about ideal types which explain observed events rather than what the actor really meant, it becomes apparent that analysis of so-called systems and system contradictions is perfectly possible in the action frame of reference. Indeed, because this language does have such strong explanatory value, it may well be asked whether talking of systems and systems-contradictions is not unnecessarily mystifying. We can *understand* means-ends action schema. It is not at all clear, on the other hand, what the properties of systems are, or what we mean when we speak of a contradiction. Thus the oft-quoted criticism of our own work, by Lockwood (Zollschan and Hirsch, 1964, p. 244 ff.), in which he suggests that both Rex and Dahrendorf write only of conflicts between individuals and not of conflicts and contradictions between one part of the system and another, is beside the point. It appears to arise from the fallacy of misplaced concreteness. When we suggest that a chain of related institutions be analysed in terms of an actor seeking goals and finding that certain other institutionalised actions constitute obstacles to the attainment of those goals, this does not mean that we are only looking at conflicts between individual actors. It means that our sociological analyses are carried out in the action frame of reference and that any question of social interrelatedness will be analysed from the standpoint of an actor. But, as we shall see in a moment, there are additional reasons why the criticisms of our own approach, as failing to analyse systems' contradictions, are misleading. We shall see this if we consider the kind of revision of Malinowski's general model of systems of institutions which have to be made if it is to be made compatible with Marxism.

Our object here is not, of course, to prove the superiority or otherwise of Marxist explanations. It is simply to try to write them and other types of explanations in similar languages, so that they can be compared. We have just shown that Malinowski's theoretical scheme can be rewritten in Weberian language, or in terms of the action frame of reference. But even if that could not be done, it becomes apparent that the attempt to accommodate Marxist insights within the framework of Malinowski's functionalism would involve a considerable alteration of concepts and ideas in a broadly social-structural direction.

What Malinowski's model suggests is this. In the first place it is assumed that there are stable forms of institutional activity, through which men fulfil their basic biological needs. All secondary institutions are seen as depending ultimately upon these basic ones, and, though their immediate function is that of servicing structural needs of the basic institutions, their ultimate function lies in themselves satisfying biological needs. The secondary institutions, however, also have the tertiary function of servicing each other, so that what we have is a stable semi-organic type of system in which all the parts contribute to the maintenance of the whole, but the ultimate reference point is outside the social system in the biological sphere. What all this means is that the structural forms of the biological base determine the form of the superstructure of secondary institutions, which must adjust to the needs of the base and to the needs of each other.

In the version of Marxism which seems from our standpoint to be most crucial, namely that of the *Theses on Feuerbach*, there are the following elements. First, the overriding fact is that man produces his subsistence and, once this is recognised, it is not the detailed fulfilling of biological needs which determines social behaviour as a whole, but rather the internal structure of the social relations of production which begins to create a whole set of social relations independent of man's will. Marx undoubtedly changed his view about the social relations of production, and saw them as ultimately determined in *their* basic form by the forces of production or the mode of production. There is some debate about what this means (see Nicolaus, 1972). It has been commonly thought to imply that the social relations of production have to have, within fairly flexible limits, a certain compatibility with the technology on which they are based and that, given a sufficient degree of technological change, they become incompatible with that technology. As against this it has been suggested that the notion of these more ultimately determining elements in the productive system itself refers to a relation. Whichever of these views is adopted, however, what may be expected in the social relations of production, the industrial firm and the economy of firms, is that, in Malinowski's terms, the institutions concerned can never be completely stable. In particular, it is taken for granted that what Malinowski calls the personnel of the institution does not refer to a stable system of institutionalised roles, but to a conflict situation, albeit perhaps a latent one.

If this were the case in a Malinowskian system, it would have profound repercussions for the system as a whole. Whereas in the simple model which Malinowski himself advances, what spread and ramify throughout the system are the consequences of the structural imperatives of stable basic institutions, in the Marxian version, however, what spreads is a conflict, in either case, roles in the superstructure support roles in the base, but whereas this leads, in Malinowski's version, to a total ordered society of interrelated role players, it leads in the Marxist model which we have in mind, to two sets of role players acting against one another in each and every institution, but acting together with those on the same side across institutional boundaries.

If this Marxist model is the one which more usefully applies to modern social systems, then the term institution ceases, in fact, to be the central one in sociological analysis. It is replaced by the term class, and that term would then seem to have a richer and fuller meaning than in the ideal type which we outlined in the previous chapter. There we simply spoke of a labour market which passed from a free-market stage to one of collective bargaining and then either to an industrial relations system in which this collective bargaining was subject to rules, or to one in which the degree of radicalness of sanctions was continually escalated and in which the conflict spread to other institutions. Now we have the notion of the classes as constituted of specific roles which have to be performed in every 'institutional' sphere in order to further the interests of the class in the most basic conflicts. By 'interests' of course, one simply means that situation in which the individual's goals may best be realised to the fullest. It refers to the product of subjective goals on the one hand, and the objective situation on the other.

The notion of classes and class conflicts here outlined is, of course, like that of capitalist rationality and its institutional consequences outlined in the previous chapter, an ideal type. Only in the ideal type, in the pure case, do the secondary or superstructural institutions actually completely reflect the conflicts in the basic ones. Most usually they have a life of their own and have to be reconciled with traditional forms in their own institutional order. Moreover, the social structure and ideas (or Malinowski's personnel, norms and activities) in these higher order institutions may well be influenced by the structures and ideas of other classes. Generally speaking, the more powerful classes are more coherent. The powerless ones are prevented from coming into being by the penetration of their structures and organisation of the ideas of the powerful.

The Communist Manifesto outlines, in its historical part, an ideal type of development, first for the bourgeoisie, whose development is already accomplished, and then for the proletariat, in this case the projection into the future of a 'similar movement' to that which occurred in the case of the bourgeoisie. The bourgeoisie emerges as a 'personnel' in conflict with the personnel of established economic

104

and political institutions, and gradually arrives at a point at which it can establish its own hegemony, so that the very moral concepts, self-conceptions and ideas of ideal social relations of other classes tend to be taken over from the bourgeoisie. As against this state of affairs, however, 'the similar movement' in the growth of the proletariat implies the development of an organised society and a counter-culture which resists the domination of the bourgeoisie, and either succeeds simply in preserving its own independence (as the bourgeoisie once preserved its own as an 'armed and independent estate' within an alien society), or it goes for hegemony. Marx believed that the latter would occur, as is clear from his references in 1864 (Marx and Engels, 1962, p. 377) to the victories of the political economy of the working class over the political economy of the bourgeoisie. In fact, however, in most industrial societies, what seems to have happened is merely the emergence of a defensive working class having its own corporate existence within the system.

It is now necessary to return for a while from this exposition of the relation between functionalism, the action frame of reference, and Marxism, to certain aspects of more recent developments in functionalism and Marxism. In particular, we propose to look at the ideas of Radcliffe-Brown and Parsons and Merton, and to some types of recent Marxism, which share with functionalism its systems-oriented approach.

The characteristic feature of Radcliffe-Brown's functionalism, as contrasted with that of Malinowski, is its lack of any external reference point or any ultimate determinant. At least, from the sociological perspective, what we appear to be being told is that every institution supports every other, and that we may conceive this supporting role as the function or purpose of that institution. We need not rehearse here the arguments against this kind of consensualism, since we have put them clearly enough elsewhere. We might only perhaps give a little more credit to Radcliffe-Brown here and recognise that his consensualism is shared by other sociologists, in one sense even by Marxists, when they see the development of a class as fully functionally integrated, and that it has value as an ideal type. There are, however, certain other aspects of Radcliffe-Brown's work which should also be noticed, and which bear upon the relation between this chapter and those which went before it. They have to do, not so much with Radcliffe-Brown's functionalism, as with his structuralism and his humanism.

In his set of essays *Structure and Function in Primitive Society* (1968), the essay on the concept of function is immediately followed by that on the concept of structure and it is evident, even in the former essay, that the function of any activity is not to be described simply as, say, political, legal, educational or economic, as in

Malinowski, but as serving to maintain a structure. Thus the Simmelian distinction between the purpose and form of any social organisation disappears. The organisation has structure, but its goal is to preserve structure.

If one goes back at this point to Malinowski's *A Scientific Theory of Culture*, one can see that there are, in fact, some overly naïve conceptualisations there. Typical is his use of the term economic. According to the theory, the economic institution has as its role the maintenance of the material apparatus. But surely the better term here is technological rather than economic. The use of the latter term makes for ambiguity, for it also refers to actions which have the characteristics of Weber's *Zweckrationalität*, actions in which there is a rational weighing of ends in terms of utility and social relations which arise out of the market. If this latter meaning is correct, however, one must ask whether the economic mode of organisation is not one which can be applied to a number of different ends, and if this is true of the economic, may it not be true also of some of the other specialised forms of activity. The Simmelian distinction between form and purpose here seems to come under considerable strain. Do not many of the purposes of social activity turn out to be the maintenance of other social forms?

If this is true, Radcliffe-Brown's knocking away of the biological base of Malinowski's theory may be more important than its too easy dismissal as consensualism suggests. It has that meaning, it is true, but it can also be construed as giving particular recognition to the forms of social organisation and the necessity of their maintenance. Along with a naïve functionalism, which takes society as having a number of interrelated institutional purposes (technological, political, legal and educational) there is a more sophisticated sociological functionalism, in which societies are seen as employing certain structural forms to meet a variety of different needs, and then needing to maintain those forms by secondary activity.

One might ask whether this additional dimension may not be profitably applied also to Marxism. There is always a fundamental difficulty about the distinction between base and superstructure, in that it seems to suggest relations unaffected by ideas on the one hand, and ideas disembodied from social relations on the other. This is a point apart from the fact that the primary social relations are concerned with production. May it not be that the notion of the Marxian base is illuminated if we recognise that it is (a) concerned with production, and (b) implies certain basic formal patterns of social relations which have to be sustained at a superstructural level?

One further point to be made about Radcliffe-Brown's work, however, is that, when he referred to structure, he referred to it in a very specific sense. He did not mean some highly abstract mathematical form, but the living network of social relations between men. In other words, the whole concept was used in a way which was compatible with the action frame of reference, which sees social relations as arising when one actor takes account of the behaviour of others and allows his own action to be affected by this fact. Radcliffe-Brown may thus be claimed for sociological humanism, as compared with Lévi-Strauss who is professedly anti-humanist and Louis Althusser, who is covertly so (through his specific rejection of Radcliffe-Brown's concept of structure). More important than the question of evaluative labels, however, is the fact that, by being humanist in this sense, Radcliffe-Brown introduces a potentially dynamic element into his concept of structure. By virtue of the fact that he is both a structuralist and a humanist, he states a view very close to our own. It is a pity that he should have tied this to a consensualist theory, particularly in its simplest organic form.

We cannot here go into all the complexities of the theories of Talcott Parsons, but we should note that something of what we have said of Radcliffe-Brown is true of him too. He is certainly a functionalist, as we have seen in his discussion of a completely institutionalised social relation. But what he sees as being institutionalised are a number of different basic social forms, and the functional problems of social systems such as role-allocation and socialisation or, later, goal attainment, adaptation, integration and pattern-maintenance and tension-management are concerned with the maintenance of these forms. Consensus, therefore, is not about the detail of social action, but about the framework within which men may act. Unfortunately, Parsons gives little attention to the forms of social conflict and his concept of human action is somewhat circumscribed and dehumanised by the fact that it is seen as simply the causal product of patterns of value-orientation which have become institutionalised as need-dispositions. Were it not for the way in which Parsonian structural-functionalism was pinned down at the base, it would in fact have some features which go far towards meeting our critique of functionalism.

Merton's famous essay (1957a), on manifest and latent functions, in rejecting the consensual basis of functionalism, goes far towards meeting some of our objections to the theories of Malinowski and Radcliffe-Brown. It certainly recognises the possibility of dysfunction. But it is odd that Merton insists on maintaining an obscure language which refers to needs of the system, rather than talking in terms of the action frame of reference. In fact, he actually sees the difficulty when he writes (p. 52):

Embedded in every functional analysis is some conception, tacit or expressed, of the functional requirements of the

107

system under observation . . . this remains one of the cloudiest and empirically most debatable concepts of functional theory. As utilized by sociologists, the concept of functional requirements tends to be tautological or *ex post facto;* it tends to be confined to the conditions of 'survival' of a given system; it tends, as in the work of Malinowski, to include biological as well as social 'needs'.

On the other hand, Merton rejects Myrdal's attempt to formulate the problem in terms of the action frame of reference, with a series of pungent footnotes to terms which he italicises. Thus Myrdal is quoted as saying (p. 37):

if a thing has a function it is good or at least essential.* The term 'function' can have meaning *only* in terms of an assumed purpose;** if that purpose is left undefined or implied to be 'the interest of society' which is not further defined*** a considerable leeway for arbitrariness in practical implication is allowed, but the main direction is given: *a description of social institutions in terms of their functions must lead to a conservative teleology.*

The italics and asterisks here are Merton's. The asterisks are footnoted as follows. The first reference is seen as unnecessarily accepting the notion of indispensability rather than substitutibility of alternative social arrangements. The second asterisked passage is simply dismissed as false, while the third is seen as supporting Merton's own rejection of the postulate of functional unity.

For our part, we would agree with Merton's notion of substitutibility. In fact we have continually made the point that forms as distinct from ends are a separate empirical topic of sociological study. On the second point, we disagree with him in rejecting, not, as he thinks, the reduction of function to intention, and sociological to individual explanation, but the action frame of reference as such. On the third point we note Merton's claimed rejection of the postulate of functional unity and therefore of the implication that functionalism necessarily implies a conservative teleology, but find this difficult to reconcile with his acceptance of the notion of the needs of the system. Myrdal's approach to the problem of functionalism, despite its looseness of formulation, in fact comes nearer to our own than Merton's, although we believe that if Merton would abandon the vestiges of language derived from the organic metaphor, his position would be near to our own.

In approaching Marxist versions of systems theory, it is useful to take as a base-line a type of conflict theory which seeks to revise Marx *inter alia*, by rejecting all hints of functionalist analysis. This is the theory of Dahrendorf (1959). Against the background of his work one can note the significance of anti-humanist forms of Marxism, like that of Louis Althusser, which are anti-humanist because they accept so much of systems theory.

Dahrendorf starts by placing conflict at the centre of things, but he immediately takes issue with Marxism because Marxism concentrates solely on conflict in industry and in the labour market. In Dahrendorf's view, the case of the labour market is only a special case of a larger category of situations in which there is power and authority exercised by one group or one individual over other groups or other individuals. Similar situations are to be found in publicly-owned industries, in fully socialist societies, and in non-economic institutions.

We need not dispute too much about Dahrendorf's point that conflicts are about power rather than simply about wages or employment, for on an abstract level it *is* true that in the labour market there is at least a potential power struggle, and industrial domination is indeed something which rests on power, especially economic or market power. Marx himself made this point by insisting that, at the moment at which the worker fully understands his situation, his struggle becomes a political struggle. We would only disagree with Dahrendorf in so far as what he is maintaining is that conflicts in industry are solely about the boss's right to give orders. This is a weak and trivial thesis, and indeed it could be argued that in this case the capacity to give orders is a matter of bargaining and that this means that power and authority relations are only a part of a large category of bargaining situations.

What is more important, however, is Dahrendorf's claim that there are a number of institutional hierarchies, and that each of them has its own theoretically independent power structure and, therefore, potentiality for conflict. This leads him on to the claim that whether or not the separate conflicts overlap and intermesh to produce a revolutionary structure is a question for empirical investigation or, virtually speaking, a matter of accident. It is difficult to believe that Dahrendorf can really mean this because it involves, not merely a rejection of Marxism and functionalism, but of all studies of the relationships between one institution and another, which writers like Weber have so patiently undertaken. The connection between institutions appears as neither causal nor meaningful, but accidental. Obviously, if Dahrendorf's theory is to be taken seriously, the element of polemical overstatement in it must be removed. What can be said is that, despite the fact that conflict in core institutions has a tendency to spread to other institutions, this spread is by no means automatic because those other institutions have a life and traditions of their own.

Finally, we turn to Marxism, understood as systems theory. This is a crude doctrine which became part of the canon of dialectical materialism as it was finally approved by Engels. It combines most of the defects of orthodox functionalism with a mischievous tendency to suggest that there can be a *material* base to society, which consists of *social* relations apparently devoid of ideal elements, and sets of ideas which float about, divorced from any institutional context. The main virtue of the theory lies solely in its claim that within an institutional complex there is a leading institution.

In its pure form the materialist conception of history, understood as sociological theory, should hold, as we have pointed out, that there are inherent tendencies to conflict in the institutional base of a society, and that conflicts originating in that base spread to all other areas. In so far as the structure of these other institutions stands in the way of this spread, changes will eventually be forced upon them. Inevitably, however, given the stubborn refusal of social systems to change in this way, alternative theories have been developed.

According to Louis Althusser, the goal of theory* is to understand socio-economic formations, and these are to be understood as a set of interrelated practices. It is not clear, however, what the structure of these practices is, and there is considerable uncertainty as to how and where change within them arises, and how it spreads. Instead of a careful analysis of the elements of a 'practice' akin to Malinowski's account of the elements of an institution, what one really has is a curious metaphysical or metaphorical notion that each practice may be thought of as a system of production. The notion has much in common with other sorts of systems theory, in which there are a series of black boxes which have inputs and outputs (Althusser, 1969, p. 166).

Compared with classical Marxism, the Marxism of Althusser, however, seeks to accord a degree of independence to the superstructure. As in Dahrendorf's theory, so here, the other practices operate independently and produce their own contradictions and conflicts. Conflict in the base, moreover, is not of itself sufficient to cause conflict and contradiction in the other practices. Neither does it produce change by itself alone. What is necessary to bring about change is a situation of 'over-determination', i.e. one in which, when many different types of institutional conflict occur simultaneously, the system as a whole breaks down and change occurs,

---

* It is unclear as to whether Althusser would wish us to say 'sociology', but it should be noted that many of his young disciples see his work either as sociology or a substitute for it.

110

particularly in the economic base, which determines the system in the last instance (ibid., p. 59).

For the outsider to institutionalised Marxist thought, this is a strangely eclectic doctrine, even as stated, and when one adds that it also seeks to establish dialogue with the structuralism of Lévi-Strauss, it seems set upon building into itself all the intellectual contradictions currently available. But such doctrines survive because they mean all things to all men, and help to rationalise a political situation in which revolutionary doctrine has to be combined with political quietism. If one were willing to compare the transient, if not the ridiculous, to the sublime, one might say that one was reminded of St Thomas Aquinas's political theory.

If we were to try to rewrite Althusser, we would have to begin by demystifying its obscure systems language. We would reinterpret the notion of the basic economic practice in terms of the social relations of production, and these we would see as based upon 'sensuous human activity'. We would then seek the 'secret of the heavenly family' in the 'earthly family', by exploring the ways in which the contradictions surrounding the business of production spread to other institutions and the way in which those on the same side of the conflict, in different institutional spheres, came to recognise each other and to act together as a class. We should also note the extent to which this tendency to class formation was inhibited because other cultural and social elements already existed which prevented the establishment of class linkages, and we should see as the most hopeful situation, from the point of view of the revolution, that case in which these obstacles did not exist, but where one conflict meshed with another. Unfortunately, this rewrite is not available to Althusser, who believes that, after the radical epistemological break of 1845, Marx, and hence Marxism, could no longer speak of human action, let alone social relations and classes, and could therefore only compare itself to a scientistic analysis of systems, their properties and dynamics. Since this kind of theory is not particularly understandable as is one stated in the action frame of reference, it is difficult to check on its abstract assertions, and the way is opened for almost any kind of dogmatic assertion.

We should now conclude this account of theories of system, structure and conflict, by summing up our own approach. It can be stated in terms of the following propositions.

(1) From the action point of view it follows that institutionalised actions may be understood as being in some degree interconnected in means-ends terms.

(2) In particular societies, particular institutions may play a leading role, so that the system as a whole moves in accordance with movement in these leading institutions. In advanced societies, since

111

the emancipation of economic activity from political and religious restraints, there can be little doubt that the leading institutions have been economic ones, but one need not commit oneself to the view that economic institutions play this leading role at all times and places.

(3) The degree of interconnectedness of institutional chains might vary in different societies and, even though they are under pressure to follow the leading institutions, 'following' ones might show some life of their own. On the other hand, the doctrine that there is no interconnection which can be assumed is as untenable as the notion that it is complete.

(4) When leading institutions are marked by conflict, what spreads from one institution to another is a tendency to conflict. The degree to which those who are on the same side of the overall conflict act together (and the degree to which it is possible to decide which *is* the same side) represents the degree to which one may speak of classes.

(5) In a class-conflict situation, where conflicts in one institution mesh with those of another, the most powerful class may seek to impose its culture and its social institutions on the other class, but meet with only limited success, the other class succeeding in counter-proposing a counter culture of its own, whether of a defensive or a hegemony-seeking kind.

(6) The forms of social action constitute an independently varying element from the institutional system understood as consisting of normative rules relating to the attainment of basic goals, but sometimes the goals, particularly of secondary institutions, might be precisely the creation or maintenance of social forms, rather than some goal which was an end in itself. In some forms of functionalism it is precisely the indirect goals concerned with the maintenance of social forms which are put at the centre of things.

(7) Sociology is bound to proceed on a formal level of analysis, as both Simmel and Weber saw, and this it must do for at least three reasons: (a) because history does repeat itself in the social forms, (b) because some of the major social functions are concerned with the maintenance of forms as well as serving other ends, and (c) because much of the sense of oppression and alienation which men experience derives, not solely from the ends to which social activity is directed, but the forms under which it is carried out.

(8) The kind of sociology espoused by Max Weber corrects the balance of sociological concern in the direction of the study of social forms, and away from any sort of global functionalism and systems theory. It also often illuminates detailed problems which are posed by such a functionalist approach. But, with this said, it is always important to explore chains of institutional interconnection.

112

(9) For many practical purposes, what sociologists do is to study the social forms within particular institutional contexts, or, to put it the other way round, to study social institutions in terms of their formal structures, which may prove not to be unrelated to the question of function.

(10) It needs to be stressed that neither sociological formalism nor functionalism of the sort we have outlined here imply a static approach. Both make possible the study of conflict, and the study of conflict is bound to mean the study of change if it is not subordinated to a concern with the problem of order as in Parsons.

It is to be hoped that this sets out our sociological assumptions on the methodological level with reasonable clarity. It may be remembered that the discussion which produced them followed an earlier discussion, from which we concluded that, although the epistemological difficulties facing the sociologist were not inconsiderable, they were still surmountable, and that there was no need for sociology to spend its whole time concerning itself with the trivia of data collection and, indeed, making that process the whole object of the sociological exercise. We are now, therefore, in a position to mount an intellectual attack on some of the most important structural problems which face men in living in the first, second and third worlds today. The way in which we conduct this analysis may serve to illustrate the ten principles just outlined.

part three

First, second and third worlds

8 The Western capitalist complex: corporations and classes

The central structural and institutional fact of the 'first' world whatever may be said about post-capitalist society and the welfare state, is still the fact that most productive functions are undertaken by capitalist enterprises, seeking profit through market opportunities, and mobilising capital, raw materials, machinery and labour to achieve this end as efficiently as possible. Such enterprises thus bring into being organisations in which large numbers of participants work under direction, and the organisation can thus, to some extent, be treated as a collective actor. The market in which such enterprises operate is no longer a free market, since conditions of oligopoly or monopoly often prevail amongst producers, and because the political authorities may take action, while not eliminating market behaviour, to prevent economic crises which might endanger long-term profitability, or to impose limited social goals on all market participants. The state also acts, through its own bureaucratic agencies, either to set up enterprises to carry out essential services on a profit-seeking, though often subsidised basis, or to provide services through its own bureaucratic machinery, using criteria of need rather than profit.

Political authority, that is to say the right to legislate about what actions are permitted and punishable, and the right to direct bureaucratic government agencies, is normally attained as the result of popular election, and political parties are the organisations of individuals which compete for control of this authority. In theory, of course, the democratic electoral process is one in which any individual can seek parliamentary office, but in fact the winning of large numbers of votes has become a sufficiently highly organised and expensive matter to prevent any but large organisations from selecting and running candidates. It is assumed, in our speaking of the right to direct government bureaucracies, that these are stable bureaucratic hierarchies responsive to a political will and not to private interests or to corruption. Looking at Western capitalist societies as a whole this is clearly a variable element.

Such a system assumes that those who have power or authority are capable of having their commands carried out, both in industrial and in government organisations. This, however, is not necessarily the case, because there are a number of variable factors involved in trying to motivate men to work for such organisations, not least of which is the factor of collective bargaining in industry. This raises the question of class conflict. To some extent there may be a ruling class in industry and/or in the larger society, which collectively possesses sufficient power and influence to ensure that its will is carried out and, on the other hand, those who combine to sell their labour may act collectively to resist the ruling class and perhaps to overthrow their rule. Obviously, in so far as there are classes and other collectivities of this kind, they will compete to control legitimate political power, but they may also deploy sanctions against one another directly, in an extra-legal fashion, to secure compliance.

Classes in this sense sometimes overlap with, and are confused with, other entities commonly called classes, but perhaps more properly called strata. These strata, unlike the classes we have mentioned above, do not enter into relations of conflict with one another, but rather form a graded prestige hierarchy. Class consciousness, in the sense of consciousness of a conflict of interests, becomes blurred, in so far as it is merged with the phenomena of status hierarchy. This process of blurring of class feeling, however, is further blunted by a kind of social contract which guarantees private ownership and profit on the one hand, and planning for full employment, and the right to collective bargaining and welfare benefits on the other. In so far as this state of affairs is achieved it might lead to a dissociation of political parties from true class groups, what is sometimes called 'the end of ideology', or it might lead to a more sophisticated kind of class-based political situation, in which parties compete for 'shares of the cake'.

This gives us an outline of one part, albeit the major part, of the structural and institutional set-up of capitalist societies. The other part, which concerns the family, community, education, and mass communications, will be dealt with in the next chapter. So far as the first part is concerned, it is obviously a studiedly naïve account, which seeks not to pre-empt the solution of problems which are at issue, and which, roughly speaking, would do for an explanation of our social system to a Trobriand sociologist, whose own world centred around such questions as yam-growing, the mother's brother, and the kula exchange. Obviously it leaves a great many problem areas to discuss.

Before we do go on to the discussion of these problems, however, it should be noted that these broad ideal types are precisely what the extreme forms of phenomenological sociology would disallow. If one confines oneself to researching into the actual meaning of a situation, for a concrete historical actor, any kind of general statement of this kind would be impossible. It is only possible if one assumes that one can make a construct which can validly explain action in a large number of cases, or act as a yardstick against which actual cases might be measured. It may also be added that empiricists might claim that we had not established our generalisations, and experimentally-oriented sociologists show that we had not proved the alleged interconnection of the complex elements in our ideal types. To this, we would reply that we do envisage that such proof could be made, and in principle should be made, but that if we want to prove something it is necessary to do a great deal of spelling out of what has to be proved before empirical work can begin. Once such spelling out has been accomplished, it should be possible to confront our ideal types with all manner of data derived from comparative studies of structure, quantitative data, and actors' theories. What we lack most of all in sociology, however, is an overall structural view, and this especially in the case of our own world, because we take it too much for granted, or study its bits and pieces in such a specialist way that we never see the wood for the trees.

On the more theoretical level, it may be interesting to note, before we go into more detail, that the ideal typical description which we have just given, reflects the balance of structural and functional approaches which we have outlined in the previous two chapters. It should serve better than the ten points made in the immediately previous chapter, to indicate the kind of balance which we mean. But now, with a certain amount of joy at having shaken off the shackles of epistemological doubt and trivialisation, let us go on to talk about important topics and, first among these, about that which we have entitled 'The Western capitalist complex: corporations and classes'. Here at last we may hope to demonstrate what it means to take a cool, sociological and 'morally nihilistic' view of questions usually treated only in an ideological way.

The first structural point to notice about this kind of society is that the capitalist enterprise oriented to making a profit in the market is the main organisational form which is relied upon for the provision of goods and services. Such enterprises, however, need not necessarily provide for all human needs, nor need they provide for their own maintenance and renewal. The result of this is that they are usually supplemented by state-sponsored enterprises which may, in theory, be subject to the test of profitability, but which, in the last analysis, will be run on a subsidised basis because they are needed.

119

Moreover, since profit-seeking industry is irresponsible, it makes no provision for such basic maintenance services as roads and railways, education, or health. The provision of these services is made directly by the state.

The irresponsibility of the provision of human needs, through the profit-seeking capitalist corporation, is in theory overcome by the fact of competition. If services are not being provided, at least within wide limits, new opportunities for profit should occur and new enterprises arise. On the other hand, an enterprise which produces a useless product should not be able to survive. This, however, is only partly true. In the first place, left to its own devices, an economy of independent entrepreneurs runs into crisis, so that, in accordance with the criteria of formal rationality or rational calculability, substantive rationality has to be sacrificed. In extreme cases, the means of production have had to be partially destroyed in order to prevent overproduction at a time when human needs went unsatisfied. As a consequence of this, the normal mode of operation of a capitalist system is that even those who believe in free enterprise are forced to demand some kind of government intervention to keep the economy out of crisis. At best, capitalists find it necessary to run 'free enterprise' within a managed economy. There does, however, remain a conflict between individual short-term interest in immediate individual profits, and the continued profitability of all efficient enterprises, and also a number of different kinds of planning or intervention, each of which favours a different interest. Thus managed, free enterprise produces politicians arguing for special interests, and also a permanent political vacancy, waiting to be filled by the demagogue who is prepared to use evidence of governmental ineffectiveness in the business of economic management to argue for a return to a free-for-all.

A more fundamental revolution of the private enterprise system, however, occurs with the improvement which occurs in the means of persuasion. The theory of private enterprise requires that individual consumers should make rational choices to maximise their own utility. What advertising has demonstrated, however, is the ultimate meaninglessness of the notion of utility. 'We don't sell women shoes', says one advertiser, 'we sell them lovely feet' (see Packard, 1957). With sufficient skill in inducing, not what Parsons called 'collectivity integrative' need-dispositions, but rather profit-producing dispositions, capitalist firms may control the needs of their buyers and not be subject to the vagaries of supply and demand at all. They decide what needs are. Moreover, as Galbraith (1962) has pointed out, since the whole process of advertising being used to ensure the continuance of a product depends upon manipulable *individual* consumers, those things which are socially consumed lag behind, so that what we have is a society with the private capitalist producer in command, the individual consumer forever straining after a higher standard of living, according to values set for him by advertising, and a relative decline in the standards of public services which do not yield a profit. At this point, capitalist power can only be limited, either by the control, or even abolition, of advertising, or by governments themselves engaging in it.

One should, of course, note that what we are saying refers to the more substantial firms, and that it it is not incompatible with the existence of a large measure of competition continuing between small firms in the interstices of the system. From the point of view of the large firms, this archaic survival of the small is a positive advantage. Their existence is a living proof of the existence of private enterprise and the legitimation of the system as a whole. On the other hand, the small businessman may find his sphere of operation restricted by the large capitalist undertakings, and start to act politically, not merely against government, but against what he sees as the evils of monopoly.

A capitalist system, however, depends not only on the market mechanism. It also depends upon the existence of corporations of a rationally-bureaucratic kind. The real importance of the corporation is not necessarily efficiency, understood in the abstract. It is that it ensures that the will of one man is carried out by many agents. But how is this achieved? If the entrepreneur has to mobilise his resources by a series of market transactions, how can he be sure that all his resources are fully at his command? Even if the market could be said to ensure an overall efficient deployment of resources, it might still be the case that no adequate chain of command existed.

The first problem here relates to the command of capital. The mobilisation of large amounts of capital means that, in principle, a single decision as to the manner of its use will be impossible. The factional politics of the boardroom, however, eventually ensure that the mass of the investors are rendered quiescent through the guarantee of regular income, while the ultimate outcome of factional struggles is domination by a few large shareholders, or their representatives. Of course, it is also true that if this process is followed through to its logical conclusions, the controllers may not be shareholders at all. Hence the question of the managerial revolution remains an issue (see Florence, 1961a, 1961b; Nichols, 1969). The important question, however, is how far shareholders can be held quiescent. In principle, it would seem that the use of boardroom positions and boardroom knowledge, by the directors, to enrich themselves rather than the shareholders, is likely to be resented, but even this may be accepted if the shareholders are convinced that their income will be regular and perhaps also high. Even if they

121

should become restive, however, their internal political power is in the company meeting, and this is astonishingly easy to manipulate. It is strange that the notion of the iron law of oligarchy is discussed so much in relation to governmental bureaucracies and trades union organisations. The sphere of its operation, *par excellence*, is the company boardroom.

Supplies of machinery and raw materials represent another area of potential irrationality, from the point of view of the corporation. Here, to some extent, there may be reliance on the market principle. But, as always, rational calculability in the market may not be enough. Actual control of the required product may be necessary. Hence firms must become integrated and, from the point of view of any individual corporation, understood as ego (why after all should he be confined to kinship theory and micro-sociology? He has a big role to play in business!), the power of decision-making amongst suppliers must be subordinated to his own. Thus, if we use the language of input-output models, our corporate capitalist ego rationalises both his inputs and the demand for his output.

The major area of difficulty for the corporation, however, and to some extent the most important sociologically, is the recruitment of labour, both at management and worker level, and, by labour, is meant human action which can be subject to the director's command. Perhaps the most important single fact in this area, however, is the effectiveness of the distinction which is drawn between management and labour.

Marxism is quite right in arguing that there is no more important sociological distinction in the modern world than that between the entrepreneur who seeks profit, and regards the labour of others as a resource, and the non-entrepreneur who must sell his labour in order to live. How then, we must ask, have managers escaped from this pathetic plight? Why do they not continually haggle over the terms of their employment, or strike for better salaries and conditions?

One thing which does not seem to be true of the industrial manager is that he behaves like Weber's bureaucrat. He has no great sense of vocation, and rarely any sort of religious motivation which leads him to rest content with labouring patiently in a corner of the Lord's vineyard without ever getting a taste of the wine. Neither has the process of social incorporation, whereby being in the firm becomes like being in a large happy family, pressed very far (Whyte, 1957). The manager enjoys the fruits of his compliance privately, and he *does* separate the affairs of home and the affairs of work, in the way which Weber has led us to expect of the good bureaucrat. The fact of the matter is that he does his job for the firm because he receives precisely those rewards which Kingsley Davis and Wilbert Moore have suggested are functional to social systems, 'things that contribute to sustenance and comfort', 'things that contribute to humour and diversion', and 'things that contribute to self-respect and ego expansion' (1964, p. 415).

Given these, why should he not be recruited to the business of using labour efficiently as a resource? Surely this is the main point about our cadre of industrial managers. Their ideology is, above all, the ideology of using other men's labour efficiently, and it is through achievements in this sphere that they attain self-esteem. This may be interpreted by some as a matter of false consciousness, but so long as they can reliably expect their rewards, that same state of consciousness will remain. One of their main problems, however, is that, at the more routine levels of decision making (not necessarily the lowest), they are wanted, above all, because, as properly programmed bureaucrats, they are a kind of machine and they can be displaced by machines. It may be noted here that when Weber described his perfect bureaucrat he may be said to have described a well programmed computer.

Finally, we turn to the so-called labour forces, that is to those men who, as Bernard Shaw suggested in his original Fabian essay (1889), have been driven to the desperate expedient of selling themselves. Are they, too, to be interpreted as bureaucrats, links in the chain of command, the final link which administers not other men but things? Clearly, for the major part of the time, they can, for, contrary to the view popularised by a capitalist-controlled press, they are not perpetually in a state of dispute. Most of the time they make the things, or do the things, which the management asks them to. They even accept, as legitimate, the orders which managers give them.

This kind of obedience, however, is regularly interrupted by negotiating processes. They have not, to any large extent, been won over to the ideology of the firm, or at least they do not see it as completely legitimate. In fact, because they are labour, bought in the labour market, they see the tie that binds them to the firm as lying, not in some kind of legitimate authority, but in what Weber called a 'constellation of material interests'.

The actual basis of the relationship between management and men, which exists when the firm is working, is a contractual one, and contracts rest upon negotiation and bargaining. As we suggested in chapter 6, the normal form of bargaining in the long-established market is collective bargaining, and that means the use of power rather than mere market sanctions to win compliance. Thus it will be a fact that, underlying the contractual relations between management and worker, which complete the chain of authority, there is a continual shifting balance of power.

The result of this fact is that trade unions do force employers to

123

pay more than they would do, simply in the interests of efficiency. It also means that there will be indulgency patterns, because part of the price which the worker exacts for selling himself is that he should win a certain amount of 'illegal' free time and perquisites, so that he can retain some sense of dignity, some sense of being his own man.

This, from the point of view of the director, is a troublesome matter, but one which, if he is wise, he will learn to accept. What is much less acceptable to him is the fact that some of his workers, not merely do not accept company ideology, but specifically accept ideologies and support organisations which aim at modifying, wrecking, overthrowing, or replacing, the whole system of capitalist entrepreneurship. From our point of view, this is not a matter for value-judgment. It is simply a fact of the social life of industry. In a capitalist industrial system which continues, some account must be taken of this fact. Workers may be offered alternatives of an apparently socialist character, such as participation in management, consultation, paternalistic provision of welfare services, or they may be encouraged to understand socialism as being a less revolutionary doctrine than they thought. On the other hand, the revolutionary shop steward will also have to make concessions in day-to-day dealings with his masters, since, if no revolution is at hand, he may be able to do no more than to preserve the negotiating strength of his union, and make the most effective bargains he can, while maintaining, in Sorel's sense of the term, the myth of the socialist revolution (1970).

We may usefully here draw attention to the difference between a sociological and a policy-oriented perspective. The latter perspective starts with open or concealed assumptions, say that inflation must be avoided, or productivity maintained. From the sociologist's point of view, these are not overriding imperatives. He simply notes that the organisation is subject to stresses of this kind and that it cannot be assumed that empirical organisations will correspond to those which are ideal from the director's point of view. He can, by no means, be expected, as a sociologist, to declare a particular industrial bargain to be desirable or necessary, just because it might promote inflation or reduce production. The industrial relations expert, on the other hand, always stands in danger of representing management interests as though they were scientific truths.

It should be added that similar considerations apply to revolutionary analysis. They are concerned to show what must be if the revolution is to occur. At this point, the sociologist must again direct attention to the possible and actual types of structures available or existing, rather than indulging in wishful thinking, or doing 'policy-oriented' research on behalf of the industrial and political left.

In broad outlines then, this is what large scale rational-capitalist

124

organisations are like. It need hardly be said that they never exist in the pure form which capitalists themselves suppose. The point is, however, that this pure form is not simply an analytic ideal type. It is an ideal which some men seek to realise in the face of contradictory principles.

Formal organisations, however, are not confined to private capitalist industry. Most capitalist societies know a range of other types, ranging from state corporations approximating to capitalist industry in that they are under some compulsion to make a profit, through bureaucratic organisations providing some form of welfare as their end product, to central and local government agencies. We may set aside the first of these, because to all intents and purposes, they function like capitalist enterprises, and are required to do so, the state acting as entrepreneur only because of the failure of private individuals to perform the necessary function.

The second type of organisation, that of the welfare department, is, in principle, organised on a different basis from that of the capitalist enterprise. Its aim is not profit, but welfare. Its rationality is substantive rather than formal, or perhaps one should say, technically rather than economically rational. The working of this principle, however, is subject to a number of important limitations. First, since the enterprise is financed out of the public purse, whether through taxation or insurance, it is subject to a scale of economic priorities, and new branches of economics are developed in order to submit the performance of these departments to tests of economic rationality. Second, however, there are those in the community who are capable of providing a private market for matters like medicine, education, and insurance, and who seek to set up a private sector in the welfare sphere, and resist as best they can making any contribution to the financing of public services. This creates a situation in which the services concerned are run at a minimum level on proof of lack of means, and carry a stigma, if not an actual punitive element. Thus the client of the public services is subject to the pressures of economic rationality, by being made aware that he is wasting public money. On the other hand, the extent to which the private sector is really private may vary. In fact, because the cost of the infrastructure of these services is high, it tends to be parasitic on the public sector, enjoying the benefits, but not sharing in the stigma. (The classic example is provided by the doctor who treats his private patient in a public hospital bed.) Third, and finally, there is the pressure on the public service, of professionalism. In principle, the professions would claim that their aims are to provide services according to high technical and ethical standards, and not to subordinate themselves to profit-making organisations. But, since this means maintaining their independence of all organisations, they are

E*

125

therefore in a strong position to sell their services at a high price to the state bureaucracy. Very often this is done in the name of professional independence and high standards, but these very claims may be simply rationalisations of economic motivations. Generally speaking, the more established professions talk more about standards at the same time as getting more money.

What we are saying here, then, is that there is a conflict between economic rationality, technical rationality, and normatively-oriented conduct. In a society in which the private enterprise, profit-seeking, economically rational principle is dominant, however, the public services represent rather feeble growths. They lack the political backing to maintain their own logic and to push it into other spheres. Clearly, the maintenance of their principles in their pure form would mean an end to commercially provided services, the use of non-economic criteria to establish the success or otherwise of the organisation, and the subjection of 'pseudo-professionalism' to the goals to which, in theory, both the organisations and the professions subscribe. It might also be possible for these services to seek to control their own supplies (e.g. by hospitals manufacturing their own drugs and equipment) and creating demand for their services by publicising and advertising them (i.e. through positive health and education campaigns), thus spreading their control in the way in which commercial enterprises do. Finally, it might be possible to extend the principle of their working so that, for instance, nationalised industries were seen as public services.

The theory of government bureaucracy in a parliamentary democracy is very simple. Through a special programme of recruitment and education, a cadre of bureaucrats is established, who seek careers in a bureaucratic hierarchy and, through each fulfilling his appointed task, make it possible for goals which are fed in at the top to be reliably achieved. In particular, these bureaucracies, in so far as they do not merge with welfare bureaucracies, concern themselves with maintaining a basic institutional environment within which private individuals and organisations can go about their business. Inevitably, however, this basic institutional environment favours some and penalises others, so that the question of what precise goals are set is left to the democratic political process rather than to the bureaucrats themselves. The bureaucrat should not make policy. He should simply carry it out.

Now, whereas the manager is judged in principle by his ability to make profit, and the member of a welfare organisation to promote some kind of welfare, the test of efficiency and quality in governmental bureaucracy is its ability reliably to carry out commands through a hierarchy of office-holders. This, above all, is the kind of bureaucracy which Weber epitomised in his ideal type.

Two types of pathology may beset bureaucracy. One is that it may subvert the democratic process, either by ruling and making policy itself, or by acting as a concealed agent of class rule. This is the kind of allegation which is made about British bureaucracy, which has strong links with aristocratic elements in the population and with élite educational institutions. The other pathology is simply that of corruption. A bureaucrat does have a sphere of office. This is as vital to the system as the chain of command to which the 'sphere of office' is subordinated. Favourable decisions may therefore be bought and the corrupt bureaucrat has something to sell. The pride of the advanced capitalist societies is that their bureaucracies are uncorrupt, but this varies from time to time and place to place, and there appear to be some areas in which corruption is more readily tolerated than others. The consequences of town and country planning in basically free market conditions, for example, mean that planning decisions enhance the value of property, and these decisions can potentially command a high price. Another area in which corruption may grow is in the sale of government contracts to suppliers. This is not merely true in government service itself but, above all, in the welfare bureaucracies and in the public sector of industry. Ironically, the way in which corrupt decisions occur at the behest of private capitalist industry is by evasion of the market principle through the avoidance of public tender.

We must now turn to the question of the political process in capitalist societies, that is to say the ultimate decision-making process about the balance between private and public interest, the maintenance of basic institutions, and the organisation of welfare. In theory, any group of individuals which has a policy in a free democratic society can implement it. Thus it is possible, in such a society, to maintain basic institutions which favour private capitalism, or institutions which restrict it. It is possible to favour one interest at the expense of others. It is possible to buy out, or simply expropriate, private owners and to restrict their attempts to integrate other organisations in order to protect themselves, or, working in the opposite direction, to sell off public assets, to enlarge the private welfare sector, and to encourage security for capitalists through monopoly and integration. It is possible, in principle, to eliminate private interests from the public welfare and industrial sector, and to extend that sector further, and finally, it is possible to support entrepreneurs against their labour force, or the labour force against the entrepreneurs.

In principle, indeed, all things are possible to a government in a society which calls itself democratic as well as capitalist, but in practice, governments, parliaments and cabinets in such societies, tend to be weak and to be able to accomplish little which is contrary

127

to the interests of major capitalist entrepreneurs. In most capitalist countries since 1945 the balance has been pushed back away from the notion of government intervention, an enlarged public sector, free welfare services as of right, and freedom of collective bargaining for labour. Whereas, for a brief period in the time of post-war reconstruction, it seemed as though parties of the left might use their established positions as a base from which to go on to extend 'socialism', in fact the public mood of that time changed, or perhaps one should say was changed, so that the sort of social contract, which was said to herald a new third type of society called the welfare state, was undermined to permit greater freedom to capitalism. Populist and labour parties seemed unable to resist this tendency.

These are, of course, broad generalisations, and there are those who might argue that, far from society going in the direction we have been suggesting, private capitalism has been steadily eroded. This seems to us untrue, but at any rate, what we have done here is to suggest the kind of questions which must be asked, to see the way in which the overall balance of the social system is tending. We are trying to indicate ideal typical tendencies and to suggest possible ranges and direction of movement within the system.

Democratic theory implies that those who can win the confidence of the electorate by their speeches will be elected. In its most idealised forms it holds that confidence is to be won by rational argument. But if the media of communication have already been adapted to the needs of commercial advertising, they will employ non-rational techniques of persuasion, and they will be expensive to employ. This means that, once these techniques are employed in politics, the individual who uses them most effectively will win his election, so that very quickly all parties are involved in using these means. Moreover, the sheer cost of doing this is such that only large and wealthy organisations can compete for the public vote.

It is interesting to notice that, in recent times, it has been assumed, in elections, that the winning of an election is primarily a technical operation, rather than a submission of basic issues to the public to be decided. Thus, in an astonishing series of events, going on at the time of writing this book, a committee acting on behalf of the President of the USA has been shown to have arranged the 'bugging' of his opponents' headquarters. The details of this operation need not concern us here, but what is interesting about it is that it is assumed, by all parties, that if the opposition's campaign plans were known, it was possible for the President's supporters, by a technical operation, to use that information to defeat it.

Clearly, the democratic process, as it actually operates, is far from that kind of decision making by a community of publics, which C. Wright Mills describes as the American myth in his *The Power Élite*

(1959a). It is very open to technical manipulation. On the other hand, we should notice that this mode of choosing governments, even in its most manipulated forms, rules out others. Laski, the leading British socialist intellectual, held, in the 1930s, that if ever the Labour Party sought to nationalise a really profitable industry, men would begin to take sides for a civil war. In fact, however, this has not happened, and the military coup, or the militarisation of government in general, has occurred primarily in backward capitalist countries, like Spain and Greece, or in conditions of economic crisis, as in Hitler's Germany. On the other hand, of course, there is no known example of a capitalist country suspending democracy in favour of the dictatorship of the proletariat.

It has been difficult to write these paragraphs about government and democracy, without assuming the existence of social classes. We must, therefore, now address ourselves to the question of the existence of a capitalist class, a ruling class, and a working class. We shall do this as we have done in our discussion of the capitalist and socialist principles above, by the development of some basic ideal types, leaving open the empirical question of the actual class situation which exists. On the other hand, we should want to claim that the principle of class and class conflict in some form, is a central one in the Western capitalist complex. This is why we have entitled this chapter 'Corporations and classes'.

Going back to our chapter on the basic social forms, we should expect, in a capitalist labour market, the development of monopolistic bargaining organisations, and the spreading of these to form nationwide classes. We also saw, in our chapter 'Structures, system and conflict', that those in conflict in industry found others who fought out the same conflict in other institutional spheres, so that the class principle became a central structural principle, cross-cutting that of the institution. The implication of these ideas for the argument of our present chapter is that the principle of bureaucracy, especially in capitalist industry, is cross-cut by the principle of class conflict.

Primarily, British experience leads one to ask, of the entrepreneurial or bourgeois class, whether it is ever a class-for-itself, not simply in the special Marxist sense of that term, but in the sense of whether it ever attains independence of older class formations and strata. This may not be the case, however, in new countries like the USA, or in countries like France, in which the aristocracy was actually defeated and to all intents and purposes eliminated, as a class, in revolution.

Clearly, the capacity to impose its will and its institutions, and its moral order on the society must depend, for any class, on the command of major sources of power, especially economic power, and

129

to that extent one would expect that, in a capitalist society, this ruling class role would be exercised by the entrepreneurs of private industry and those whose alliance they can win. In the case of a pure entrepreneurial class it will be necessary, if it is to unite to pursue collective goals, that it should establish its own educational institutions in which its children, as well as others entering the class, can be educated in its way of life and ideology. Educational establishments are thus always vital to such a class.

In many societies which have come to be dominated by capitalist industry, however, an aristocratic element of the population remains in being and controls both élite forms of education and other positions of power and influence, e.g. in politics, government and the professions. Such an element may then become transformed in its own nature through participating itself in shareholding and entrepreneurship in capitalist industry. At the same time as this is going on, the bourgeois, or entrepreneurial, class might gain admission for its children to élite educational establishments and to other exclusive social centres, so welding together, not merely a capitalist class, but a ruling class which is successful in claiming a high degree of legitimacy.

Whether a simple bourgeoisie, or a bourgeoisie allied with a traditional aristocracy, however, in a capitalist state there will be a ruling class and that class is likely to control at least one political party as well as exercising considerable influence within others. Because of the complexity of the relations between old and new, however, even the class's own party will be marked by sub-class tensions and, given that there are a number of choices open as to how the basic institutions of the society are to be run, some of them more 'socialist' than others, it will also be possible for members of the ruling class, or those indoctrinated in their establishments, to penetrate the radical, labour, left-wing, and socialist parties. In those cases, where a ruling class party is not easily distinguished, it may be either because the ruling class controls all the parties, or because factors like religion and regionalism and education create divisions within the ruling class. None the less, given the unequal distribution of power and influence in the society, there will always be some expression, in political party terms, of a ruling class and a capitalist class influence.

On the other hand, the structure of the society is bound also to be influenced by the role of organised labour. In discussing the sociological nature of capitalist corporations, we emphasised that labour was organised into the system through contracts negotiated in collective bargaining. We also saw, however, that workers' organisations laid a basis for political action, either through the formation of political parties concerned to ensure that the basic institutions of the society were pushed in a left direction, emphasising planning for full-employment, the extension of welfare, and freedom of collective bargaining, or, alternatively, through parliamentary or extra-parliamentary organisations attempting to actually change the total system of ownership in the society. There is, however, no known case in which the latter strategy has been successful, and what tends to happen is that the actual class behaviour of the working class is a resultant of conflicting pressures, based on the one hand on the strategy of moderate parliamentary pressure and reformism, and on the other, on disruptive activity not limited in its means or ends by a desire to preserve the overall economic system.

In certain circumstances, particularly in countries with expanding frontiers, or with opportunities for settler colonialism, trade unionism and resultant working-class politics may not be much in evidence. Opportunities will appear to exist for all in an open society. And even where there is trade unionism of a significant kind, a large part of the population, which certainly does not belong to the entrepreneurial class, will see the social order more in terms of an open-class system or a three-class status model, rather than a two-class power model (Bott, 1957). None the less, a basic trade union element affects the political structure of most of the advanced capitalist societies, and though it may not produce revolutionary or hegemonic parties, it will, none the less, maintain a strong corporate existence, which will at least be capable of effective defensive action. In any capitalist industrial society, one of the most sensitive areas of politics will be the law relating to collective bargaining. In times of capitalist ruling class ascendancy, attempts will be made to abolish this right, but the cost may prove too high if defensive working-class action is provoked. It is probably only in cases of extreme economic crisis that the full consequences of suspending collective bargaining will be faced. In this case, some sort of authoritarian political rule, as well as an authoritarian industrial system, will be necessary. In such cases, the organisation of the working class on a military basis, inside or outside industry, might occur in extreme cases.

The question of the working class as a factor in the life of a capitalist society is a more far-reaching one, however, than can be shown merely in a discussion of industry and politics. The bourgeoisie and their allies became a class through their capacity to think in terms of free economic enterprise for themselves, and through élite education. The working class consists of people for whom all other life problems centre around the question of getting a job. Out of this there arises a sense of social solidarity, a set of norms, and a common culture which is expressed in hundreds of regional industrially-based communities. In between these two worlds, however, there is the world which is inhabited by the petit bourgeoisie, which

131

seeks escape from the limited horizons of the working-class world through upward mobility, yet which does not see itself as in a position of power, or in a position of commanding its own market situation. Yet this class tends to lack any real social and political identity as a class, because it has no common political goals, no capacity for collective action, and no characteristic sanctions which it can employ. Thus the organised working class, based in industry, but expressing itself in working-class community, commands more of a political initiative than the petit bourgeoisie ever could. C. Wright Mills set out, in his *White Collar* (1967), to demonstrate the political impotence of the petit bourgeoisie, and no subsequent study has refuted his thesis.

What we have been seeking to do in this chapter is to look at some of the major structural elements in late capitalist society. We do accept, in some measure, the 'end of ideology' thesis, which suggests that the transformation of this system from the revolutionary left is unlikely, but we do not see it as a type of society so different in its essentials from earlier capitalist society, so that it merits a wholly new name, even a residual one like 'post-capitalist', and we would insist, that, if the society has its social contract between the classes, that contract rests upon profound conflicts and contradictions. In the next chapter, we shall consider some of the ideological mechanisms through which those conflicts and contradictions are contained. In this chapter, we have tried to do justice to the industrial and political sociology of both Marx and Weber. In the next we shall try to do equal justice to that of writers like C. Wright Mills.

9 The Western capitalist complex: the engineering of consent

We have spoken of capitalist and industrial society, and these are two of the terms which are used, both to describe our own type of society, and to point to some of its ills. Another term, however, is 'mass society', and this is so important a term in its own right, as well as indicating an aspect of capitalist society, that we find it necessary to devote a whole chapter to it. Strangely, none of the major sociologists used this term and it is not one of the types used in any of the major typologies of social systems. Even Durkheim does not use it, even though he, above all, provides the framework in terms of which our analysis will be carried out.

Before making clear our own Durkheimian perspective, it will be as well to locate it by comparing the usage of the notion of mass with other usages, because there are few areas of study in sociology in which a term is used with so many contradictory overtones. We shall show how it has been used, both to defend aristocratic and authoritarian institutions and to defend democracy, and how the usage of the term changed as the theory was exported from Europe to America.

One of the major points of origin of mass society theory is Gustave Le Bon's *The Crowd* (1909), which, though it lacks theoretical structure, is a work of some historical significance. Not merely was it, in itself, a late nineteenth-century rejection of the French Revolution and democracy, but it also came to be the main intellectual stimulus of Joseph Goebbels, Hitler's propaganda minister, who is said to have remarked that Gustave Le Bon had assigned the same central role in sociology to the crowd as that which Marx had assigned to classes, and that on this level, history had proved Marx wrong and Le Bon right.

Complementary to the theory of the crowd and the theory of the mass in Europe was the theory of élites. This notion was specifically

133

used as a critique of Marxism, and argued that democracy and the politics of the left was subject, just as much as authoritarianism and the politics of the right, to oligarchical tendencies. Pareto (1963) saw the only consequence of democracy or revolution as lying in a circulation of élites. Mosca (1939) saw a political ruling élite or class as inevitable in a democracy, and Michels (1958), in perhaps the best known study in political sociology, showed how the German Social Democratic Party had been dominated by oligarchies, despite the fact that, almost before all other parties, it claimed to be a party of the people.

The crowd, in Le Bon's work, consists of an unstructured plurality of people who, because they live in unstructured situations, behave in an infantile and regressive way. In this state they are readily subject to manipulation by demagogues. Le Bon applied this theory, not merely to the mob in the street, but to parliamentary assemblies and newspaper publics. It was easy to see how it could be applied, together with élite theory, as a double critique and condemnation of the left. The people, released from the rule of their established leaders, were seen as responsive to demagogues, who used them for their own purposes. These demagogues used democratic slogans, but as soon as the old rulers had been overthrown, they were in a position to take over and new forms of élitism and oligarchy were established.

This kind of doctrine did not have much impact amongst politicians and intellectuals of the left until the rise of fascism and the mass movements of the right. Then it appeared that, whereas in the past it had been assumed in democratic, as well as Marxist, theory, that the parties of the people would be rationally structured so that the officers of the party would be responsive to the real needs of their followers, articulate them clearly, and fight for them in politics, now one had the intrusion of the masses into politics. These masses, however, were not seen as manipulated by élites, they were seen as not allowing responsible and reasoned argument and debate by responsible and reasonable leaders. Thus one has the curious anomaly that a writer like Mannheim (1940), representing social democratic thought in his time, saw the main danger in modern society, not in the manipulation of the masses by élites, but in the capitulation of socially necessary élites to the masses.

In the USA, the first developments of mass society theory were amongst rural and urban sociologists concerned with the difference between rural and urban society, and seeing the latter as involving liberation from conservative traditional restraints and the emergence of a new transitional phase, from which a more stable social order was likely, in the long run, to emerge. This was the optimistic view of Park, and it was maintained by Herbert Blumer, even though

Blumer saw, in the transitional behaviour of the mass, much of the irrationality which Le Bon had seen in the crowd (Bramson, 1961).

Meanwhile, the refugees of the Frankfurt school had found their way to the USA, where they envisaged, not merely the breakdown of capitalism and the coming of fascism, but also the massification of society. This position, however, was challenged by American writers, on the basis, not of general sociological theory or any typology of societies, but rather on the basis of media research. According to this research, the readers of newspapers did not simply take their opinions from the papers which they read. They were far more influenced by local opinion leaders who acted as a kind of filter of what was disseminated from above. This led to the conclusion that America was basically a plural society, and that an attack on it was being made in the name of mass society theory by the left.

One of the leading defenders of American society was Edward Shils. In a significant article in the *Sewanee Review* (1957), he drew attention to the fact that the critique of mass society, which had once been a prerogative of the aristocratic right, was now almost entirely carried on by Marxists. These he listed, concluding his list with the name of the English writer Richard Hoggart who, he suggested, though not actually a Marxist, was none the less a socialist of Labour persuasion. Shils's own interpretation of mass phenomena (1956), like the movement in support of McCarthy in the USA, was that the newly mobile masses and the newly rich could not stand 'the torment of secrecy', that is to say, they would not allow élites privacy and the right to deliberate on governmental matters without interference. In this study, as in his article with Michael Young on the British coronation, Shils showed his own markedly aristocratic leanings. It was precisely the existence of symbols like the monarchy which helped to hold society together (Shils and Young, 1953).

Along with this went another important contribution by Lipset and Trow (1970), involving a study of the Typographical Union in the USA. This was intended as a refutation of Michels's notion of the inevitability of oligarchy in workers' organisations. Thus, if Shils had saved America from the charge of being massified, Lipset now defended its institutions from the charge of oligarchy. Taken together, these notions could be used to argue for the notion that the USA was a truly pluralist society, in which there were neither irresponsible élites nor unreasoning masses.

This was precisely the conclusion drawn by W. Kornhauser (1960). Kornhauser argued that, while the democratic critique of mass society had emphasised the availability of the masses for exploitation, the aristocratic critique had emphasised the accessibility of élites to pressure. If one combined the dimensions of availability and non-availability of masses with accessibility and non-accessibility of

135

élites (see Figure 2), one then saw that there were four types of society.

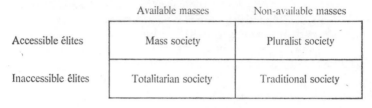

	Available masses	Non-available masses
Accessible élites	Mass society	Pluralist society
Inaccessible élites	Totalitarian society	Traditional society

FIGURE 2

There are several points of interest here. One is that Le Bon's, Mannheim's, and Shils's fear of a situation in which élites are too accessible is set on one side and the situation in which élites are accessible is positively welcomed and regarded as partially achieved in the USA. The second is that the kind of society which the left criticises as a mass society is called totalitarian, and identified with Russia. The third is that the kind of situation which is identified as a mass one, is one in which demagogues manipulate the masses against the established authorities. In line with the combination of the theories of Le Bon and Pareto and Michels, which we mentioned earlier, this society is seen as on its way to being 'totalitarian'. Thus the danger to the USA is that its masses will be released from their formal organisations and become responsive to demagogues, and the potentially dangerous elements in American society are people like students and those in isolated occupations who are outside normal structured life, whereas the family man who minds his own garden, joins a union and one of the orthodox political parties, and goes to church, is the very stuff of which the non-available masses are built.

The striking thing about Kornhauser is that, starting out with the declared intention of combining aristocratic and democratic theories, he ends up by demanding a kind of total orthodoxy as a protection of the masses against exploitation. Similarly, Smelser (1962) succeeds, starting from a different point of view, in representing every movement of social change, from Christianity to the working class movement, as arising from situations of strain, in which leaders exaggerate the extent of the difficulties which men face, and unite them behind beliefs in mass movements.

By contrast with these notions, there is another school, by no means confined to the left, which sees precisely Kornhauser's orthodoxly organised man as the unit of mass society, and those who stand outside such organisations as the upholders of structured democracy. The most important writers in this tradition in the USA are C. Wright Mills and Robert Nisbet, and in England the literary critics, Richard Hoggart and Raymond Williams. The whole of their body of ideas makes sense in terms of, even if it does not specifically draw upon, the sociology of Emile Durkheim.

Mills was the American pupil of the Frankfurt school. In his joint work with Hans Gerth (1959) he writes:

> all current work that comes to much fits into one or other
> of two basic traditions: Freud on the side of character
> structure and Marx, including the early Marx of the 1840s
> on the side of social structure.

Thus he reflects the recurring Frankfurt preoccupation with reviewing Marxism in terms of Freud, to explain irrational politics, and politicising Freud to rid his theories of their class-bound and clinic-bound limitations. For Mills, as for Adorno (1950), Marcuse (1955) or Fromm (1960), the irrationalities of politics are to be explained in terms of personality disturbance, but personality disturbance in turn is to be explained in terms of social structure.

Whether the notion of personality disturbance is a valid one is an important issue to which we should return in a moment. It is not, however, in any way important to Mills's notion of the mass society, in his *The Power Élite* (1959a). The main question there is that of the means of political control. First he describes the ideal of American democracy, which is that of a 'community of publics', who discuss issues rationally, reach a decision, send their representative on to make their views known at a higher level, and so on upwards, till eventually Congress discusses the matter and acts out the will of the people. But this is, so far as America is concerned, a matter of myth and fairy tale. America is actually a society which is approximating to the ideal of a mass society, even though it had not, in Mills's day, yet reached that point.

Crucial to the concept of the mass society is that of the way in which communication occurs between the people and their rulers. The important questions are (1) Do as many people get the opportunity to offer opinions as receive them? (2) Do those who receive opinions from above get the chance to answer back? (3) Do people have the opportunity to meet freely to discuss their own ideas? (4) Are people who meet in this democratic way spied upon, or is their private world influenced by those charged with moulding their opinion?

There were still, Mills believed, important vestiges of democracy in America, but more and more actual political decisions about such matters as peace or war, the level at which the economy should be run, and so on, were being taken by small groups of men at the top of the three main institutional hierarchies in corporate business, in government, and in the military. This small group took decisions and then, given their nearly total command of the media, 'engineered the consent' of the public to them.

Exactly how this is regarded as being done by Mills, except in the negative sense of closing the channels of opposition and imposing opinions by sheer repetition, on men who would otherwise behave rationally, is not clear in *The Power Élite*. It is, however, clear from Mills's comments elsewhere, on Parsons, that he has in mind a process of manipulative socialisation and the use of symbols. Thus, after quoting a central passage from Parsons's work, Mills goes on (1959b, p. 37):

> Now, what Parsons and other grand theorists call 'value-orientations' and 'normative structure' has mainly to do with master symbols of legitimation. This is, indeed, a useful and important subject. The relations of such symbols to the structure of institutions are among the most important problems of social science. Such symbols, however, do not form some autonomous realm within a society; their social relevance lies in their use to justify or to oppose the arrangement of power and the positions within this arrangement of the powerful. Their psychological relevance lies in the fact that they become the basis for adherence to the structure of power or for opposing it.

It would seem, from this, that Mills is offering us a manipulative model of society in which, instead of there being patterns of value-orientation, which exist because they integrate the collectivity, there is, instead, a process by which the masses are persuaded, against their own interests and perhaps against their rational wills, to accept the entitlement of the power élite to govern, and the validity of their ideas. This model should, if it is to be spelled out in detail, say something more about structure and, if not about personality, at least about the plasticity of the human person.

A different approach, which comes near to doing this, is that of Robert Nisbet, in his book *Community and Power* (1962). In this, Nisbet criticises what he calls, in a peculiar usage of the term, the 'alienation' of suburban man, not from the point of view of democracy, but from that of traditional organic community. It is the more interesting for that and helps to make Kornhauser's point that the mass society differs both from democracy and from traditional society.

Suburban man, according to Nisbet, has been forced into a totally privatised existence, based upon the isolated conjugal family. In a traditional organic community, different aspects of life were woven together and, as a result, men had 'hard property' and took significant decisions about their total lives. Now, man has a job away from home and his home is away from his job. The sole relationship between the two is the salary which, in broad outlines, determines the range of his private decision making. This is a range which is left to him after his firm has made the major decisions which affect his life.

At home there are no great decisions which need to be made. Lacking hard property means that his home is his by virtue of a number of legal and financial transactions which are made on his behalf. If he possesses other property, he does so, equally simply, in the sense of handling pieces of paper, probably on someone else's advice. There is little he can do to occupy his human and independent self, other than work in the garden, decorate the back room, or perhaps go to the parent-teachers' association.

This, then, is the alienated and privatised man, and it is he who is the stuff of the mass society. Nisbet adds little about the process by which he is manipulated and his consent engineered, for his standpoint is that of one who wishes community to be significant rather than someone who, above all, wants democracy to work. None the less, it is significant that his mass-man is the opposite of Kornhauser's and far more like Mills's. Kornhauser's man is the man who occupies himself with real community affairs, rather than with remote aims, and who lives in a world of relatively small-scale neighbourly community, which articulates with the larger society through representative institutions. Nisbet shows us what this world of community is really like. His suburban man, like Mills's mass-man, is caught in the trap of privatisation. Power, he knows, lies elsewhere, and the best that he can do is to watch its operation on the television set in his living room.

Before we explore some of these structural notions further, we can gain some further insights from the work of the two main theorists of the mass society in Britain, namely Hoggart and Williams. Hoggart (1957) makes one point which no one else, to our knowledge, has made in the whole mass society debate, namely that manipulation takes place through the use of working-class values. Williams puts the notion of mass manipulation and the middle-class notion of service together, in contrast to his own rich conception of the common culture (1960, 1961).

In an evocative and nostalgic portrait of working-class community life, in Hunslet, Leeds, Hoggart indicates what some of the key values of working-class community life are, when contrasted with those of the middle classes. Moreover, he shows that they are values which are real in the sense that they are realised in concrete institutional contexts of an intimate and domestic kind. But as the new classless mass-media emerge, they do not, and probably cannot, appeal to these values at anything like the same level of concreteness.

139

In a striking phrase, Hoggart tells us that the springs of action have been unbent. Yet, although they are unbent they are still used. It is precisely the notions of solidarity, fair play, and tolerance, which are used to justify the undermining of many other values of great cultural importance. But, of course, they are not used in their real culturally-embedded sense. The whole operation is a kind of confidence trick, though one which is performed inadvertently, for the truth is that the media-man often has no values of his own. He is solely concerned with his audience and circulation figures.

Williams's picture of the world lost is that of a small semi-rural working-class community. Perhaps not working class, though, for there is a common culture which binds man to man in terms of a set of shared meanings. But, when one looks at the nineteenth century, one sees it as a record of the destruction of these common meanings, despite the protests of writers of the right and left, whose words are drawn from a more common organic culture, and are used to protest at its violation. Finally, in a world of individualism and class rule, when the common culture no longer exists, there emerges the emaciated middle-class idea of 'service' in which men, no longer capable of really understanding and communicating with their fellow men, now have dealings with them as alien beings, whom they serve because they cannot know them. Hopefully, Williams posits, in his later book (1961), the notion that just as the workers have won legal and political and social rights, so they will, through the long revolution, regain their cultural heritage. It is an interesting utopian ideal.

Now undoubtedly, both the work of writers like Shils, Smelser and Kornhauser on the one hand, and Mills, Nisbet, Hoggart and Williams on the other, are affected by ideological considerations. Also, however, both have some value as ideal types. Our own preference is for the work of the left school, simply because we cannot accept the right-wing adulation of traditional élites and the traditional order (which is present even in the work of Kornhauser, as a point of contrast with his isolated man dissociated from ortho-dox society). But what is important is not simply our preference. It is the task of placing the theory of the mass society in a framework of social structural, cultural and social psychological theory. For guidance on this, it is necessary to return to the work of Durkheim.

The problem which Durkheim asks us to consider is that of the kind of structural framework within which human beings are to live now that extended kinship no longer provides one. Like Comte, Durkheim (1964a) believed that it must be provided by the division of labour, but the division of labour could lead to total social dislocation, and Comte had seen the state (albeit a moral state staffed by sociological preachers) as being the agency which would

140

hold the social world together. Durkheim takes Spencer's side in believing that this cannot be done without tyranny, and is therefore forced, like Spencer, to fall back on the division of labour, taken by itself as the integrating principle (ibid., p. 374).

Saying this, however, Durkheim must transform the notion of the division of labour. It is not simply an external fact. 'The image of the one who completes me' in an act of social or occupational exchange 'becomes inseparable from mine' (p. 61), so that we are bound together in a morally significant community. The division of labour, he tells us, is a moral fact. It produces, not an individualistic market place, but organic *solidarity*. This clearly includes Williams's shared world of meanings, the common culture, but it also includes a social psychological dimension. Selfhood and social order are combined and the integration of self is the product of the integration of society.

Durkheim none the less realised that this state of affairs, organic solidarity, did not prevail in his own times, and he sought to describe what he saw, first in terms of the concept of the anomic division of labour, and then more generally as anomie. The first conception is a structural and political one, drawing attention to social dislocation and the degree to which an isolated individual cut off from community is exposed to state tyranny. It is not unlike that of Mills and Nisbet. But the second conception is a more psychological one. Anomie is seen as invading the soul. The individual in his state of social isolation is disturbed on the personality level, and in some cases at least, he finds life intolerable. This line of thinking has hardly been developed by Durkheim's successors. The questions which it raises are these. 'Does the structural dislocation of modern society make man psychologically ill or disturbed?' and 'has the sickness of modern man, if such it be, anything to do with the fact of tyranny and mass manipulation?' A fully closed version of the Durkheimian model would have to posit (a) that there was a collapse of community and of social organisation on the middle level between the family and the state, which itself left man powerless to control the state, (b) that this social dislocation in some sense made men disturbed or sick on the personality level, and, (c) that in this state men were particularly open to manipulation and to the processes which Mills called 'the engineering of consent'.

Now, most of the main mass society theories seem to imply that the mass-man is a disturbed man, not exercising rational choice and having a different psychology from the rational man. But no one has proved this clinically. All too often, the implication is built into what is basically an analysis of a political structure, or it is simply an unsubstantiated value-judgment. Let us see, therefore, to what degree the fully closed Durkheimian case could be made.

Freudian social and psychological theory does not impute the cause of psychological disturbance to any organisation other than the family, and, indeed, it is assumed in most psycho-analytic writing, that provided the isolated conjugal family operates efficiently, a rational and healthy individual will be produced. Even in the work of Fromm, the most sociologically-oriented of writers of the psycho-analytic school, this is true. What Fromm tells us, in *The Fear of Freedom* (1960) is that the reason why men behave pathologically is that they lack adequate conditions of ego-growth to be able to cope with freedom and individualism. No cause of this inadequate ego-growth is suggested, except within the family. True, Fromm envisages consequences in the wider sphere of the behaviour of those who lack the necessary ego-growth to face their freedom, but he does not claim that the nature of the wider social structure makes men sick. Even in his book *The Sane Society* (1955) he may speak loosely of a sick society, but he does not suggest that social institutions of a wider sort are the cause of personality disturbance. Curiously, however, in this latter book he claims to agree with Durkheim's conception of anomie.

In fact Fromm is also odd in his use of 'alienation' as a psycho-analytic term, and appears amongst sociologists as someone who uses that term in a psychological sense (just as amongst psycho-analysts he appears to belong in the camp of sociology). But anomie, in Durkheim's sense, and alienation, in Marx's or in Nisbet's sense, do not really refer to straightforward psychological states at all. If they refer to diseases they are diseases of society as much as of the individual. What then, exactly, is the nature of this social disease?

For Durkheim, it refers to a lack of moral involvement with other individuals with whom one interacts, as well as a sense of normlessness in one's action. For Marx it is a sense of the social world as alien, as not belonging to the self. Thus the terms do have a great deal in common, despite what we have said elsewhere (1973a, p. 137) about anomie implying suffering from lack of social involvement, and alienation implying suffering through lack of freedom. It is also the case that, even though it may be impossible to diagnose individual cases of anomie and alienation as one can, say cases of paranoia or schizophrenia, these are none the less significant aspects of the relation between the individual and society.

Some similar notion seems to be implied in Mills's concept of the mass-man and Nisbet's concept of alienated suburban man. The relationships over which he has a sense of command are distinguished sharply from others over which he has none, and the existence of the latter does not merely imply political impotence, it also implies a lack of moral involvement. The privatised man is less than a man because so many of his relations are of this kind. Being too often only a victim or a spectator, his quest for community though it may often be misdirected, is a desperate attempt to regain the sense of moral significance which he has lost.

Secondary social relationships beyond the family are not merely a political means. They are things which men yearn for in a society in which they are not available. Nowadays, a minority intellectual and political movement sees marriage and the family as positively destructive of mental health (see Cooper, 1961) and calls, amongst other things, for open marriage, which is not to be conceived of simply as a continuation of the free love movement. It is at least arguable that that might be both socially and personally destructive for those who participate in it. What is important is that married adults and parents should not be cut off from other morally signifi-cant relations, that a man and woman, after marriage, and after the birth of children, should continue to participate in wide circles of group life. In so doing, they would not merely revitalise democracy, they would also revitalise themselves.

Unrevitalised, as we have said, alienated and anomic men can only enter into social relations with the larger world as victims or spectators. They have no control over the economy, and such matters as the continuation of their employment, or the price of their homes, are matters which they must leave to the government, having no more control over these facts than can be exercised at five-yearly intervals in the choice of politicians, and that choice may still leave them several removes away from actual power. They have more information about the world than ever before and indeed the world of politics and revolution flashes in on the television screen almost continually. Most children, aged ten or so, in 1973 have tucked away in their minds mental pictures of the revolutionary events in Paris and Prague in 1968. Tanks and grenades they take to be part of the normal furniture of the remoter world beyond their homes. But they are spectators only of these events. They know that they cannot affect them and, what is more, the organisation of these events into some kind of coherent picture is something which will have been done for them in the editing of the television news.

The perception of the larger world of politics on the part of ordinary powerless people is an important topic for sociological study of an empirical kind. But such study would be aided by ideal types, and to this end we suggest the following. First, there is the individual who knows that he is impotent in these matters, and sees any attempt to involve him in political activity as a threat and a potential source of danger. He withdraws from any attempt to in-volve him in political conversation and prefers to discuss neutral questions which do not threaten to introduce unpredictable con-flicts between him and others. Discussing the performance of a sports team with fellow fans is a good example of this. The more dangerous areas will crop up in conversation only when they impinge directly on the life of the local community. What one should do if a large number of members of the community are, or become, unemployed, what one should do about one's children's schooling, the price of houses – these are legitimate topics, it is true, but even they are not to be discussed in terms of general principles.

Second, there is the individual who has completely accepted, and become involved in, the trivialised world of entertainment. He lives vicariously through the performance of the football hero, the pop singer, the family entertainer. The studio audience represents him. He likes to have it there to speak, or perhaps only to applaud, on behalf of the ordinary man. Such a world has its own satisfactions, and those who purport to despise it are often surprised, if they become involved in it, how apparently satisfying it can be. Thus, the outsider who dismisses football, or some other spectator sport, as a form of escape, will find, if he participates as a spectator, that many of his fellow spectators do not regard the match as escape at all. It is only there that one really lives. It is like Durkheim's world of the corroboree (1964b), exciting, thrilling, and sacred, as compared with the dull, grey, profane world of everyday life.

Third, however, there is a significant minority in the population, who refuse to be trivialised. They read the quality papers, and in Britain they listen or watch the state-run broadcasting networks which are more serious in tone than the commercial stations. They believe that they should seriously search for the truth and get both the facts and all the alternative opinions. But in a way these, more than others, are open to manipulation. The trivialised man cannot be touched by the ideologist. He has cooled himself out of participation. But the man who wants to know can very easily be given a pre-packed account of the world. If he believes that there are two sides to every question, he can have those too, and still not be allowed to know the truth.

In short, what we are saying is that each of these types, the deliberate cynic, the fully trivialised, and the deadly serious, can be contained within the system of ideas which those who have power determine to be permissible. The only way out lies in the possession of independent knowledge of, and actual participation in, the world of politics.

The latter course, however, would bring the individual into touch with the structures of formal politics. And coming into touch with these structures could mean coming into touch with oligarchy. Once a party system is established in a society, there is little chance of independent political action. The only real choice is a choice between rival oligarchies. Strangely, whereas Michels's work was once taken to be anti-democratic, and the argument of Lipset and Trow to be one which restored faith in democracy, there are many today who would argue that it was Michels who perceived the problem, and Lipset and Trow who, by wishing it away, helped to entrench the oligarchies which existed.

Particularly difficult is action through political parties based on trade unions. There is a sense in which these are bound to be oligarchic in nature. Trade unions themselves are fighting organisations and, to be prepared to fight, they cannot afford the luxury of too much democratic debate. But, if unions become involved in politics, as they are bound to do if the basic institutional framework of collective bargaining is to be preserved, the oligarchs who are the trade unions' professional negotiators will also control the political party, Above all, they will be concerned to ensure that the party is not controlled by intellectuals. But in any case the intellectuals concerned may be careerists who have seen that in a society in which politics is labour-based, many political career opportunities lie with the party of the workers. So the great majority of those who are politically active amongst the working class find that if they do ever influence party decisions, these decisions may well be overthrown by the parliamentary élite or an oligarchy of union bosses who exercise a veto over policy. In the British case, Robert Mackenzie (1963) saw the role of Labour's parliamentary élite, but was strangely silent on the role of the union oligarchy.

What we have described in this chapter is essentially the complement of the previous chapter. There we described the structures of capitalist organisation and the inherent tensions between these and state organisations on the one hand, and between them and the class struggle on the other. In effect, what we said there was that, despite the welfare state, and despite the role of working-class organisations, the rule of a corporately well-organised capitalist class, working in terms of capitalist rationality, could be maintained, unless conditions of economic crisis of a kind not hitherto known occurred.

This kind of situation in a capitalist society, however, is greatly stabilised through the structural transformations which have produced élites on the one hand and masses on the other. We cannot see the social system of the Western capitalist complex, as Parsons does, as one in which there is an appropriate value system which, if it is internalised, makes the system work for all concerned. Rather we see it as one in which the rationalities of a ruling class are applied to the system by, on the one hand the exploitation of the impotence and irrationality of the masses, and on the other by oligarchies, who ensure that decision-making power in the society does not become dangerously diffused. This is essentially the manipulative model of the social order which Mills sought to describe.

145

To say this is not, of course, to express approval or disapproval of the system. It is merely to set out a hypothesis of how it works. For those who do disapprove of it, however, the picture is a very pessimistic one. This is a social order with an enormous capacity to resist change. It may be, of course, that technological and economic developments in the future might expose new instabilities, but so far, despite Marxist prognostications, these developments have not occurred, and the system remains strong. In the meanwhile, the one small hope of change lies in a growing number of individuals achieving sufficient sociological understanding to be able to see how oligarchy works and how ideas and beliefs are imposed on them through the media. Such a change would, of course, also have the effect of liberating individuals on the personality level from the subjective experience of alienation and anomie.

Some who read those last words will ask whether we are, by our limited perspective on change, actually helping to sustain the system, or whether what we are saying is itself so much ideology. This is a danger. But there is at least an equal danger of being utopian in Mannheim's sense* and seeing change wherever we look. What we *have* done is to try, in broad outlines, to expose a social structure as we believe it to exist. The apprehension of the nature of that social structure may, in fact, be painful compared with the optimistic account of the functions of existing structures and values for the system as outlined by Parsons. But here we are in the position which, as we suggested in our discussion of the work of Habermas, might occur in psycho-analysis, if understanding did not, of itself, lead to liberation. All we can say is that it may be its precondition.

* In our final chapter we refer to utopian perspectives in a sense different from Mannheim's. There we are seeking to show that, despite the pessimistic picture of the contemporary world which we have drawn, there are some *realistic* prospects of change. The point of what we call moral nihilism is to reject utopian thinking of the kind to which Mannheim refers and attempt to project realisable ideals.

10 The second world: central economic planning and political mobilisation

We have seen how the capitalist world, despite the prevalence of market relations, at every level, between man and man, does none the less develop its own characteristic corporate and group structures. Most notably, industry and commerce is conducted by formal corporate organisations and, cross-cutting this, there is a conflict between organised capital and organised labour as well as between classes. The one point, however, to which corporate action does not fully extend is that of the relation between corporations, and between corporations and the individuals with whom they deal. Here we still find market relations, even through the horizontal and vertical integrations of industry, and the command exercised by corporations over consumers, through advertising, means that they are somewhat limited here too. The characteristic motive force of this whole system is the profit seeking of those who exercise command over the major corporations, although the ideology which is propagated by the powerful, and which has a certain rationale, is that the market principle operates to ensure an efficient allocation of resources, both in terms of formal and economic rationality, and in terms of substantive and technical rationality.

The tensions within such a system, and the sense of suffering and lack of self-fulfilment on the part of those who take, rather than give, orders, inevitably lead to the emergence of a utopian belief that a situation is possible in which men do not suffer alienation, even though large-scale industry continues. This situation is seen as depending upon the overthrow of the power of the entrepreneurial class and the elimination of the profit motive, and their replacement by a planning agency or planning agencies directed by 'the people' and working to meet human needs rather than making profit. Such is the goal of all socialist and anarchist movements, which are an inevitable part of the structure of capitalist societies.

Separately from this, another type of structural alteration for, or development of, Western capitalism might be envisaged. This is that the logic of the corporate system of social organisation within industrial and commercial firms should be extended to the whole society. Thus, instead of the market principle being relied upon as the main means of attaining a substantively rational allocation of resources, and meeting of needs through formally rational or rationally calculating behaviour, a single bureaucratic organisation could be set up which could set for itself goals of a substantive kind and, treating the separate corporations as its own subordinate agencies, direct them all to work in accordance with a rationally conceived plan. If the market principle was used at all, it could then be used in a subordinate way and allowed to operate only in so far as it could be shown to achieve a substantively rational outcome. Under such a system there need be no guarantee that the goals set would necessarily be for the benefit of the greatest happiness of the greatest number, and there would be an open question as to how arbitrariness of action could be avoided and objective tests applied to the performance of the system and, most clearly of all, 'alienation', far from being relieved, could be increased.

The question which faces a world in which socialist revolutions have taken place is whether movements of the type mentioned in our second paragraph actually bring about situations of the type mentioned in our third. If it is argued that they do not, then it must be shown, either that organisations of the type mentioned do not necessarily come into being following the overthrow of capitalism, or that, having come into being, their operations are checked by other agencies which we have not yet discussed. In addition to this there is the question of what structural differences are likely to exist in a society in which central economic planning is established without an intervening capitalist stage, which would certainly be the case where the system was established, not by a workers' revolution, but by a largely peasant-based movement.

But, *per contra*, it may be asked whether there is not an internal dynamic in capitalist society or industrial society, such that it is in any case likely to move in this direction, regardless of whether or not a socialist or workers' revolution occurs. That is to say that, in some respects at least, the achievement of a totally planned system with a bureaucratic administration is the culmination, rather than the denial, of processes initiated by earlier capitalist societies. Max Weber was aware of this, although he was doubtful as to whether the totally planned economy was possible, because of the impossibility of the planners making the necessary calculations in so complex a system. Parsons, on the other hand, while in no sense welcoming the achievement of total economic planning, argued that Weber was wrong on this technical question (Weber, 1947, Introduction and chapter 2). On a very different level, Durkheim opposed what he called the forced division of labour because he believed that the integration of society had to be accomplished through a kind of moral complementarity between groups and individuals, which was just what bureaucratic relations prevented.

Sidney Webb is an outstanding example of many socialist intellectuals, who advocated socialism because it involved collectivism and planning. As he put it, in his early Fabian essay (1889, p. 58):

the perfect and fitting development of each individual
is not necessarily the utmost and highest cultivation of his
personality, but the filling in the best possible way of his humble
function in the great social machine. We must abandon the
self-conceit of imagining that we are independent units, and
bend our jealous minds, absorbed in their own cultivation,
to the subjection of the higher end, the Common Weal.

It should be noted here that a double dissociation of socialism from working-class utopianism has occurred. In Marx's own time, Hess and the True Socialists had argued that socialism was a doctrine which had no connection with the proletariat. They did, however, still see it as a means of freeing man from his condition of alienation. In Webb one has the final celebration of comprehensive state bureaucracy for its own sake.

Notions such as these were undoubtedly a part of those sections of the Marxist movement which ever actually captured governmental power, and they were greatly strengthened by the application of rational-bureaucratic principles to the organisation of revolutionary parties. Lenin had conceived of a tightly organised political party, based upon a high proportion of full-time members and upon committed members only. He held that the party needed members who were prepared to devote to the revolution not merely their spare evenings, but their whole lives, thus stating, in an even more extreme form, the ideal of bureaucracy, enunciated by Weber, of separating home and work-place. It was more than likely that men used to this type of organisation would have a taste for bureaucracy when they took control of the government. The only question for them was which bureaucracy should be paramount, that of the government or that of the party.

Another Marxist notion which was of some importance for the development of the bureaucratic planned economy was the notion that, where there was a backward bourgeoisie, they should be forced to carry through the revolution by proletarian leaders who would then maintain the revolution in a state of permanence through the dictatorship of the proletariat. From this it was only a short

F

step to arguing that, where there was no adequate development of capitalist organisations, industrialisation should be accomplished by the planners.

One may well ask the question, although the answer cannot be given at all decisively, whether the planned economy as a basis for industrialisation was not inevitable in industrially backward countries like Russia, China and Cuba, and that a political situation only had to be created which opened up a gap for them, for the new central agencies to be set up. Those who staffed these agencies would pay tribute to the revolutionary heroes and their ideologies, but this would be largely a means of legitimating their rule. Still more would this be the case when the new order was established, not by a peasant and proletarian revolution at all, but by an alien army.

The first problem which faces us, in understanding the sociology of the centrally planned state, is what relationship is likely to exist between the new economic bureaucracy and the state. In so far as there is truth in the Marxist contention that the state in capitalist society arises as a means for the protection of the property of the ruling class, or for that matter, in so far as our own thesis about the state as the agency which laid down the rules for the operation of capitalism was true, there would be no need for a state in the new society. And, indeed, the state as such, regarded as separate from the planning mechanism and the party does appear to play a much more shadowy role under communism than it does under capitalism. This is why the prime minister in the USSR at least, although himself a party functionary, is of relatively minor importance, compared with the secretary of the party.

This brings us to the question of the role of the party, its internal structure and its relationship to the economic bureaucracy. Quite clearly there cannot be a political party in this sort of society which is akin to the political parties of the capitalist world, for, if parties are more than collections of individuals and have a social base in organisations within the society, representing sectional interests, there are no recognised and acknowledged sectional interests in the centrally planned society. The party in such a society is therefore a social phenomenon of an entirely new kind. Indeed, we would go so far as to say that it is one of the very few major social inventions and bears comparison, in its importance as an invention, with capitalism and bureaucracy themselves. Moreover, the new type of party has a role to play in an entirely different context, that of the formerly colonial states, so that it can be regarded in the Simmel-Weber sense as one of the detachable social forms.

In theory, and undoubtedly to some extent in practice, a revolutionary party is the guardian of the interests of the class which brought it into being. It is the means whereby the goals of the planners are not left to be settled on a basis of some arbitrary whim, but must conform with some ideal such as serving the working class, the most numerous class, or the greatest happiness of the greatest number. Moreover, as we shall see, the party concerns itself, not merely with setting the goals of the economic bureaucracy but also seeing that they are carried out. Potentially, therefore, it represents a double check on economic arbitrariness, sinister interests, and incompetence.

The reason why we say that this is so in theory, rather than definitely the case, however, is that the party's capacity to perform these functions is limited by its own internal structure. This leads us to the question of democratic centralism, or centralist democracy, both in revolutionary parties which have not yet won power, and those which are victorious. It is this question which is the most central one in the communist world today, and, in so far as it can be shown that there is a good chance of democracy yielding to centralism within the party, one must admit that the notion of a built-in guarantee of socialist ideals, under communism, is hard to defend. Not merely the economic bureaucracy, but the party leadership, may be the means whereby the 'revolution is betrayed'.

As a party engaged in revolution, there are certain obvious tactical considerations to which the party must pay heed. Not being organised for the winning of parliamentary elections, and therefore not needing a mass base, it seeks to make up for its lack of numbers by an improvement in its qualitative reliability. When a policy is decided upon, it must be reliably carried out and this implies an adequate chain of command. If it does not have this, if it becomes a kind of democratic debating society, the party is not able to act decisively in either industrial or political situations. Thus there must be a goodly proportion of full-time officials, paid officials, and a totally committed membership, ideologically trained in their party duties and seeing all questions from a party point of view. Moreover, the party must be able to enhance its strength by penetrating other organisations, which it can then manipulate for its own purposes, because even a minority can control an organisation if it operates as a well-drilled faction. And the other side of the same coin is that the party must be able to protect itself from penetration by police spies and *agents provocateurs*, and must have the means of discovering them and expelling them.

A party of this kind is well equipped for political action when a suitable historical conjuncture presents itself. Usually, the only more efficiently organised body in the state is the army, but if the army cracks or becomes disloyal, the leading officers of the party have a power to act such as no one else has. They know that they can give orders and that they will be reliably carried out in many different situations. If they have a nationwide basis they are in a position to organise the nation, and no other organisation which relies upon a voluntary membership and ideological appeals can compete with them. In fact, to somewhat overstate the case, if organisation is adequate, ideology can be dispensed with, for, in the absence of other adequately prepared organisations, they can take power by default. If there is a political job to be done, people may, in difficult circumstances, turn to those who have the means to do political jobs rather than to those who have beautiful ideals and nothing else.

At the moment of revolution all the tendencies which we have mentioned are reinforced. Then it is not merely a matter of having a party line. It is a matter of having an organisation at least as strong as anyone else, and hence being in a position to meet counter-revolution. Ideally, for this purpose, the party should have its own agents in the police and the army. Before the revolution the duty of these is to undermine loyalty. As the revolution proceeds, their duty will be that of educating and winning over some of their fellows and helping to purge the rest.

Finally, the structure of the party as a permanent institution has to be determined. In its new role it grows in size and in resources, but if it is to be a reliable instrument, its internal discipline has to be maintained. Now the conflict between the bureaucratic and democratic principles becomes apparent. Democracy demands that the officers of the party should be subject to elected assemblies, but the role of the party branch as an agency of the party and its policies, demands that these party branches should be at least well informed and instructed, and this means that they should be influenced, if not controlled, by full-time officials. This leads, in fact, to a situation in which the full-time officials appointed by the party secretariat are usually elected to represent the branch as its delegates to higher levels. Finally, the party secretary confronts a democratic assembly consisting only of his appointed officials. If there is opposition at all, it may occur when some fairly major underling seeks to give his own orders to his own apparatus-within-the-apparatus. If he does, however, he is likely to be removed from his post before the next conference.

The previous paragraph is probably somewhat exaggerated as an account of the operation of the communist party in the Soviet Union today. There is pressure on the local party official by his branch and there are probably always ways in which a dissatisfied branch can play one official off against another. It is also probably true that the secretary cannot go too far in opposing his own central committee and its executive. But clearly this was not always so, and it may well be asked whether anything has changed so fundamentally that another secretary might not regain something like Stalin's status and strength.

Of course the crux of the matter here is that of what sinister interest the secretary might represent. The matter is not really simply one of the 'cult of the individual' or of personal despotism and tyranny. What matters is whether a new class emerges whose privileges are defended in the name of the substantive rationalities of party policy. This is difficult to determine. Stalin for example, declared his opposition to equality-mongering. Whether this was necessary in order to achieve an adequate policy of incentives, we cannot say for certain. But it was also consistent with giving special privileges to the new intelligentsia and technocrats.

Whatever the situation *within* the party, however, there remains the question of its relations with the economic bureaucracy, from central planning level down to the level of the local plant. In the nature of the case, a workers' party, or one which claims to be a workers' party, cannot simply take over the system and convert all its members into managers. Therefore, it is bound to be the case that there are rank and file workers who are reliable party members, and managers who are not, even though they may have technical expertise. Thus the party represents a valuable instrument which can act to ensure that the plan which implements party goals is not sabotaged by the incompetence, corruption, or self-interests of the managerial class. Though this may interfere with the technical rationality of industry, from a management point of view, it does also mean that the attainment of party goals is subject to a double check.

One possibility which may occur, however, is that the manager of a plant will succeed in corrupting the party members whose job it is to watch over him ideologically. Stalin was well aware of this danger and spoke of the danger of management and party members developing 'family relations' with each other. The terrible consequential decision was that the party member should be watched over by the secret police. This decision was terrible, not simply in itself, but because the logic of it implied an infinity of secret police corps, all keeping watch over each other. Moreover, the introduction of police into this situation meant the escalation of penal sanctions and, though there appears to have been no absolute necessity for the institution of penal sanctions of the scale and degree which Stalin introduced, it does introduce a qualitatively new element into the life of the party and of the economy.

The idea of a second check on the party need not necessarily be entrusted to the secret police. It is only necessary that there should be some disciplined body subject to the party secretariat, who will see to it that party officials do their duty. Thus, whatever else the

153

cultural revolution and its accompanying Red Guard represented in China, it represented this. It was not simply a spontaneous revolt of the young, which produced platoons of marching young men and women with their red books raised above their heads. The party to watch the party seems to have been created. In the Chinese case, this same Red Guard had the responsibility of policing the economic bureaucracy and the army, the latter role being especially important in a country where the army had itself conducted the revolution. As an alternative bureaucracy it had to be kept in check.

The next structural problem which we have to face is that of the relation between the party and other organisations in the society. Such organisations flourish in capitalist society, where some come into conflict with the purposes of capitalist corporations, some act as political lobbies influencing or shaping the policies of political parties, and some exist in quiet irrelevance to the purposes of capitalism. They also exist in the planned society, but to a much greater extent they are prevented from coming into conflict with the main purposes of the society, as represented by the party and, indeed, are assigned an important positive role from the party's point of view. It is this aspect of communist societies which gives a certain credence to their being labelled as 'totalitarian'. Since, however, this term is much abused in political ideology, we would prefer to use the term 'mobilised'. What we wish, above all, to suggest about non-political and non-economic organisations and associations in the communist world, is that they are mobilised by the party and given an essential role in the society.

The first crucial question to be faced was that of the role of the trade unions. It must be apparent that the kind of social change brought about by central economic planning in no way alters the fact that individual men work for wages and must sell their labour in order to live. Even if we allow that the state and the party and the central planning agency serve the purposes of the working class in some ultimate sense, it is still the case that the individual worker confronts a large and even 'alien' structure to which he must sell his labour. Quite naturally then, he forms organisations to defend his special interests, which can be conceived of as existing even within the context of these larger purposes.

In a post-revolutionary society, however, these organisations will at first occupy a peculiarly ambivalent position. They are, of course, particularly prestigious, in that in fact, as well as in mythology, they will be seen to have had a special role in the revolution. Yet they do represent special interests against those of the whole society, and have great potentiality for subversion. It is conceivable that in some planned societies, given that there is a sufficiently reasonable or compliant trade union leadership, a certain freedom to haggle over wages and conditions may be given. But the long-term plans of the planning agency need a fixed wages policy, and in the sphere of wages as in every other sphere, the society is based upon the formal rationality of bureaucracy. Thus the usual compromise is to look to the party as the means for bringing the unions under control. They may be allowed freedom, but the party will penetrate the leadership and see to it that that freedom is responsibly used. At the time of revolution, in all likelihood the penetration will already have happened. The point now, however, is that the party representatives in the leadership are identified with the purposes of their society and have the highest prestige in the leadership.

The incorporation of unions to win compliance by the workers on matters of wages is the more possible because trade unions also serve other functions. They are in one respect guilds of workers, and they are also friendly or welfare societies. Durkheim, had he known the communist revolution, might well have seen them as having the important moral role which he assigned to occupational associations. Naturally, then, the party will assign a positive role to the unions in these respects. One need not posit any malign intentions on the part of the party in order to say this. It simply is the case that, if there are in being organisations well equipped to undertake friendly society and welfare work, there is a positive advantage in this work being undertaken independently of the state and the party. So far as education and ideology are concerned, however, the party will see the unions as valuable agencies of adult education for 'social responsibility' and moral control and integration in Durkheim's sense. They may, indeed, be used to push a basically bureaucratic society in the direction of organic solidarity.

Our critics may point out that the process of incorporation of the trade unions is something which happens *de facto* in capitalist societies anyway, and that it is misleading to emphasise these features of their role in the communist world, for the main difference is that there, at least, they are not incorporated to serve the purposes of their class enemy. There is some truth in this, but here we would point out that the process in communist societies is far more deliberate and far more concerned with ideological control. If the politicians of the capitalist world encourage the union leaders to 'sell out' they do not, to any great extent, seek to ensure the moral and ideological support of the rank and file. In a communist society, however, this is thought to matter, and given that it is, it becomes a powerful tool in the hands of the party leadership, for good or ill, from the workers' point of view.

This discussion of trade unions in communist societies has the pre-eminence which it has, in our discussion, because the first communist revolution in Russia was one in which the unions were

155

sufficiently important to play a central role in everyone's thinking. In other circumstances, such as revolution by a peasant army, farmers' and peasants' organisations, as well as the army itself, might be looked on by the party as presenting similar opportunities and threats as those presented by the trade unions in Russia.

Once the revolution has been established, other ways may also be found of accommodating special interest groups, and at the same time using them for party purposes. One thing which at times the party has been able to do is to appeal especially to women and to youth. Women it could claim to be liberating from the family hearth in order to give them a role as independent workers, and in the case of young people, it was able to offer unprecedented opportunities for change and social mobility. While offering these things, moreover, it could use women's and youth organisations as educational and ideological agencies. These therefore became another sphere for penetration by the party, another sphere in which individual party members might find a special vocation for doing party work.

Religious organisations presented a different kind of problem. On the one hand they seem, at least from the point of view of the belief system of the party, to be 'on the way out'. The processes of secularisation, implicit in the rationalisation of the modern world by capitalism, are carried still further under communism and, given the clear formulation of ideological objectives in communist thinking, it is natural that a definite move in the direction of anti-religious propaganda should occur. But this does not necessarily mean a total suppression of the churches. For one thing, religious belief, though it may be dying, dies hard, and an outright assault on folk superstition would quite unnecessarily antagonise a very large section of the population. Second, it should be recognised that the Christian church, as well as other religious organisations, often embodies ideals of social solidarity and mutual aid, which are specifically denied under capitalism and whose maintenance the communist party finds entirely worthy. Finally, given that this is a society singularly lacking in ritual, and that there does appear to be a cultural and psychological need for ritual as such, the church can perform a role which no other organisation can afford to play.

Finally, we come to the question of formal education and intellectual freedom. The first thing to notice here is that free philosophical and sociological enquiry of the kind undertaken, for instance in this book, is not permitted. There is no need for them, the party ideologist would say, because they are, in any case, at best gropings after truth, which are clearly grasped in Marxism (or whatever official ideology the planned society might have). Thus there is no need for intellectuals who stand outside of society in a disenchanted way, and comment upon it. That appears as a decadent phenomenon in a society which has lost faith in itself. Whatever other aspect of Marxism is likely to be developed, one might notice, there is not likely to be any encouragement of that kind of reflexiveness which radical Western sociologists urge upon us.

The question of intellectual enquiry, however, is not merely one relating to organisations outside the party. It is a vital matter within the party itself. It also affects the functioning of economic bureaucracy and understanding its significance there is probably the key to the whole matter. In principle, the planners have to achieve the substantively or technically rational goals of the society by the most efficient means. Their knowledge and culture therefore should be confined to technical matters. But one central technical matter is the use of the market principle as an element in economic planning, and this is a notion fraught with ideological consequences.

One thing which could happen in a communist society is that, once the market principle has been introduced in a limited way, there will be a tendency for its role to be enlarged, and for those who exercise an entrepreneurial role to enlarge it still further. They will be encouraged by, and will encourage, others who urge a free market in intellectual ideas on a wider basis, and very quickly there will be an accelerating process which is likely to be exploited by those, inside and outside the society, interested in overthrowing the planned social system. Thus it is necessary to be vigilant on all points at once. Managers must be prevented from exercising too grand an entrepreneurial freedom, and intellectuals must be controlled and organised within the party itself.

So long as the planned economy is viable, it is unlikely that dissident managers and intellectuals will 'get away with it'. They have no solutions to offer to the problems of the economy and society better than those on offer already. And, apart from economic matters, they are usually regarded as only defending their special interests anyway. Thus the Soviet Union has had little truck with intellectual speculation, either at home or in its dependencies abroad. It has used the most severe penal and military sanctions against them, and has been remarkably successful in maintaining intellectual order. On the other hand, some communist countries have seen the danger of total intellectual restriction, on largely the same utilitarian grounds as did John Stuart Mill, and have sought to find a niche for the intellectual. The usual form is to allow intellectual freedom, even to do sociology, but also to run party intellectual agencies and journals, which keep up a continuous critical commentary of work done.

On the other point, the communist world has made advances along

F*

lines pioneered in the West. This is in its use of the media and related institutions. Control of the media of mass communication is complete and this means that there is a capacity to restrict actual information to a degree unparalleled in the capitalist world. Moreover, news is systematically slanted by propaganda, so that, both in his picture of the world, and in his fundamental belief system, the citizen of the communist country is more completely subject to the control of his rulers than are people outside. The surprising thing, however, is that the control has, on the whole, been political rather than concerned with controlling and stimulating economic wants. The latter, it might be thought, would be an important instrument in a planned economy, and a logical extension of what capitalist corporations do in the face of the threat of competition. But the main style of communist propaganda is to create a relatively simplistic picture of the world in which party leaders receive adulation while the forces of good and evil in political matters, both at home and abroad, are presented in the most simplistic, if not childish, terms.

We may now ask whether the planned industrial societies of a communist kind are, in fact, a unique phenomenon in world history, and whether they do relate in some way to the utopian hopes of the working class. Two important negative views worth considering here are those represented by the so-called convergence thesis, and that argued for by Karl Wittfogel in his *Oriental Despotism* (1957).

The convergence thesis, as it has been presented, suffers from two great limitations. First, it has usually been advanced by empiricist writers whose criteria for understanding a society are mostly derived from the consideration of quantitative data, whereas such quantitative data tells us little about actual social structures. This is a more fundamental point than that which is sometimes made, namely that ideologies are different and that differences in ideology alter the working of institutions. Second, the convergence theorists have assumed that, even if the communist countries are not moving to a capitalist industrial pattern, it certainly is not the case that convergence is towards the communist forms. Our suggestion here is that convergence is to some extent in this direction, that communism represents the logical completion of the process of bureaucratisation and rationalisation in the world, and that there is much which happens as a result of *de facto* class domination under capitalism, which happens as a matter of deliberate policy under communist party rule. None the less as we have seen, the party is, as we put it, a new social invention, and gravely disturbs the balance of bureaucratic order which would exist if planning by itself were to operate under the sole rule of economic planners, oriented to nothing but growth, or for that matter to conservation. What may happen in the future is that capitalist societies which are in crisis, which can no longer achieve growth, or are faced with an ecological crisis, may be forced to accept greater and greater measures of planning. This might none the less leave them with a total institutional set very different from that of the communist world.

One point to be considered about an evolutionary transition to economic planning is that it would involve the same personnel as existed in the capitalist system which went before. The new economic controllers would be the same men who had sat on boards of directors, while the working-class leaders, who ran the dictatorship of the proletariat, would be the self-same trade union bureaucrats who had negotiated wages and run the labour movement under capitalism. The fact of revolution and the fact of a disciplined and centrally organised party in the existing communist countries, which are more than satellites, makes that kind of perpetuation of class and élite power impossible.

Wittfogel's argument about Russia is that it was traditionally an oriental despotism, in which the features of political freedom, to be found under feudalism, did not exist. The Russian form of this oriental despotism was a variant of the most fundamental form, which was to be found in the so-called 'hydraulic societies' faced with a need for large-scale irrigation and other public works. Leaving aside the technological determinism of this argument, however, there is still a Weberian version, namely that Russia, with its servitor nobility, was characterised by a patrimonial rather than a feudal system of administration. In either case, the characteristic feature of oriental despotism, or patrimonialism, was a set of techniques designed to prevent underling administrators from getting out of line. At its most extreme, this set of techniques involved the purge, including a high incidence of homicide, or induced suicide. This was particularly true in Imperial China. Wittfogel's argument is that, in the case of both Russia and China, what one had was no workers' utopian revolutionary society, but in essence a reversion to type. The prima facie case for this argument is strong, most particularly when one reflects on the operation of the purge under Stalin. But to say that the structural forms of history repeat themselves in different contexts is not to say that the same social system as a whole has re-emerged. The fact is that there is an element of rational-bureaucracy in the Soviet Union and in China, and a commitment to substantively rational goals, which is quite lacking under oriental despotism.

Lastly, we should ask whether there are signs that the planned economies and social systems of the communist world represent the fulfilment of the utopian sociological ideals of workers' movements in capitalist countries. The answer to this is that clearly it does not.

159

They are influenced by those ideals, both in ideology and in practice, but they are also the product of the logic of individualism, and of their own internal logic. We therefore should see it as our task, as sociologists, as moral nihilists liberated from the normal naïve policy-oriented and ideological perspectives, to describe and to analyse the workings of this new structural form. In so doing, we help to expose its painful reality and help men to see wherein, in such societies, the limitations to their freedom and self-fulfilment lie.

In saying this, we do not really depart from a Marxist perspective, and one hopes that if this chapter is ever read in the communist world, it will not merely be treated as anti-communist propaganda. We believe that history does not cease under a system of economic planning and that new forms of alienation arise there. An ideologically instructed communist should accept this, for to him the present state of affairs is a transitional one only, and the overcoming of alienation is something which has to be achieved by further revolutionary transformations. Marx's occasionally expressed belief that it could only come about with the abolition of the division of labour is probably correct. It is also absolutely utopian. What we envisage is that mankind will always have to struggle against the social forms he has created and that, if the supersession of capitalism does mean liberation in many respects, new challenges now face man. They will not be responded to immediately and the responses may not be successful. Indeed, as we see it, the communist system is immensely viable, and its viability implies that for many generations men will suffer under communism as men have suffered under capitalism, and for many this will mean imprisonment and loss of freedom of thought and initiative, just as under capitalism the nature of the social system has implied oppression and economic exploitation of the workers. But men have not yet found a form of social living for which someone does not have to pay a price.

11 The third world and the institutions of colonialism

The world of the capitalist corporation, of free labour, of the class struggle, workers' revolution, the planned economy, and the welfare state, did not come into being in total isolation from the rest of the world. Most of the major European countries developed their economic systems after a period of 'primitive accumulation', in which the amassing of profits in colonial enterprises played a large part. The USA incorporated into itself a colonial world based on slave labour, and the Russian revolution was based upon its own primitive accumulation from a peasantry who stretched far beyond the bounds of Russia itself into remote parts of Asia.

The economies and related social structures which were set up in the colonial world were of an entirely different character from those in the advanced industrial societies. In some cases strong traditional social structures remained, and the 'expansion of Europe overseas' consisted, in their case, primarily of an initial act of conquest and then the drawing of feudal tribute in return for 'protection', without any radical alteration of the existing structure. More frequently, however, traditional civilisations were overthrown or destroyed and the people who were shaken out of them by the conquest became labour in new colonial economic enterprises. Moreover, the new colonial societies were rarely homogeneous because colonial and traditional rational and tribal boundaries did not coincide, and because various types of workers, traders, settlers, administrators, preachers and teachers, were brought in to live with the natives.

The ideal typical description of colonial society cannot refer, however, to a static structure, or even a range of static structures. At the centre of things, at the beginning of colonialism, there is a certain pattern of social relations of production, usually based on unfree labour, but around this core there is a series of cultural and

161

social accretions which give the society its characteristic style, or feel, or tone. Usually, within a fairly short term, colonial societies develop an ethnically plural character. This basic situation, however, changes with fluctuation in the world market for commodities, with the formal emancipation of labour, and with the attainment of formal political independence. Market fluctuation may mean more or less intensive exploitation of labour and greater, or less, dominance of the economy in determining the social structure. Labour emancipation will mean the development of a new kind of class and stratification system, depending upon the relations which develop between the newly emancipated workers and their descendants, and free immigrants and natives together with theirs. Finally, political independence will involve problems of national integration, or, to put it another way, inter-ethnic and class conflict threatening political breakup. In every case the end product, colonial society, confronts the first and second worlds from a position of economic weakness, and the terms of trade and the balance of power tend to widen rather than to close the gap between the affluent nations and the wretched of the earth.

The problems which confront individual men and women in these societies are quite different too from those which confront individual men and women in the second or third world. In the first world, men argue about economic exploitation, prices, housing, and other welfare benefits. In the second world, the pressing issues are those of political and intellectual liberty. In the third world they are ever-present poverty, disease, and violence of a kind which the first and second worlds no longer know. We shall return to all these questions under the heading of 'Public issues and private troubles'. For the moment, however, our task is to develop a more detailed typological portrait of the third world.

The European and American sociological traditions are surprisingly silent on this question. The account of social systems given, either assumes a model of social integration, albeit in terms of a system of status classes, or it is based upon the Marxian concept of class conflict. It says nothing of ethnic pluralism or the race war. Industrial sociology assumes free labour, even if, in the Marxist tradition, it chooses to emphasise that the labour is less free than it looks and is dominated by market power. Moreover, when this sociology is tinged with moral outrage and reforming zeal, it concentrates on a series of European events, such as the right wing overthrow of democracy in Spain and the Spanish civil war, or the use, by the Germans, of concentration and extermination camps to deal with other Europeans. It has little to say about, little comprehension of, little interest in, the fact of plantation slavery and its consequences, and nothing at all about the hundreds of colonial and neo-colonial

wars which have gone on in the twentieth century and which cul-
minate in the twenty-five year-long war in Vietnam.

In fact, of course, the most striking single event in world history,
in the last five hundred years, the event which would stand out before
all others to an objective observer from another planet, is the fact
that the more advanced and 'civilised' nations began, in the fifteenth
and sixteenth centuries, to explore the rest of the world. By a curious
convention, inexplicable on other than racist grounds, they say that
their seamen 'discovered' America and India at this time. Having
discovered them, they revived old Roman traditions of exploitation.
Companies of adventurer capitalists formed to finance wars, to
hold existing kingdoms in subjection and to wring feudal tribute
from them, simply to plunder and destroy others, and where there
was unused land free or cleared, to put either the natives, or men
imported like cattle from other parts of the world, to work as slaves.

Now, very little of this history can be fitted into the categories of
European sociology. Durkheim's main problem, it will be remembered, was the division of labour, understood as a moral fact, which
integrated man with man in a new way. The Marxist tradition was
concerned with the development of the bourgeois mode of production, which involved the exploitation of labour through the operation
of the labour market. Weber concentrated on questions of legitimate
authority, and particularly the case of rational-legal authority with
bureaucratic administration, within which the peculiar Western type
of capitalism could flourish. In fact, of course, in the colonial world,
the division of labour was not a moral, but a very external and imposed sort of social fact. The exploitation of labour was far more
direct than that which could be accomplished through the labour
market. It rested, in fact, upon sheer military force. Finally, neither
on the level of the political and legal framework, nor on the level
of the economic enterprise, was there that peace and inward discipline which made Western capitalism such a smooth, if disenchanted,
process.

In fairness, however, it should be pointed out that Weber, and
to some extent Marx, had a conception of the social world outside
Europe. Since, however, Marx had a theory of historical stages,
where he either saw non-capitalist social forms as pre-capitalist or,
while noting the colonial consequences of capitalism, concentrated
on analysing the dynamics of the system in its home base, Marxist
sociology characteristically turned its back on the colonial world,
and it is to Weber one has to look for any kind of understanding of
society conceived in imperial terms.

Weber's insights into the world of colonialism do not derive
very directly from his analysis of modern colonialism. His researches
on this theme are, at best, scattered and spasmodic. But he did

163

recognise that the Western type of capitalist system was peculiar, and that its understanding presupposed its being placed within a wider context of possibilities. This led him to a wide-ranging comparative and historical programme which included a study of Chinese (1964), Indian (1968b) and Jewish civilisations (1967) as well as, to some extent, of the Islamic world (1963). Even more important, however, being concerned with the question of the evolution of seigneurial proprietorship in Europe, and whether this was a German or a Roman institution, he became familiar with Roman systems of agricultural production and, more widely, with the system of Roman colonialism.

Weber was not alone in noticing that European feudalism (meaning, not seigneurial proprietorship in the manor, but the relation between superior and inferior rulers) was not a widespread phenomenon. The most usual social form was that of a patrimonial administration operating under a traditional authority and ensuring a flow of revenue into the royal coffers. But such a highly centralised system lent itself to incorporation within a feudal order. The existing authority was 'protected' by his conqueror, and in return he paid tribute to him. Such was probably the main social form of the ancient empires. The empire of Augustus, however, also went far beyond this. The collection of the revenue directly, and not through a feudal underling, became a major Roman industry, and created a new adventurer capitalist class in Rome. Moreover, prisoners of war were enslaved and put to work on plantations outside of Rome itself, to ensure supplies to the capital, including a permanent dole for its plebeian citizens. On this basis, the imperial administrative structures which were established could not take on the simple patrimonial model, which Augustus's experience of the Ptolemies might have led one to expect, nor did it remain second-hand and feudal. It had to be systematic and thus, for the first time in history, one saw the emergence of bureaucracy, operating under an emperor endowed with legal authority.

Weber, in fact, never put together this total picture of the Roman world. He was simply interested separately in the non-peaceful forms of capitalism and in the forms of domination. The synthesis which he was looking for was finally achieved in modern capitalism. He might have noticed an earlier synthesis achieved in Rome,which was even more relevant to the understanding of the modern world. But, even given this limitation, one can begin to find, in Weber, some of the concepts of social structure which are useful in the analysis of colonialism. Clearly, although he might be said to have had a theory of progress in his notion of the ever-increasing rationalisation of the world, he was neither surprised nor shocked to find history repeating itself in bits. The adventurer capitalists of the ancient world had invented a social form. So had the slave-owning landed proprietors of Rome. As soon as the cultural shell of the peculiarly European cultural complex was broken, such forms were very likely to recur as natural possibilities.

The story of the British, Portuguese, Spanish, French, Dutch and Belgian empires is a story of the establishment of new forms of feudalism, of the creation of privately financed armies, of private enterprise government (both of them versions of adventurer capitalism) and the setting up of slave plantations. In a complete sequence, what one might envisage is this: first the subordination of an existing ruler and his agreement to terms of tribute. Second, the establishment of direct rule through adventurer capitalist companies, which broke the ruler's resistance, put him on a pension, and then proceeded to collect the revenue directly. Finally, the establishment, not merely of revenue-collecting institutions based upon the existing productive systems, but the setting up of new forms of production which let in, along with the adventurer capitalists, a new type of capitalist, interested in agricultural, mining, and occasionally industrial, developments, using forced labour.

In time the adventurer capitalists became the *rentier* class of colonial society and, with political independence, they are likely to be bought out or forced out. The role of the producer capitalist, however, is likely to be more permanent, and lays the foundation of a social order which endures through colonial times and, to some extent, beyond them. This, therefore, is the point from which we will begin our own analysis.

The exact style of each colonial structure would, of course, depend upon the nature of the colonisers' social institutions, and upon the particular resources available. A common social form, and one of the most spontaneous and natural, was the establishment of the manor, in which a conquering settler put native peasants to work for him for a goodly portion of their time, or simply a claim to a certain amount of forced labour, unrelated to settlement. When, however, such structures came to be used for more than the provision of the master's own *oikos*, and oriented to market opportunities, they took on a new role. As Weber saw, the manor is one of the most universal of institutions, but it can, given appropriate market circumstances, be developed in a capitalist direction, involving either rent farming in an estate system, where tenant producers are exploited through rent, or the development of the plantation system, using some type of forced labour (Weber, 1961, ch. 6).

At this point colonial sociology becomes involved in a complex and many-sided argument about the relative role of ideological factors, such as law and religion on the one hand, and economic and ecological ones on the other, in determining which type of systems

165

emerged. We cannot expect to resolve these issues here. All that we
need do is notice that the more advanced capitalist societies readily
adapted their agricultural production to the systematic exploitation
of market opportunities, whereas the more feudal colonisers went
'instinctively' for a manorial type of order. What happened subsequently, however, depended upon the total market situation (so
that the British settlements in North America and the Caribbean
subsided at times to a semi-manorial state, whereas, under pressure
of market opportunities, the plantations of Brazil and Cuba became
activated in a capitalist way) and it was also limited by the conception
of the labour relationship inherent in the culture. (An introduction
to the full complexity of the issues involved here can be gained from
such writers as Elkins (1959), Genovese (1965, 1969) and Genovese
and Foner (1969).)

In any case, it is important to note that labour in colonial circumstances was forced labour, and not simply labour exploited
through the market. Its availability depended upon the fact of
direct or indirect military conquest. But if it is the case, as Weber
suggested, that capitalism demands formally free labour, as a part
of its inherent drive towards rational-calculation of costs, how
could slave labour ever be compatible with capitalism? Prima facie,
it is highly irrational to keep slaves in times of low demand and
underemployment, and one would have expected this conclusion
to be drawn quickly from economic experience. In fact, however,
several features of the slave plantation situation ensured its historical
survival over a number of centuries. One was that there was, despite
local and temporal fluctuations, sufficiently sustained demand to
keep slaves reasonably fully employed. A second was that, despite
humanitarian prejudice, it is possible that really effective mobilisation of the sanctions of force may be an efficient way of using labour.
But, third, the ego-satisfactions accruing to the slave-master are
such that they might well compensate for the apparently uneconomic
nature of his enterprise.

On the other hand it should be noted that slavery did not survive.
When industrialisation came to North, and later to South, America,
emancipation came too. Capital was invested increasingly in a
kind of enterprise in which free labour was essential and in the long
run the slave system was repressed. But this did not, by any means,
imply that all forms of forced labour were at an end. Indeed, they
were perfected with the introduction of contract labour.

Undoubtedly, the most important social invention within the
colonial system, after the chattel-slave, was the coolie. He was, of
course, within limits, a free man. He was paid wages and his bond to
his employer was for a limited term only. Moreover, at the end of his
indentures he had the opportunity of either setting up as a peasant

166

proprietor or returning to his own country. Such was the rationalisation which was used by those who used this form of labour, and indeed it was partly true. But it was also true that employing such labour was a highly efficient way of getting the best of both worlds, of having, on the one hand a labour force which was not free to leave at short notice, yet being able to calculate labour costs more exactly than was possible with slave labour. The logical extension of this would be a shorter and shorter term of indentures, coupled with a total denial of labour mobility during the period of employment.

In fact the use of indentured labour was pioneered in the plantations of Mauritius, Guyana, Natal, Malaysia and Fiji and, when gold-mining was introduced in South Africa, this also was seen as a suitable sphere for such labour. Chinese coolies were therefore imported, but when this policy was ended, the mine-owners turned to the question of the most efficient way of mobilising the native labour force.

The situation in South Africa, was in many ways, a unique one. The discovery of mineral resources in a temperate climate promised the possibility of establishing a settler society, but the cost of working the mines with settler labour was prohibitive and some sort of in-dentured labour system was required. The native population had, by this time, been confined to so-called native reserves, and these reserves, overcrowded and eroded as they were bound to become, offered a source of indentured labour, which did not suffer from the one great disadvantage which India and China suffered from, namely that of distance and transport costs. It was therefore possible to set up a system of short-term contract labour, so that able-bodied men were recruited in the reserves and transported to closed labour compounds for a period of nine months at a time. This labour force became less and less free as time went on, through the introduction of a money tax and the individualisation of tenure in the rural reserves, and by the cutting-off of the compounds from town life. At the same time, costs were kept as low as they could be. Not only was there no problem of unemployment benefit, all social costs were borne by the workers' family. As we have shown elsewhere (1972, 1973b), though free native labour was also used, the contract labour system and the restrictions which it implied affected the whole labour system of the country.

As functionalism and Marxism would both tell us, the structure of a society and its internal dynamic will, in large measure, be determined by the economic base but, quite crucial to the understanding of colonial society none the less, is a recognition of the special role and the special interests of subsidiary and marginal groups which are attracted to the society once it has been established.

In the first place, there is always likely to be some miscegenation, and there therefore emerges a half-breed population whose legal and social status is in doubt. Very rarely are such children assigned to the servile population. They may be legally merged with the freed slaves, and yet kept socially separate from the ruling group, as in the USA, where a colour line was always drawn between white and non-white, though not between coloured and black. They may be set totally free and achieve social status in accordance with their social positions and degree of colour, as in some parts of the Caribbean and Latin America (Hoetink, 1967). Or finally, they may be assigned to an entirely separate legal and social category of an intermediate level, as were the Cape Coloureds in South Africa (Patterson, 1953; Dickie-Clark, 1966). In all cases, such intermediate people tend to work as labourers, craftsmen, or factory hands, although they may also be found in other occupations.

The second obvious group in most colonial societies are what may best be called secondary colonialists. The basic economic structure is already established, but the servicing of the needs of the free and unfree populations alike offer opportunities for the kind of petty traders, which, on the whole, the main colonising society does not produce. Thus groups ethnically distinct from the main colonial population, like the 'passenger Indians' who followed the indentured Indians to South Africa or Guyana, and also settled in East Africa; the Syrians and Lebanese who took up trading in West Africa; Portuguese and Jews who moved in to the Caribbean; and the Chinese in Malaya, all came and settled permanently, often to the point of losing their links with their native society. They formed a very distinct and, by virtue of their ethnic identity, very recognisable element in the colonies, and could perhaps be called its *petit bourgeoisie*. This population also took up petty activity in mining, agriculture and manufacture.

A colonial society also has its missionaries and its administrators, who form a distinct element from the capitalist entrepreneurs and employers of labour. The missionaries occupy a peculiarly ambiguous role. They claim to be where they are because they wish to convert the heathen. This will not do as an explanation, however, since their enthusiasm for conversion has varied at different stages of the colonising process. In fact they both serve to protect the native population from some of the grosser forms of exploitation and, through their educational activities, prepare them for it. What they may be said to do is to carry through a process of ideological rationalisation, which serves to reconcile colonialism with the professed religious and ethical ideals of the colonising society. Thus the missionary population may produce all kinds and conditions of men, from those who are almost solely concerned with submitting the natives and the workers to a spiritual discipline which makes their economic and political discipline more effective, to crusading priests like Las Casas in Latin America in the early days of Spanish settlement, or the line of priests from John Phillip through to Trevor Huddleston in South Africa. Socially they tend to merge with other settler groups and sometimes they, or their children, actually join them. In one case in East Africa, we found it reported that a missionary finished up as a freelance gun-runner. (Perham, 1956). But, far more frequently, one finds that the missionary's son becomes an administrator, and his grandson a settler farmer.

The officials of the colonial government must, to some extent, remain distinct from the capitalist entrepreneurs, for, broadly speaking, their role is to set the terms of fair competition and dealing between entrepreneurs, and to protect the metropolitan interest which may be threatened by the rapaciousness of the capitalists and settlers. This led, in the British case, to the enunciation of the doctrine of trusteeship on behalf of the native population which, although it was often betrayed in practice, and finally abandoned altogether in Rhodesia, did actually do something to separate the administrators from the colonialists. They were deeply dependent on these other colonialists for their social life, though, and it was not always possible for them, in countries like Kenya, to be loyal to their masters, and to their friends (Buell, 1965).

Finally, it need hardly be said that in some countries, notably those with a temperate climate, a free group of metropolitan-born settlers arrives as farmers or workers. If there are enough of them they will seek to establish a new nation based upon a modern economy, and using free labour. But in some cases, most notably in South Africa, this new nation, so like the Australian or New Zealand nation in all other respects, has to co-exist with the kind of unfree economy and society we have been describing. In this case, of course, governmental power passes to a coalition of settler workers or farmers, who pursue a policy of 'apartheid' which means, not social separation, but the maintenance of settler political supremacy and the separation of two social worlds from one another, so that the new nation (in the European sense) can grow and flourish in the midst of a colonial world. A fairly substantial minority of metro-politan-descended settlers is necessary to win the position which the white South Africans have won, but their success has inspired other settler groups to make a similar bid for power. These have included, not merely the smaller groups of settlers in Algeria, Tunisia, Kenya, Nyasaland, Zambia and Rhodesia, but even groups of Creoles descended from freed slaves, who have themselves become a kind of social 'white settler' even though they are black. There is also the case of the six northern counties of Ireland, where what

169

appears as a religious conflict has all the elements of a 'white settler' situation.

The emancipation of labour in different colonies has had different consequences and, in some cases, one form of unfree labour has only been replaced by another. In some countries it has created a situation where the colonial power has to rule, not one, but two populations, who are by then, to all intents and purposes, the 'natives'. In this case there is a serious problem of pluralism and, *inter alia*, these two groups will compete for economic privileges, privileges in education and privileges of entry into the civil service. The Marxist expectation that, as workers, these groups will unite as a working-class-for-itself, is always frustrated because the necessary connections required to establish such a class-for-itself are already blocked by the existence of ethnic group linkages.

What is the appropriate way of conceptualising the relationship between ethnic segments of this kind has been a considerable source of dispute. Clearly a Parsonian account of stratification fails to work here, because that depends upon the existence of a unitary value system, which is lacking. Neither does the Marxist notion of class, for reasons outlined above. Still less does the notion of racial antagonism, for this poses, rather than solves, a sociological problem.

The most important contribution to an analysis of this type of situation (i.e. specifically the situation in which there are two 'emancipated' groups of workers, ethnically distinct from each other) is that of M. G. Smith. Smith apparently moved in his conceptualisation of this notion, from an initial formulation of ethnic difference to an emphasis upon the binding together of the society, through political domination to a final recognition that the 'political institution' must be taken to include forms of *economic* domination (Smith, 1965; Smith and Kuper, 1971). In the first formulation there is no political problem at all. In the second, colonial domination appears as essential to holding the society together, while in the third, a neo-colonial situation can be envisaged in which the maintenance of metropolitan economic domination keeps the two groups working together in the same industries.

Curiously, however, Smith is so preoccupied with pluralism as a general theory that he has little to say in his general theory about those societies in which there is not the complicating factor of a second labour force. This is the case, for example, in Barbados, where a small white settler class has not entirely prevented miscegenation, so that there are Barbadians of every hue, from completely white to completely black. In general, social privilege attaches in a graded way to whiteness, but as Smith does say, social position whitens men, so that a black man whose social and economic achievement is considerable would be seen as white. In such a society, in any case, there is the possibility of a unitary value system and a status ordering of the Parsonian sort. The interesting point about it is that it is possible, with a status order, for it to be expressed in racial and ethnic terms, just as it is for economic exploitation where the classes may also be races. Cox (1970) was no doubt right in insisting that the race problem had some relationship to the class struggle in the Marxist sense. It may also, in certain situations, be related to the status order.

One feature of most colonial situations at the time of labour emancipation is the fact that the economy is in a state of collapse. If it were not, the central and determining feature of social structure might lie in the social relations of production and the class struggle it engenders. But where the economy is dormant, the whole society takes on a sleepy character and both the nostalgic culture of the wealthy and the folk culture of the poor, and the culture of poverty become elaborated. In this sense one gets a new kind of pluralism and different groups, mainly fulfilling different occupational roles, take on the character of castes or estates, or something different from both of these, in the form of a characteristically colonial estate system. Eventually, individual members of the society may come to recognise the whole of these co-existing culture patterns as constituting the culture of their nation. But it is also the case that the myth of the national culture in this complex sense may not survive independence. Thus, for all the fact that the outsider might have seen East African society and culture as having a very important Asian component, this has not prevented the expulsion of the Asians from Uganda.

The slackness of the economy at the time of emancipation may be followed by its reconstruction on new lines. But when this happens, the formerly unfree workers and their children find themselves at a serious disadvantage. Long conditioned to a servile status, having been deprived of their own culture, and having a self-image of themselves as inferior imposed by their masters' culture, they may not merely lack the skills, but also the will, to undertake industrial training and compete. Though this point has been used in a somewhat dubious ideological and political way, particularly in the USA in relation to the Moynihan report (Yancey and Rainwater, 1967) it is one which does have some truth in it, and serves partially to explain why the Negro, not only in the USA, but in Brazil (Fernandes, 1969) has been forced into unemployment and poverty. When one adds to this the processes of formal and informal discrimination, it can be seen that, even after emancipation, the slave and his descendants will be at the bottom of the heap economically and socially. Legally free citizens they might be, and

171

in Brazil at least, not subject to a formal colour bar, but their chances of employment, housing and education are such that, statistically speaking, they clearly are the most disadvantaged section of the new society and find it impossible to break out of their ghettoised situation.

In the USA, which presents us with the best example of an unfree labour force undergoing emancipation and then being faced with developing industrial opportunities, there has been more of a development of a black middle class than in any other country (see Broom, 1967), but, the point originally made by Warner (1936) remains true. However, much as the blacks may develop their own internal class system, and some of them improve their life chances, there remains an impenetrable barrier, of a caste-like kind, between black and white, which no compensatory education, employment, or housing programme appears capable of overcoming. Whether this will always be the case in Brazil, which did not ever have a simple line of colour-distinction, remains to be seen. It does not appear to be an adequate answer, though, to those who suggest that Portuguese traditions, or some other cultural factor, make a breaching of the colour-bar possible, to say that, as a matter of statistical fact, most blacks fare badly economically. It could be the case that, if they did progress economically, they would not suffer the same kind of discrimination and segregation as do America's blacks.

Racism, the doctrine which, in its present form, suggests that some groups are biologically inferior to others, is a part of most, but not all, colonial situations. It clearly was so in the case of the USA's slavery, and is still a factor in South Africa, where black and coloured people are legally discriminated against. It may well be less so, however, in some of the French, Spanish and Portuguese territories, though there is evidence, from all these territories, of its existence (on the Portuguese territories see especially Boxer, 1963). In its most extreme form it is associated with a barrier to marriage between black and white, which effectively secures a white monopoly of political and economic advantages.

Of at least as great importance as labour emancipation in colonial societies is the attainment of political independence. Here the important questions are, 'Who succeeds to governmental power?', 'By what means do they rule?' and 'What factors, other than governmental power, hold the various social segments together?'

The answer to the first question is in part that group which is most successful in organising a national liberation movement, but in part that group which can give the best guarantee to the former colonising power that its interests will be protected. Ethnically speaking, the failure of nearly equal ethnic groups to create a united national front holds up the attainment of independence, partly because the colonial power might, in the last stages of colonialism, divide and rule, but sometimes because it really is difficult to find a clear and undisputed claimant to the succession. The simplest solution is to give power to the majority, and this conclusion is inescapable if it is clear that minorities have no real means of defending themselves. In the outcome, what one has in some cases is the domination of one ethnic group by another, as in the cases of Guyana and Malaysia and, in other cases, a minority which had hopes of the succession will be cruelly denied it, as with the Creoles of Freetown in Sierra Leone.

Separate from the ethnic pluralism question is the question of class and stratification in the liberation movement. As Fatma Mansur (1962) has shown this usually goes through several stages. At first the independence movement is controlled by a minute professional middle class, much concerned with ensuring their own future promotion to government office, but in the long run a westernised élite, often of traditional native descent, appeals to the 'masses' and organises the peasants and the urban lumpenproletariat and unemployed youth into a single movement. Thus one may well expect that most successor governments, whether representing only a segment of the society or the whole of it will have this character. The question then looms as to whether the political leadership will seek to, or be able to, emancipate itself from its mass following.

That the leadership will want to do this may follow from the fact that it is offered suitable rewards for itself if it serves neo-colonial interests, or alternatively that it sees opportunities of booty for itself in the management of the national economy. The story of most post-colonial leaderships is a story of transactions between these leaders and various old colonial and neo-colonial economic interests. In some cases these transactions may become confused and intertwined with the attempts of the world's super powers to buy support, for strategic reasons. Thus, when there are crises and coups in colonial territories, the real beneficiaries may not be the participants but the cultural, economic and political interests which they represent.

As we saw earlier, it is a mistake to suppose that post-colonial societies are held together by the sheer fact of political domination. In so far as they are, they are likely to be very weak, because power begets its own opposition, and if that opposition can be externally financed and armed, it will not be held down forever. On the other hand, what often is the case is that the institutions of the economy or the social relations of production bind various groups together, either by their involvement in the same industries, or through the fact that one group has a measure of economic power, and another political power (e.g. the Chinese and Malays in Malaysia).

173

Another question at issue in all post-colonial societies, however, is the type of authority exercised and the form of administration which it uses. The assumption of some of the colonial powers was that rational-legal authority and bureaucracy on a European model would be established and survive in the form of colonial parliaments and civil services. When these failed, as they usually did, except where the experience of imperial rule was longest lasting, as in India, this was usually put down to the intrusion of Weber's other two types of authority, namely the charismatic and traditional forms.

In fact, the notions of charisma and tradition have been somewhat overemployed in the Western sociology of the third world. What usually happened was the emergence of a political party which, in its present form, approximated to that of the communist party of Europe, but which could not always establish its own disciplined branches and cells, and depended instead on a variety of traditional and class interests. Such a party, not merely governed the nation, in an important sense it *was* the nation, or at least it was the means of political mobilisation.

Not every country has a Lenin, however, and the traditional, or middle class, connections of the new colonial rulers were such that they very often failed to organise the party as a revolutionary nation-building instrument. In that case, whatever reliable bureaucracy there was would be able to take over power, and the most likely candidate for this role would be the army.

It should not be thought, however, that the crises and coups of the post-colonial world were solely the result of internal contests between individuals and between organisations. Wherever there are resources to be exploited in a third world country, capitalist corporations, and governments of the capitalist countries will be concerned to exploit them, and a means to that end may well be support, of a financial or military kind, for a revolution or a coup. The other side of the same coin is that even the politician who genuinely wants to develop his country, apart from gaining booty himself, will be tempted to take short cuts. He may achieve visible economic growth in the form of capital investment, but only by agreeing to an outflow of revenue which is ruinous to his country's future, and, politically speaking, he may find financial sources for strengthening his party's hold on power, but at the cost of true political independence.

When all other structural factors have been analysed, the fact which stands out in nearly every post-colonial society is this. Far from them being developing countries, they will be subject to economic processes of de-development, which positively offset nearly all the growth which they may achieve. And, even where real income per head rises, the relative position of these societies, *vis-à-vis* the first and second worlds, will be worsening. In these circumstances, China, as a backward country which held off colonialism and proceeded to raise itself economically through its own efforts, provides a startlingly appealing model. But there are no other definitive examples of this kind, of truly independent development, and the basic structure of most third world countries is determined by the needs of a concealed economic neo-colonialism backed by any available political method. Thus the revolution of the third world is likely to be a revolution not merely against the advanced countries but against its own leadership. We return to this question in chapter 13.

part four

Social structures and moral perspectives

12 The moral disintegration of the enlightened world

Durkheim envisaged the future of industrial society as a future of moral integration, in the sense that individual human beings would enter into morally significant relations with one another, that the corporations so formed would each be guided by its own group ethic, but that these ethics would be complementary and that individuals and groups would have fixed goals, the limits of which they would not seek to transcend. The English utilitarians thought almost exactly the opposite. The individual, for them, could and should follow his own self-interest in the market, and nations should pursue theirs (through free trade). Thereby, the happiness of the individual and the wealth of nations could increase almost without limit.

In an odd way, Weber brought these two ideals together. The pursuit of wealth through the capitalist enterprise called for the coming into being of the bureaucratically-run corporation, but both a continuous capitalist enterprise and its bureaucracy were only possible subject to a certain kind of ethic which, if it propelled the individual in the direction of the kind of morality which Durkheim called egoistic, none the less was an ethic, namely that of dedication in a calling. On the other hand, once capitalism was in being, it would, as it were, kick away the institutional ladder up which it had climbed. As he wrote (Weber, 1952, p. 181)

> Victorious capitalism, since it rests on mechanical foundations,
> needs its support no longer. The rosy blush of its laughing
> air, the Enlightenment, seems also to be irretrievably
> fading and the idea of duty in one's calling prowls about
> in our lives like the ghost of dead religious beliefs.

In this disenchanted world the sole virtue left was organisational efficiency.

The British Fabians and the Social Democratic movement took

these ideas further. Individualism, the great engine of capitalist progress, must be transcended. The world not merely of the individual, but of the great collective actors, the corporations, must be made subject to the public good or to substantively rational goals. In essence these were the goals of the welfare state. At a later point the notion was elaborated of a new social citizenship which transcended social class, even though it might have been won out of class struggle. Thus there was a new social contract, on the basis of which the substantively rational goals of the welfare state, the mixed economy, planning for full employment, and free collective bargaining, were established.

Meanwhile, Marxism rejected all of these goals, while at the same time proposing its own 'enlightenment' or its own means of overcoming alienation. It envisaged a kind of freedom as the natural human condition, which was at first sight at least the very opposite of Durkheim's subordination of the individual to the group, yet it saw bourgeois freedom in the market place as the selfish freedom of civil society, which had to be transcended. Bureaucracy and capitalism it saw as the complex structural forms of alienation and, in any case, capitalism was for it, headed for crisis and disaster because of its own internal contradictions.

Marxism's own enlightenment lay in the role to be played by the proletariat. Weber was to become disenchanted with bureaucracy, but seventy years before, Marx had considered the role of bureaucracy and the state, as these had appeared in the work of Hegel, as the means of transcending the alienation of civil society, and he had never been enchanted. The bureaucracy was not the universal class. That role was reserved for the proletariat which, through its antithetical denial of the whole capitalist bureaucratic order, would promote the final class struggle which would end all class struggles. Thus the proletariat makes its appearance in Marx's critique of the Hegelian philosophy of law (1967a, p. 249):

Where then is the possibility of German emancipation?
Answer: in the form of a class with *radical chains*, a class in civil society, that is not of civil society, a class that is a dissolution of all classes, a sphere of society having a universal character because of its universal suffering and claiming no *particular* right because no *particular wrong* but *unqualified wrong* is perpetrated on it; a sphere that can invoke no *traditional* title but only a human title, which does not partially oppose the consequence but totally opposes the premises of the German political system; a sphere, finally, that cannot emancipate itself without emancipating itself from all the other spheres of society, thereby emancipating

them; a sphere in short that is the *complete loss* of humanity and can only redeem itself through the *total redemption of humanity*. The dissolution of society as a particular class is the proletariat.

In his later works, especially in the Address to the Communist League (1962b), Marx was more cautious. The liberation of society by the proletariat would not be immediate. It would depend upon a prior stage in which, under the dictatorship of the proletariat, the basis of the capitalist class would be destroyed. Then, however, after a dangerous period of raw communism (Marx, 1959), true communism would be achieved and would be marked by, amongst other things, a withering away of the state.

At this point our argument about Enlightenment ideals comes full circle. We started by putting Durkheim first, because in some ways he was the most utopian thinker in the whole sociological tradition, and we then saw how, by successive stages, men had got disillusioned with other ideals, with capitalism based on individual and corporate self-interest, with bureaucracy, and with the welfare state. Finally we come to the notion of proletarian revolution. But if proletarian revolution releases man to act in freedom, this does not simply mean bourgeois freedom. For man in his liberated state will not be driven for ever by the desire to fulfil his needs without limit. He will seek that kind of fulfilment through a moral and social life which Durkheim originally envisaged. That is, as Durkheim (1959) saw a socialist ideal. His mistake lay only in believing that somehow it could be achieved within a world of capitalist corporations.

Now our own position in this book has already been made clear. In the latter half of the twentieth century we cannot naïvely accept any of these Enlightenment utopias. We raise the question as to whether those successive structural ideals about which successive social thinkers became enthusiastic were not entirely mistaken. Is it not possible that the structures which men hailed as ideal or liberating were the very ones which were leading men to chaos and disaster? We live at the beginning of that period of chaos and disaster and we are increasingly forced to ask whether any of these social ideals represents anything but a kind of mad exultation in the face of the abyss.

Looking back over the perspectives we have mentioned, it is clear that, belonging, as most of them do, not to the Enlightenment itself, but to its heritage in the next generation, they are frank about recognising that even the highest achievements of this civilisation have their underside. We shall now seek to show that those aspects of social structure which were recognised with foreboding

G

have now attained fulfilment, that the internal contradictions of the system place it in crisis so that totally opposite forces are unleashed and that the system, in any case, loses faith in itself and undergoes moral disintegration. What begins to take shape is not, in fact, a new enlightened age, but its exact opposite, a new Dark Age. If we cannot save anything of the optimism of the Enlightenment – and we can see no slick formula for doing so – sociology and social thought should be devoted to discerning the problems of this new age and, having discerned them, find ways of mastering them.

On the most superficial level the problems of our time are the problems of economic crisis and of impersonality. But these essentially are parts of the self-image of our age, part of the way in which our media intellectuals avoid the issues which really face us. More mischievously, however, in so far as they trap us into believing that the terms of the problem must be so narrowly set, they force on us structural solutions which involve an intensification of underlying problems. This is the basic criticism which we would make of policy-oriented research which, through its very devotion to doing something practical here and now, becomes a means of entrenching social structures which would otherwise be removed.

It is useful, none the less, if we do place the problem in a larger perspective, to begin by looking at those disenchanting aspects of the modern world which enlightened but disillusioned sociology has noted. The first of these is the consequence of the liberation of self-interest as the basic imperative of social order. What we have to say is that self-interest, or the market principle, sometimes corrupts the substantive rationality of social institutions; sometimes it fails as a means of providing for human needs; and sometimes it creates conditions of dangerous social irresponsibility.

The social ideal of capitalism is that every good and service should become a commodity. This should be true, not merely of soap and sealing wax, of coal and steel, of education and health, but also of such matters as sex and love, political representation, and salvation. In fact, as we have seen, it fails in providing for an economic infrastructure as well as for social needs. But, despite its failures, the basic principle operates and, as soon as there is any weakness in social organisation, exploits its opportunities.

The natural tendency of the upstart capitalist is to buy his way into, and out of, every situation. Thus, in most so-called developing countries, the nascent bourgeoisie openly seeks to corrupt the civil service by buying privileges. The pride of Western European capitalism, however, has always been its moral uprightness, its acceptance of the fact that all forms of force and fraud should be outlawed in economic transactions, and that capitalist operations should take place within a framework of rational law. Yet, as the moral ladder

182

which made capitalism possible is kicked away, these limitations no longer operate. The customer, the shareholder and the government may be tricked and cheated, not merely occasionally and deviously, but so systematically that trickery and cheating become businesses in themselves. The form of trickery and cheating which is used against the customer is called advertising. That which is used against the shareholder is called company promotion, and includes the use of holding companies and takeover bids, which are means of making a business out of other men's business, and making the richest of profits in the process. And finally, trickery against the government is called public relations, and involves the buying of those services of councillors and members of legislatures, which really belong to those who elected them.

A Conservative prime minister has felt constrained, in Britain recently, to refer to the 'unacceptable face of capitalism'. But a question must soon arise as to whether it can have any other face and whether it can be controlled merely by reform of company law or the control of advertising or public relations. What is striking at the present time is the way in which what might once have been regarded as ethically dubious activities have new and respectable names. It seems clear from the American example that such activity penetrates into the highest levels of government and that where there is a scandal revealed, the difficulty is to find anyone who is sufficiently clean to investigate it. Some make the mistake of believing that today's corruption scandals are of minor importance compared with those of earlier times. What seems to be the case, however, is that they are better organised and have some of the technical rationality of bureaucracy about them. What is perhaps even more striking is the degree to which those in government do deals, not merely with orthodox business men, but with what Merton called 'innovators' that is, with the leaders of the well-organised crime world. Thus, not merely fraud but force comes to play a legitimate part in the working of the economy.

If commercial principles can be applied to the business of organising what should be a rational process of decision making, they can also be applied in other 'sacred' spheres, like sex and religion. We have spoken, in earlier chapters, of the significance of privatisation and the role of the family and organised religion in this process, and it will clearly be a matter for discussion, in a later section on utopian perspectives, whether this privatisation can be overcome. What passes, in the advanced capitalist countries, as a discussion of the permissive society, however, very often represents nothing other than the pursuit of commercial opportunities in the sphere of sex and religion.

So far as sex is concerned, it has always had a deviant commercial form in prostitution. But prostitution appears as one of the more dignified older professions by comparison with the various forms taken by the commercialisation of sex today. The barriers to public sexual exhibition, to pornographic films and literature, and to sex shops which sell the various items of equipment required in normal and deviant sex, have all quite suddenly come tumbling down, as did the barriers to certain kinds of gambling in previous years. But in the case of the sexual revolution, supply probably exceeds demand. The public are told that 'the permissive society' exists and, in this very particular field, those concerned with advertising quickly realised that even criticism of their activities counts as a form of advertisement.

Closely related to the question of sex is the question of the use of soft drugs and of this we may say more later, when we turn to the question of revolution and drop-out. But the world of drug-induced experiences, like the world of pop music, is an important sphere of commercial activity. There are said to be capitalist enterprises in being with brand names and advertising campaigns in readiness to go into operation as soon as marijuana is legalised. Along with this, however, goes the notion that there is an overlap between the world of pop, the world of drugs and the world of religion.

The business of religious revival was long ago put on to a capitalist basis and, quite outside the ordinary church, as well as far removed from the world of the simple evangelical preacher, there arose the religious crusade in which all the massive techniques of capitalist public relations were put to a new use. For, whatever it meant, quite large numbers of people were saved in this way and then referred to their own churches for further religious treatment, while the preacher and his entourage became very very rich.

But the white collar and tie world of this kind of revival is now, in part, superseded. Religion has become 'pop'. One can become a Jesus-freak, or, if one wishes a more exotic type of religious experience, one may get it from a well-publicised guru. There are those who see in these developments a new religious hunger in a secular society, and the experiences which are cultivated in these organisations are seen as on a par with other religious experiences of the past. One other possible way of looking at the matter, however, is that capitalist business has now invaded the last sacred areas of men's lives. The crucifixion of Christ becomes the subject of a pop musical.

The capitalist enterprise, therefore, may be seen as still finding new areas of activity, and what is loosely called secularisation proceeds apace. But at the same time there are some needs which it cannot supply because demand is not effective. This includes the infrastructure of industry itself, where no spontaneous collective

184

action is taken to ensure that demand is effective, until eventually failing industrial enterprises in fields like fuel and transport are 'nationalised', that is to say, run by the state, very often on a sub-sidised basis so that the taxpayer in general, rather than industrial consumers only, bear the costs of non-profitability. It also, however, includes the provision of health, education, housing and other forms of social welfare benefit for the poor. Here the service can be pro-vided commercially at whatever level required if the consumer is prepared to pay for it. But this means that it can only be provided for the rich. The poor must be provided for by the state.

In all of these spheres, one notes the phenomenon of private affluence and public squalor (Galbraith, 1962). It is precisely on the social level that capitalism fails, whether this social level refers to the industrial infrastructure or to the provision for basic human needs. In the latter case, the separation out of the needs of the poor will be met in conditions of public squalor. It is particularly worth noting that, despite the brave slogan of the welfare state that benefits should be equal and as of right, the increase in available wealth succeeds in pushing the social services back to what we call in England a Poor Law basis.

The final indictment of capitalism as a system, however, lies in its irresponsibility. The notion of conservationism is, of course, one fraught with ideological overtones. Some mean conservation of their rural luxury from the poor and the townsfolk. Others mean the halting of industrialisation in the third world, so that the first world's resources are conserved. But, amongst other meanings, there is this simple and inescapable one, that the resources available to man to maintain his existence on this planet need not be inexhaustible or available in suitable forms at the right moments in history. This requires planning. But capitalism is not only not capable of planning. It has no checks in and of itself to prevent the overexploitation of resources and, indeed, has a built-in tendency to overexploit them. The world of a supermarket is a world in which the resources of the world are being squandered, even if the customer is kept in a stupified and happy daze.

The world of capitalism, however, is also the world of bureau-cracy and, if one considers man as a worker rather than as a con-sumer, the main problems which face him are those of the quality of his relations with his fellow-man. Each of the separate aspects of bureaucracy which Weber mentions proves, in fact, to involve some form of human deprivation. A man is required by the system to have only defined and official relations with his superiors or inferiors, for this is what formal rationality demands. He can have no property, and, therefore, in all likelihood, no self-fulfilment in his job. He must record all his official acts in the files and therefore

185

make himself dispensable and disposable. He must separate home from work, and therefore lead a completely schizoid existence. So much is this the case that the leaders of the corporations themselves have proposed, instead of cold bureaucracy, the glad hand of the corporation seen as a family substitute. But this programme, one possible interpretation of Durkheim's proposal for a society based on occupational groups though it may be, has never got very far. Men actually prefer to sell *part* of themselves to the corporation and behave like automatons, and to keep their real selves for their private life.

In fact, of course, the position of the organisation man is considerably less secure than it once was anyway. Since all that is said about rationalisation and predictability implies that bureaucrats are ideally perfectly programmed men, they can often be replaced by perfectly programmed machines. In this case the skilled bureaucrat is displaced and new posts become available, either for machine-minders or for professional scientists and technologists. This could mean a transformation, in the long run, of historical bureaucracy in the direction of professionalisation or proletarianisation, but in the meanwhile it does little to enhance the rewards of the bureaucrat's job.

The 'real selves' which are kept for private life are, however, pretty threadbare. As we have seen, they involve the privatised world of the family, the home and a small amount of communal and associative activity. Such a situation might be rewarding in those happy cases where members of a family find intra-familial family relationships completely enriching, but it will usually mean, either great precariousness of relationships of a personal kind, or total boredom. All that is left then is a spectator role in the larger world which is paraded before him.

This rationalisation of the world, the division of home and work-place, and the emotional impoverishment of both, has inevitably produced a romantic reaction. The inherently unsatisfying nature of employment, and the limitations |on emotional life within the family, lead to the cultivation of the non-rational emotive aspects of life and, generally, to the development of a counter-culture based upon anti-bureaucratic values. Generally speaking, the so-called student movement bases itself on this culture. Mainly it is quiescent, representing merely a drop-out movement rather than a revolutionary one, but at times it may have an anarchistic or socialist character. It is also strongly tied in to other aspects of protest in capitalist culture, particularly the anti-war movement.

When we speak of moral disintegration of 'enlightened' society, one of its most obvious aspects is this. For what the counter-culture does is systematically to deny the legitimacy of major social values.

In some cases it is an almost completely *counter* culture, in that it denies every value of the corporate capitalist world. Amongst a minority, this might even mean committing acts of anarchistic violence, and this raises the question of whether it presages actual revolution. The answer to this is uncertain, but at least it prevents the kind of value-consensus which might be expected in a Durkheimian social system.

The response of official society is to seek to accommodate the new way of life in terms of pluralism and, to a large extent, this is successful. Moreover, capitalism, seeing a demand for romantic cultural styles, sees a new opportunity for profit, and so helps to spread it, if not to universalise it. At this point it becomes difficult to distinguish the authentic and inauthentic versions even of a drop-out, let alone a revolutionary, culture.

A most important question, however, is the relation between the mental agonies, anxieties, and protest of the middle class and their adult children on the one hand, and the more conflict-ridden relations between organised labour and capitalism on the other, not to mention the relation between the unemployed and permanently poor and the main society.

From the standpoint of bureaucracy, organised labour is at the disposal of the corporation, measured and calculated in terms of the time taken over movements. Trade unionism and the political labour movement intervene, however, to ensure that the worker's standard of life and the conditions of his work are protected against such calculations. The result is a set of agreed values, both inside industry and outside, regarding workers' rights. But such values rest only on a fragile truce and upon a balance of power. If the balance of power is upset, or if the capitalist employer can no longer negotiate and make concessions, it may well be that the right to collective bargaining, and even the right to form unions, may be withdrawn. If this does happen, organised force may have to be used against the working class.

In fact, what the experience of revolution from the right, in Europe since the First World War, has shown is that, in the event of such an authoritarian regime being established, it does enjoy a measure of working-class support. More than that, it has proved possible, in times of economic crisis and unemployment, to organise working men and the unemployed alike against scapegoat groups rather than against the ruling class. In the case of Nazi Germany, such a movement eventually captured political power. It was financed, no doubt, by the capitalist class, but it also lived a life of its own and enjoyed both working- and middle-class support.

In the case of Nazi Germany, the mass movement created by the Nazis itself overthrew most of the values of rational-liberal capitalism, and helped to usher in a new barbarism. For the most part, however, the trade union movement has worked within the framework of rational bureaucratic organisation, taking action through collective bargaining to defend and enlarge the rights of its members and, if necessary, fighting to defend the right of collective bargaining itself. But, by virtue of this fact, organised labour does become part of the total system, and one of the most conservative parts at that. When, therefore, it is faced with a romantic irrational middle-class protest, or one which its members see in this light, it fights, not with this movement, but against it. It is for the maintenance of a prosperous economy, for corporate values, and for patriotism. Thus, the prospect of a drop-out movement sparking off working-class action appears to be very limited.

One question which may be posed is whether the counter-culture of the drop-out movement and of students is, in any significant sense, not merely anti-capitalist, but socialist. It uses the slogans of socialism clearly enough and, in a country with a revolutionary tradition, like France, the student movement and the workers' movement did momentarily come together in a revolutionary situation. But there is much that is merely romantic and anti-rational about the student movement. It seeks participation in the management of educational affairs, as trade unions do in industrial matters, but, in doing so, either seeks participation for its own sake, without the guidance of any political policy, or simply seeks to undermine existing academic standards without offering alternative ones. The institutions of the teach-in and the anti-university have, by now, clearly failed to become a positive force.

We should not be misunderstood here. It is certainly understandable that, faced with an educational content which is likely to be ideologically loaded in favour of the bureaucratic and capitalist *status quo*, students who are, in any case, unlikely to find satisfying employment after graduating will engage in protest, and it is conceivable that a socialist student movement might arise. But in many cases of so-called student revolt, there has been a romantic, rather than a political-rational, rejection of capitalism and bureaucracy. This, coupled with the dissociation of the working class from the student, leaves them as a free-floating and potentially mobilisable element in most capitalist societies. They might also, through their somewhat facile rejection of their curricula, cultivate a kind of irrationalism of unpredictable significance. Amongst other possibilities, one should not exclude that of the emergence of a movement which shares some of the characteristics of fascism, even though it may employ vulgar Marxist slogans.

The most striking point of social breakdown, in most capitalist societies, however, has been their failure to integrate their immigrants

188

as well as the new poor, so that these together constitute a distinct deprived group. In the case of Europe this has meant a temporary migrant labour system, with workers living in hutted camps. In France it has meant the accommodation of the Algerian, as well as the Portuguese, worker in *bidonvilles*. In England it has meant the emergence of immigrant lodging houses. But it is in the USA that the problem takes a particularly ominous turning.

The black population of the USA's cities are not, of course, immigrants, except in the sense of being migrants from the quasi-colonial south to the northern cities. They are not, however, in the position of the European immigrant, who functions as a sought-after replacement worker in areas of employment which workers in the host nation reject. The black worker in the USA's cities stays in the USA because he has no other home. But he does not even have the rights of the replacement worker. Many live in a nearly permanent state of unemployment, and they live permanently in the ghetto. The concentration of pathologies in this area, and the anger and contempt felt by the young black American towards his white fellow countrymen, means that a large part of the central city areas have now become dangerous for whites to walk in. Thus there is a new urgency about the problem of the blacks in the cities in the USA, and the urgency lies, for the whites, in the fact that they can no longer walk safely on their streets.

The problem which is being faced by the major American cities is not, however, entirely a new one. The ghettoes have been there for generations. The problem is that their inhabitants are now making war on those who put them there. Robert Blauner, in a perceptive study (1972), has described the ghetto as representing a kind of domestic colonialism, and this is one way of viewing the matter. If it is correct, then the present urban riots are roughly equivalent to a colonial war of liberation. We may, however, note that similar phenomena to those of the American ghetto are to be observed in any city which is basically unplanned. The natural processes of competition for land use, which Park and Burgess (1925) had noted in Chicago leave behind, in the centre of the city, all those too weak to survive in the struggle to settle in the most desirable areas. More-over, something similar may happen even where housing is a matter of rational-bureaucratic allocation, as in England. There, a spon-sored urban migration takes place for the established working class, but this leaves behind the underclass who lack political leverage in the allocative system (Rex and Moore, 1967). Thus there can be a concentration of pathologies in the central city areas (or, in some countries, in the peri-urban areas), which requires only prolonged unemployment amongst the young active males, and a deterioration of relations with the police, to spark off something like the American urban riots of the late 1960s. Certainly there has been an astonishing change in the nature of capitalist cities in the twenty-five years which followed the Second World War, and cities are tending to be no longer inhabitable because they are at war with themselves.

We have so far traced the way in which normal capitalism undergoes moral degeneration, as a result of the implication of the profit motive, the extension of bureaucracy, the breakdown, or potential breakdown, of the collective bargaining system, and the segregation and suppression of the underclass of those whom the society cannot employ. We believe, moreover, that the processes referred to will continue to operate. But in some circumstances, when the system breaks down, new kinds of barbarism may be unleashed, which cannot be put down simply to capitalism. Neither can they be seen as confined in all respects to the non-communist world. We refer to the use of prison camps, of torture, and of military repression.

The Nazi party in Germany was perhaps a product of capitalism in crisis, but in many respects it was a denial of many of the structural principles of capitalism. The Nazi party adopted the Führer principle as its basic principle of organisation and, at first sight, this may appear to be simply the essence of bureaucracy. There was, however, a deliberate use of the notion of charismatic leadership on the one hand, and of the 'laws' of crowd psychology on the other. It was, therefore, based upon a virtual cult of unreason. But it was also based upon violence.

The Nazis might be said to have invented a system for the artificial manufacture of charisma. A cheering, saluting mob of supporters in a stadium would greet the leader, whose arrival and whose speaking would be theatrically arranged. But, if there were still dissidents, the party's hired strong-arm men would be at hand to deal with them. Charisma flourished because opposition was impossible, and this was not a matter confined to public rallies.

When a para-military political party controls the streets, as the Nazi party did, and the actual military refuses to intervene, there is little hope of opposition of any kind and there is little chance for dissent. Socialism of a rational kind, concerned with protecting workers' rights, or setting up a planned economy, must be ruthlessly suppressed. So also, given the alliance of the party with the large employers, must trade unionism, and very quietly the prisons fill up with the working-class enemies of the regime. They are quickly followed by intellectuals and, given that opposition is driven underground, a secret police has to be created to root it out. Very quickly, too, torture, as a means of accomplishing this rooting out, becomes accepted as normal. In fact these techniques were not only accepted as normal in Nazi Germany, they were perfected and spread to many other parts of the world as well.

The one truly unique phenomenon under Nazism was the concentration of the large Jewish minority in camps and, at first as a matter of fact, and then deliberately, the acceptance of a policy of genocide. In the case of the German Jews, this scarcely credible policy was justified by treating the Jews as a scapegoat and holding them responsible for the evils of capitalist crisis, even though the party was actually helping to sustain capitalism in that crisis.

Some of these aspects of Nazism, however, do have at least some analogies in other societies, and not solely in capitalist ones. How else can one explain the phenomena which now go under the name of Stalinism? If Hitler artificially created his own charisma, the cult of the individual was not lacking in Russia, and very quickly, in all communist countries, the adulation of the leader and the control of public opinion through propagandist use of the media, became the norm, although one might distinguish between the total irrationality and contempt for truth in the Nazi case, and mere ideological distortion in the case of Stalinism.

The Russian communist party was, of course, a much more rational instrument for achieving political objectives than the German Nazi party, and it did embody the bureaucratic principle, but it also had its enemies to deal with, both external and internal, and it was faced with the need to root out conspiracies in a way very similar to that which faced the Nazis, even though the enemies were different. Moreover, once the system of police persecution and terror was under way, it gathered momentum to a degree which could not be explained by mere individual paranoia. Tens of thousands were imprisoned in labour camps and, amongst these, a whole succession of those whose own careers reached their zenith in the secret police when they were consigning others to the camps.

It is true that, following the death of Stalin, many of these abuses were checked, and nearly all political prisoners released. But the explanation of Stalinism, offered by the communist party leadership, has never been convincing sociologically. These were surely more than the aberrations of one man. From our perspective, then, we ask whether there is not an inherent danger, if the class tensions of capitalism are ended by either class, of a resort to methods which represent a total denial of all the enlightenment ideals which capitalism and communism have, at various times, professed.

The practices of mass imprisonment, of torture, and the use of the weapons of political terror, have spread widely in the modern world. So has the cult of the individual political leader with a synthetically created charisma. In some colonial wars, moreover, policies have been adopted, involving the resettling of minorities, which come close to the Nazi policies which led to the practice of genocide against the Jews.

191

The final question which we should ask in this review of moral disintegration and a descent into a new barbarism is, what is done about unwanted minorities and about dissident satellites? On the first question, that of unwanted minorities, one has noted the *de facto* segregation of the American blacks, and one has only to look at immigration policies in other countries to see that the idea of concentration camps is not far away. In fact, the revolt of the ghetto might be a last revolt before the ghettoes become plain concentration camps. Moreover, there is so much racist propaganda, of an open or concealed kind, permitted in some Western capitalist countries that one cannot help predicting that the blacks in the USA and Britain, at least, might not suffer in some degree the fate of the Jews in Nazi Germany. It is not merely the blacks of the USA who use violence against the whites. Violence in the other direction is a feature both of the current American, and of the British, situations.

On the other hand, there is the question of maintaining the ideological loyalty and military reliability of the satellites of the super powers. On the whole the communist leaders in Russia are better at this than are the Western capitalist countries, since they do have, in their satellite communist parties, efficient instruments of control. But, faced with the prospect of open debate, which might lead to a change of system and a change of sides, neither of the super powers has hesitated to embark on military intervention. The Americans tend, on the whole, to use bombers, and the Russians, tanks. It may perhaps be added, however, that such actions are more capable of being smoothly and quickly carried out by the Russians because their political control at home is so complete. The Americans face, not merely a democratic anti-war movement, but a morally disaffected population amongst their educated young.

We now begin to see how the smooth and stable social systems of capitalism and communism, which we described in earlier chapters and which their own ideologists see as ideal systems, have in fact begun to break down, so that we live more and more in a world in which fraud and force are the rule. What is most striking about their contemporary use is how respectable and normal they have become.* But, in order to understand the full extent of the barbarism of the modern world, one has to turn to the attempts of the third world to liberate itself from bondage to the first.

---

* Cf. the evidence supplied to the Watergate tribunal, which reported that White House agents in the USA had carried out a 'feasibility study' to assess the chances of successfully burgling a psychiatrist's office.

13 The revolution of the third world and the new dark ages

European Enlightenment sociology not only has a theory of its own structure, it also has a theory of revolution. That theory is provided by Marx's political economy, which described, not how prices moved and resources flowed from one part of the system to another while none the less the system remained stable and wealth grew, but rather how, inevitably starting from the central contradiction of surplus value, other contradictions arose until the whole system was in a state of crisis and the forces of political revolution put an end to it. Unfortunately, however, so far the capitalist economy has not worked this way. As we have seen there is no instance, in the more advanced capitalist countries, of economic crisis leading to a worker-based revolution. What the working class have usually achieved is a kind of countervailing power which leads to a social contract but when this has broken down it has usually led to a revolution from the right, which puts an end to the freedom of labour.

Meanwhile, of course, Marxism also needs a theory of imperialism and colonial revolution, since capitalist operations extend beyond the metropolitan countries to every corner of the globe. Here, however, Marxism seems caught in a dilemma. It could say that this was where the revolution was likely to occur and that it had been precisely the ability of the metropolitan economy to stabilise itself by living off the fruits of colonial exploitation which had enabled it to survive. But, built into Marx's own theories, was the notion that *the* crisis which would produce change was one based upon a long process of the development of contradictions under capitalism and that only the urban working class of the advanced countries had the maturity, the consciousness and the organisation to constitute a truly revolutionary class. In the colonial situation there would have to be a bourgeois revolution and the establishment of a capitalist economy before the forces of a socialist revolution could begin to

193

gather. In the meanwhile, there could be only the development of some kind of bourgeois nationalism or occasional peasant revolts which would, if European experience was repeated, at least lead to some kind of Caesarism or Bonapartism.

In fact, of course, things have not happened this way at all. While European economies have been stabilised, the backward colonial countries have been in a state of perpetual turmoil, revolution and war. What is called communism at least occurs, not in the advanced countries, but in underdeveloped capitalist ones like Russia, and in frankly peasant ones like China and Cuba, and though, in each case, a communist party, acting as a vanguard, moves into a commanding position, the movement is based squarely on the support of the peasants. On the other hand, nationalist movements have arisen and have found themselves fighting, not with the organised working class of the metropolis or, indeed, very often in colonial cities, but against it. And finally, the revolution has been conceived in racial terms as a revolt of the poor black nations against the white, including as *its* vanguard the blacks of the most advanced industrial countries.

It seems possible to us that the underlying secret process behind all this may well lie in economic factors. Lacking the necessary expertise ourselves, we can only call in our colleagues for this political economy of imperialism and the colonial revolution, but in the meanwhile we can record the evident structural changes on a social and political level, noting that sometimes at least they have a dynamic of their own. We should also be prepared to recognise that, when exploitation is based on naked force, conquest and compulsion, rather than on the labour market, its overthrow may occur through a political struggle which circumvents complex economic changes.

What then are the actual revolutionary events which we have to record? They include, first of all, the establishment of communism in several economically and industrially backward countries. They include national liberation movements which have political independence and what we might call 'nativisation' of their administrations as their primary goal. They include guerilla armies and urban guerillas in both the remaining colonial countries and in the long-established independent ones. They include black power movements in the USA and the other formerly slave-based countries. They include people fighting neo-colonial wars directly against the metropolitan powers (above all, the fight of the Vietnamese people against the USA, which has had an exemplary significance). And finally, they include peoples who are martyred by what are often externally sustained civil wars which reduce their countries to barbarism.

Structurally, of course, these separate revolutionary developments are very different from one another, and to talk of a single third world revolution may be misleading. None the less, on an ideological level, attempts have been made by politicians and writers in all countries to generalise their experience, and in some ways it is an important and significant fact that consciousness outstrips structure. If, by a class-for-itself is meant a self-consciousness group, we might say that, in Marxist terms, the forces of the third world revolution had produced a class-for-itself without yet producing a class-in-itself.

The first important question at issue is that of the role of the peasantry. Clearly Marx had assumed that the peasantry, as such, were not able, of themselves, to unite for political action. Indeed they were not, in the true sense of the term, a class. When the revolution occurred in Russia, moreover, Lenin worked on the basis, first of united action by the peasants and workers, led by what was, in essence, a workers' party, and then through united action by workers and poor peasants against rich peasants. In Stalin's day this involved the process known as the 'liquidation of the Kulaks' which was a class war against the richer peasants and, to some extent, a war of town against country.

Stalin, naturally, refused to accept, given his own experience, that the Chinese could win their revolution by depending upon a peasant-based army. But one of the major facts of world history is that Mao Tse-tung proved him wrong. Instead of class war of town against country, Mao Tse-tung envisaged a situation in which his army got control of the countryside and, allying itself with the peasantry, gradually surrounded the towns and starved them out before trying to capture them. Following this, even the process of industrialisation bore the marks of peasant thinking. Instead of primitive accumulation, through the exploitation of the peasantry, to finance large-scale industrialisation, emphasis was given to small-scale industrial enterprise, which could be carried on as well in peasant communes as in urban backyards.

The whole Chinese model was one which was much more exportable than the Russian, and it appealed most particularly in those countries where peasants had embarked upon armed revolution, especially Cuba and Algeria. Significantly, however, these two countries produced, not merely politicians, but ideologists and theorists, who took the revolutionary thinking of the third world well beyond the point at which Mao Tse-tung and the Chinese experience left it.

Cuba provided a new model of liberation by a peasant-based army, and, in the first place, it was not a communist revolution at all. It did, however, come to terms politically with the communists and therefore produced political problems with which the Cuban leadership had to deal. These problems were thrashed out at the Tricontinental Conference in Havana in January 1966 and the

Conference of the Latin American Solidarity Organisation in 1967. While most of the Latin American communist parties supported the Soviet Union when it was subject to criticism, Cuba did not, and it was argued by some, not merely that the Soviet Union's support for reactionary dictatorships was opportunist, but that in some cases the organised working class, led by the communist party, was actually the enemy of the revolution. By then, Guevara had disappeared from Cuba to spread the notion of peasant-based revolution, and Régis Debray, a French communist philosopher working in Cuba, wrote (1967) of the revolution-within-the-revolution, that revolution was essentially a recognition of the new role to be played by the peasantry as compared with the working class.

The problems facing the Algerian revolution were different and they were dealt with in a far more systematic way by the third world's most significant theorist, Franz Fanon. Fanon had grown up in Martinique and had originally been influenced by the Martinique leader, Aimé Césaire. Césaire had himself resigned from the French communist party on the grounds that it subordinated the interests of the Martinique liberation movement to those of the French proletariat. The same was clearly true in Algeria.

From the point of view of communism in its European form, the destiny of the Algerian peasants and workers was to work with the French proletariat for the overthrow of French capitalism. Moreover this was something which it seemed could best be done by trade union struggle and parliamentary methods. The impending Algerian revolution, however, was a revolution with a leadership drawn from the national bourgeoisie and the peasantry, and a following drawn from the peasantry and the lumpenproletariat. It also turned deliberately to violence, rather than relying on peaceful trade union and parliamentary methods.

Fanon, like many of his contemporaries, had to choose between these positions, and he chose for the Algerian revolution. The theoretical justification for this was that it was simply not true to see the position of the poor colonial peoples as the same as that of the metropolitan proletariat. The white worker was often a *colon* who underwent nothing quite like the suffering and the exploitation of the native. When it came to the point, the difference between settler and 'native' was a far more important division than that between bourgeois and proletariat, and certainly the Algerian native worker had more to gain from following his own national bourgeois leaders into revolution than playing politics with the French communist party.

The question of violence was also a central one for Fanon. It was not, however, simply an abstract question for him. The fact was that the oppression of the colonial peoples was the most complete kind of oppression of all, namely that which led men to despise themselves. Moreover, so long as they lived in normal society, they survived only by living in a world of fantasy. The act of violence was a rational act to eliminate the cause of oppression and also to make men psychologically healthy by releasing them from their fantasies. The French communist conception of revolution would not enable them to achieve this.

Finally, however, Fanon was not prepared to give unqualified support to the national bourgeoisie. They were the potential agents of neo-colonialism. Thus, the Fanonist doctrine is like that of Marxism, a doctrine of permanent revolution. The colonial power has to be expelled and political independence won. But the danger of neo-colonialism only begins at this point, and one must expect that, in the newly independent countries, political struggle will go on. There are no short cuts to freedom to be obtained by collaborating with metropolitan capitalists. The people have to free themselves, and they must beware of the danger of their own national bourgeoisie becoming an exploiting class, either as agents or in their own right.

In fact, the major problems of the colonial revolution arise precisely in those countries where there has been a peaceful transition to political independence through a movement largely led by an educated élite (even if this is not, in a strict sense, a bourgeoisie). The new leadership in these countries may begin to act as the paid agents of foreign political or economic interests, or they may use their political position to milk the publicly-owned sectors of the economy (especially such bodies as marketing boards) for a large private income.

The matter is not, however, as simple as that of a class struggle between an exploiting bourgeoisie or political leadership. No colonial country, having recently won independence, is in a position to take over and manage large-scale industrial undertakings. Even if it is entirely uncorrupt, and wishes to bring such undertakings under public control, it is still deeply dependent upon retaining the goodwill of foreign experts and technicians. So, acts of political judgment have to be made and, between those who simply sell their countries to foreign capitalists, and those who attempt to pursue completely socialist policies, there are many political types. And, wherever one judgment is made or one policy pursued, it is possible that there may be alternatives. A political leader may, therefore, soon find that he has enemies with sources of finance, prepared to pursue policies which give a better deal to outside interests. This is, in essence, what most third world politics are about.

There is a point of some comparative interest here. In talking about the structure of the societies of the first world, we suggested that, in a capitalist society, the state bureaucracy organised the arena of market operations, and that political parties fed policies into that bureaucracy, which would favour one party or another. It is of the essence of a neo-colonial situation that external interests operating in the colonial territory find and finance their own political allies to create an arena for their colonial operations.

The dangers to which formerly colonial nations are exposed in this way are generally enhanced by the divisions which exist within the nation. Amongst these are ethnic and regional divisions as well as those between modern and traditional sectors of the society. As we saw, in an earlier chapter, the withdrawal of the colonial power may be followed by the handing over of power to one or other of the ethnic segments in a society. Whether this is a majority or a minority, it still means that there is a deprived ethnic group. In many cases, even where there is no integrated system of ethnic castes or estates, moreover, the nation may be compounded of large tribal groupings. And, finally, traditional rulers, who were vassal rulers under colonialism, now find themselves threatened by the party of national unity, whose local branch or cell undermines traditional rule.

It is easy to see how an outside power, or an outside corporation, which feels that it has had an unfair deal from the colonial government, would naturally consider whether or not there was not some other grouping in the country which, if it had power, would give a better deal. Thus secession, revolt and civil war become real possibilities, because such sectional elements may be given money and, having obtained money, can obtain men and arms to challenge the government. The mercenary soldier thus becomes a permanent part of the neo-colonial scene and remarkably large sums of money are available for the pursuit of very long and expensive wars indeed, like those of the Congo and of Nigeria.

The scale of brutality, suffering, and hardship, which a colonial civil war engenders, reminds one of mediaeval times in Europe. Inter-tribal 'genocide' becomes a matter of course; unarmed villagers are subject to air attack and can only run into the bush to hide from bombs, and as communications collapse thousands of men, women, and children may die of starvation, even though it usually remains possible for the newspaper correspondents of the metropolitan powers to obtain gourmet meals in not too distant hotels while they prepare their copy.

This situation of barbarism, following the collapse of national government, usually ends on some kind of feudal basis. The weak seek protection from the strong and no one is totally innocent. Eventually a politician, a colonel or a chief holds all other powers in feudal dependence, or, if he seems not to, may have them publicly executed. Thus the urbane diplomats of the metropolitan powers dine with a man who has executed a dozen or so enemies before breakfast, and see what can be done to protect their own national economic interests.

The politicians least likely to become involved in neo-colonial corruption are those who have the hardest fight to win independence, and this usually means those who have had to win independence by military struggle. In these cases the patterns of guerilla warfare and of revolution have usually been influenced by China and Cuba. But even in these cases one does find neo-colonial influences and other influences at work. There is scarcely a liberation movement whose armies, as well as political parties, are not split, and money which gives an advantage over political rivals might well flow into their movements as it does into political parties elsewhere. This money often comes from economically interested parties, but it also comes from rival revolutionary sources (e.g. Russian, Chinese or Pan-African). It is hard, therefore, to envisage a process of liberation which can take power without its members attacking one another, as well as the common enemy, and as time goes on the conflicts between Trotskyists, anarchists and communists in Spain, or between rival groups of guerillas in East Europe, will pale into insignificance by comparison.

A further point to be noticed is the plight which awaits settler elements when settler dominated colonies are liberated. It should always be remembered that these countries have huge differences in the standard of living of their rich and their poor, and it would be surprising indeed if some of the leaders of the liberation movement did not covet for themselves some of the privileges of the former ruling element. On the other hand, however moderate and gradualist the Westernised élite leadership of the liberation movement might be, it is extremely unlikely that it will be able, if liberation occurs, to prevent looting, plunder, and vengeful murder on a colossal scale. One must therefore expect that there will be atrocity stories pouring out of every such territory as it is liberated. These will, of course, be grossly exaggerated by pro-settler journalists from the metropolis, but they will certainly have some basis in fact. There is no reason to suppose that a liberation movement can be carried through solely by saints.

Before one talks about the bloody cost of liberation, however, it is important to notice that most guerila movements are desperately weak. They know that the withdrawal of white troops from Vietnam took twenty-five years to achieve, and they do not expect to win more quickly and more cheaply. In the meanwhile, the best weapons which the weak can use against the strong are those of terror. We now accept that international air travel will be delayed as passengers are frisked by special security guards, that the plane may be hijacked, that ambassadors and businessmen may be captured and held to ransom, that the post must be carefully inspected lest it contain a letter bomb, or that our wives may be killed by an explosion in the supermarket.

Amongst the leading exponents of these techniques are the Palestine liberation movements. Here one has a people which has lost its homeland and stands no chance of regaining it. It has suffered a quite catastrophic military defeat, which it is unable to reverse, even by the risky process of involving the super powers. Therefore, all that it can do is to make life systematically unpleasant and dangerous for anyone who appears sympathetic to its enemies, without worrying too much about whether or not innocent by-standers are hurt. From a position of somewhat greater strength, the Irish Republican Army 'Provisionals' have carried their urban guerilla warfare from Belfast in Northern Ireland to the cities of England.

Terrorism and anarchy, however terrible may be its consequences for its victims, has a certain romantic attraction for its participants, particularly since the carrying out of a terrorist venture involves a very high risk of the loss of one's own life, indeed in some cases the commission of the act may involve one's suicide. It is also true that, just as in the class struggle in the advanced countries, as Marx and Engels noted in *The Communist Manifesto*, 'a section of the ruling class cuts itself adrift and joins the revolutionary class, the class that holds the future in its hands' so also, in the case of the third world revolution, there are idealistic young people in the metropolitan countries who will risk all for a cause. As we have seen, such group-ings, alienated from the values of their own society, might in any case commit violence against it, but the third world's struggle gives them a positive cause. What this means is that the respectable bourgeoisie of the metropolitan countries might find in the future, not merely that there are terrible deeds committed by violent men in far away places, but that their own children, or their friends' children, might also be involved in murder.

A very special set of problems besets those who are the descen-dants of slaves in the Americas and elsewhere. This is that, inde-pendently of the question of their freedom, they have a problem of cultural identity. They live in countries which are not their own, and have been educated into a culture which is not their own, and one which, in the image which it has of them, systematically degrades them. Thus it is essential that this cultural situation should be changed and that an African, or black, identity and consciousness should be cultivated. This, then, is one aspect of what is called black power.

Black power, however, has a different meaning to this. It also refers to a political programme. That political programme must necessarily take one of the following forms:

(1) Zionism, i.e. a 'return' to an African homeland.
(2) Secession within the country of residence.
(3) Revolution with a view to actually installing black rulers in place of white, and subordinating white workers to black rule.
(4) Organising a black political movement with the objective of sparking off a more widespread socialist revolution which will improve the black man's status.
(5) Imposition of a reign of terror on a white ruling group who, it is assumed, will none the less continue to rule.

Most of these possibilities exist both in the West Indies and in the USA. We should look at them separately, however, because the black man in the USA does not only act for himself or see himself as acting only for himself. He is in the vanguard of the third world revolution, because he conducts that revolution in the homeland of one of the world's super powers.

Most Europeans today probably regard the West Indies as consisting of black men's countries, and it may appear to the newcomer as absurd to regard them as anything else, since most men's skins are reasonably black. Yet one cannot live long in any of these territories without recognising that their social leadership was, and to some degree still is, white, and that their institutions appear as white men's institutions. Barbados boasts that its legislature is one of the oldest in the British Empire, but this boast by the social élite wins little applause from the black population, because the legislature was a legislature of white planters and it still has the feel of whiteness about it. Similarly, to the uneducated rural Jamaican, even more than to the educated adherent of black power, Jamaica is not really home. But if the place where one lives is not one's own, the belief then arises that there must be some such place, and both the religious Ras Tafari movement, and subsequent black power movements have raised this possibility (Nettleford, 1971).

Trinidad has had both socialist and black power movements, and it is difficult to distinguish the two. Guyana, on the other hand, is a country where black power means domination by Afro-Guyanese rather than by East Indians. It is somewhat difficult, therefore, to be quite sure what anyone in these territories is talking about when black power is mentioned.

In the case of Trinidad there was a quasi-socialist intellectual movement in being, which was concerned with the liberation of the

201

Trinidad economy from its position as a mere point of reference in a chain of transactions within multi-national corporations. This movement was extremely critical of the regime as being neo-colonial. But it did not, however, speak explicitly in the name of black power. Later, however, after certain incidents abroad, involving the conviction of Trinidad students, there was a protest march across the island, led by a black, former student leader, aiming at organising all *workers* under the banner of black power. Here one had the phenomenon of a young middle-class black man appealing to Indian workers to act against a black prime minister in the name of black power. This clearly is a situation which contrasts very sharply with that in Guyana, but which shows how intertwined black power is with socialist and working-class ideology.

As yet there is little sign of a great social reversal in the West Indies, as there could be in the name of black power. If such a reversal occurred, one could imagine whites being denied access to various clubs and public places, being discriminated against in housing, employment and education, and forced to live in segregated areas, as is to a large extent the case for West Indians living in England. In fact, far from this being the case, the white man in the West Indies still enjoys privileges in a black man's country. Where a racial supremacy version of black power has arisen, it has been directed, not against whites, but against East Indians.

The situation of the American black rioting in his ghetto and striking terror into the hearts of the white population hardly applies in the West Indies, where the white population is so small, but it could well apply in the equivalent for the West Indian of the northern cities of the USA for America's blacks, i.e. the United Kingdom. Black power is talked in the cafés and the schools of Notting Hill amongst both the West and East Indian young and, although such race riots as there have been have taken the form of attacks by white on black, militancy amongst the blacks is growing, and when questions arise of working together with, or separately from, white liberal and socialist allies, the increasing tendency is to reject co-operation and to trust a racially based movement.

Much of what happens in the British West Indian community, and in the West Indies itself, takes its cue from the USA, even though the USA has drawn a number of its militant black leaders from the West Indies. To understand what is happening in that black world which lives symbiotically with white America and Europe, therefore, one must understand the model of cultural and political action which is disseminated to blacks from the USA. Amongst other things, one should note that America's blacks are among the most educated, the most literate, and the most literary, in the world.

Before we look at the details of black American political action, we should return to the general point about culture and identity. Quite clearly, given the degrading old Negro image in American culture, American films and American schoolbooks, it could hardly be expected that American blacks would be doing anything less than they are in order to assert their own cultural identity. Black culture and black studies in American schools and universities, therefore, have a very genuine core. It is also the case, however, that, through the white use of the technique of accommodating to a threat in terms of pluralism, black studies are actually encouraged in universities and schools. What passes as black studies in many quarters contains a great mixture of lies and nonsense and offers, therefore, many opportunities for intellectual charlatans, while not seriously enhancing black dignity. On the other hand, one may well expect that, given the untruths of self-confident racist myths built into American culture by whites in the past, a counter-culture amongst blacks who are not so self-confident is more than likely to involve ideological distortion and untruth.

The rational, liberal and socialist approach to the situation of the American black in the past was to deny the relevance of colour to questions of human rights. Thus the National Association for the Advancement of the Coloured People sought to use the guarantees of rights allowed to all men under the American Constitution to overcome segregation, discrimination and inequality. What this tended to show, in the long run, however, was that although law was rational, it was also far too slow to liberate anyone.

The most popular black movement in the USA before 1939 was Garveyism. Led by a Jamaican, this movement stimulated black achievement in many spheres and posited the notion of a return to Africa. Pan-Africanism was also a notion preached by W. E. du Bois, even though he in turn became a communist. Today, however, Garveyism and other forms of black zionism, appear to be dead. Its nearest expression is to be found in growing black American support for liberation movements in Africa as though they were their own.

The use of legal redress as a method of gaining rights for the black population was transcended with the growth of street demonstrations and direct action and passive resistance under the leadership of Martin Luther King. This, of course, represented an actual increase in black militancy at the time, a point often now forgotten when white America claims to venerate King, not because he fought injustice as he saw it, but because he opposed the use of open violence in that fight.

Young American college students, led by the Trinidad-born Stokeley Carmichael, were not prepared to limit themselves to methods used by King. They openly claimed to be in favour of the use of violence and called for the creation of a 'new Vietnam' within the USA itself. King himself had opposed the war in Vietnam, but the new call was, although essentially rhetorical, a call to civil war in the USA.

The rhetoric of Carmichael, however, was reflected in a much more significant development in the streets and amongst common people. Poverty and unemployment had already driven many young blacks to crimes of violence. The growing use of drugs, moreover, increased both the need for money and the need for crime. But in Watts, for the first time, open fighting with the police, and systematic looting of shops began. The Watts experience was repeated in the 'long hot summer' of 1967, in dozens of other cities. Everywhere, young unemployed American blacks were at war with the police. It was hard to say where this might stop. Either America would find a way of dealing with the grievances of the blacks, or the spasmodic rioting would go on until American cities became uninhabitable for whites or the American government would use drastic and racist methods of repression. Which of these courses will, in the long run, be adopted it is difficult to say. Certainly at this time, there is no sign that America has found a way of living with a free black majority. Something of a state of war exists already. It seems more likely to become more, rather than less, violent in the future.

Two other black American movements should be noted. One was that of the Black Muslims, the other that of the Black Panthers. The former simply denied ruling class white values by adopting a non-white religion, and succeeded to some extent in creating cultural autonomy for the blacks. The latter also denied ruling class values, by calling itself a Marxist-Leninist party, aiming at using a black revolution to spark off an anti-capitalist one. The Panthers were brought almost immediately into conflict with the police and a number of them were killed. Their skill in dramatising their conflicts with the police, however, especially in relation to the Soledad brothers, and the trial of Angela Davis, helped to focus the sharpness of the American race war (Davis, 1971). It seems unlikely that it will do more than this, however, and there are certainly doubts whether it will ever produce any real linkages with a general American revolution. So far it has hardly even succeeded in winning the full support of the peace movement or the student movement. The real power to change the United States of America still lies, probably not with its black intellectuals, but with the young black unemployed in the ghettoes.

We suggested earlier that the American blacks might claim to be the vanguard of the third world revolution. The claim is also made by Chinese communists and by the leaders of African and Latin American liberation movements, but all problems come together in the American war in Vietnam and in her eventual forced withdrawal. Here the greatest military power in the world was deployed against a small non-white nation. But the people, and particularly the students, of America revolted against the war and so, to some extent, did the blacks. There was also truth in the notion that the burning and looting of American cities was creating a new Vietnam in the USA itself. Most of all, however, there was a capacity to resist, shown by a colonial people organised by a communist party and a communist army, which had never been shown before. Little wonder then that Vietnam became a focal symbol for all those engaged in the third world revolution everywhere.

Apart from all other issues, the consequence of the Vietnam war was to bring the world communist movement, the anti-colonial movement and the revolt of the blacks together in a single cause. The link could have been closer, it is true, if there had been mass defection from the American army by black troops. None the less, troops of all races in the American army fought unenthusiastically and began to produce, within the army itself, those kinds of cultural dissent which were prevalent in their home country, even to the extent of the formation of peace groups. And, while all anti-colonial movements were encouraged by the success of the Vietnamese, the American blacks began to see their own cause as an anti-colonial one.

Now it is not our intention as sociologists to suggest that there is one unitary third world class in revolt against the colonialists, producing, on a world scale, that kind of struggle which Marx had foreseen in a more limited way in the industrialised countries. This is the view which is suggested, both by Fanon in his book *The Wretched of the Earth* (1965) and by Segal in his *The Race War* (1966), but these are manifestos rather than sociological analyses. A sociologist may note the manifestos as themselves social facts, but he has an inescapable duty to point out the actual structural situation as well as the myths and utopian sociologies, in terms of which that situation is interpreted.

What we must say here, therefore, is that there is no single and unified third world revolutionary movement in being, and that the formation of such a movement, or even a few such movements, and their ultimate success, is something which must take a very long time, perhaps hundreds of years. In the meanwhile, it has to be recognised that, although there are some real alliances between real liberation movements established, there are also a number of purely nominal alliances and a number of movements which claim to be part of the revolt of the third world, but which actually represent sheer vested interests which have nothing whatever to do with liberation. Feudal emperors, dictators, and self-seeking bourgeois politicians all gather together under the banner of anti-colonialism as a matter of political convenience to themselves, but the true meaning of their presence at international conferences is more a sign of the divisions in the liberation movement than of its strength.

There is, of course, no going back to colonialism. For one thing, the former colonising powers would not wish it, for at this stage of history the colonies would be more of a liability than an asset. Moreover, it should be remembered that, however orderly the metropolitan systems were which arose on the basis of colonialism and, for that matter, however orderly their systems of colonial administration, the fact was that from the point of view of the colonial people they were systems of social destruction, of exploitation and plunder. Neither, however, can one go back to the pre-colonial order, although in some cases this appears an attractive possibility, because pre-colonial society had a kind of social peace about it before it was destroyed by conquest and capitalist rapacity.

But in saying this, we do not have to be idealistic about the present state of affairs either. The period of social upheaval which follows colonialism may be a long dark period fraught with much brutality and bloodshed. Neither is it to be thought that the colonising powers can themselves escape the consequences of the undoing of colonial relations. The revolution, the bloodshed, and the violence will take place, not merely in African, Latin American, or Asian jungles, but in their streets too, and to some extent it must contribute, if it does not give the final push to, the moral disintegration which we described in the previous chapter. We are thus living, not with a new idyllic set of social institutions such as Enlightenment sociology envisaged. The fruits of the 'liberation' of man from earlier forms of social order are now evident in the brutality and anarchy which more and more we take for granted. When half-a-million Chinese in Indonesia are massacred, a British politician notes only the political decline of the Indonesian prime minister, and rejoices that stability has returned to that part of the world. It is this bland acceptance of mass murder as a daily thing which really shows where the social processes, which the Enlightenment hailed with naïve joy, have actually led us.

But, last of all, let us emphasise that here, as elsewhere, while we have been nihilistic enough to reject the substitution of naïve wishful thinking for sociological analysis, we do so, not simply out of a kind of political masochism; we do so in order to take the true sociological measure of the task of those who seek happiness and self-fulfilment for men in the post-colonial world. We have to see what can be done, taking the social structures and the liberation movement which we have, to destroy the last vestiges of colonialism and to find our way out of the anarchy and brutality which post-colonial society, as well as neo-colonialism, have produced.

14   Public issues and private troubles

There are some who will say, when they read this book, that it is not about sociological, but about political, questions, and that the real problems of sociology are those of more subtle and intimate human relations. Or again, we will be accused of leaving out the individual and not recognising that the whole purpose of studying society is to relieve suffering, which, in its final form can only be an individual experience, to be rectified by alteration of the immediate world of social relations. This perspective is that which C. Wright Mills rightly sums up as being concerned with what he calls 'the personal troubles of the milieu'. To quote him (1959b, p. 8):

> Troubles occur within the character of the individual and within the range of his immediate relations with others; they have to do with his self and with those limited areas of social life of which he is directly and personally aware. Accordingly, the statement and resolution of troubles properly lie within the individual as a biographical entity and within the scope of his immediate milieu – the social setting that is directly open to his personal experience and to some extent his wilful activity.

At its narrowest, what this perspective does is to limit the area of control of wilful activity of the individual to his own personality, and many of the techniques of social casework, based as they are upon Freudian theory, are concerned with the achievement of personal equilibrium, or what is sometimes called a mature set of attitudes, even if this means taking a heroic stance *vis à vis* a world in which social relations have been fractured and the individual has no basis of personal support. The social worker intervenes temporarily and regards himself as ultimately successful only if the client is able to stand on his own feet.

208

A more sociological approach to 'troubles' is that which looks at the problem, not merely as one of personality disturbance, but as one in which the immediate structure of social relations around the individual has been fractured and needs repair, or, if we may put it that way, the replacement of a part. Such an approach is suggested by a brilliantly suggestive essay by William Goode on the incomplete family (Merton and Nisbet, 1963, p. 390).

Goode looks at a number of contingencies which might befall the family and render it incomplete and therefore leave individual members without the support of normal social relations. Especially illuminating is the deliberate contrast which he makes between divorce and bereavement, but he also indicates the main structural features of other incomplete family situations, including illegitimate motherhood, forms of willed and unwilled departure of a spouse other than divorce, such as work-desertion, military service and imprisonment, prolonged physical and mental illness of one or more parents or children, and unemployment.

In each of these cases the total situation of the individual may be one of disgrace (as in illegitimacy or imprisonment), prestige (as in the case of military service), or ambiguity (as in the case of divorce). In each case different significant role partners will be missing, or a set of services may have been withdrawn. The task of the social worker could then be defined, not simply as that of getting the client to pull himself together, but of restoring the social fabric by a variety of techniques. These might include winning reconciliation with, and support from, a relative or friend who has rejected the client's disgraceful behaviour, or finding substitutes for such a person, building upon the relatively temporary support accruing to a bereaved person at the time of a funeral, and trying to make it permanent, replacing the services of a husband-breadwinner through welfare payments, or those of a mother through the crèching of a baby, or generally finding substitute networks of friends and relations to constitute a new social milieu.

Now Goode's actual contribution here was the analysis of a sociological problem of the incomplete family.* The discussion of social work techniques which might cure the condition through a sort of socio-therapy (as distinct from psycho-therapy) is our own. But it is appropriate to respond to his analysis in terms of such proposals because this is still a case in which troubles are seen as

* It should not be thought that we mean to imply here that Goode confines himself to the problems of the immediate social milieu. His *World Revolution in Family Patterns* (1963) indicates very clearly how aware he is of the extent to which family structure is affected by wider socio-economic systems, while his *After Divorce* (1956) shows clearly that he is aware of divorce as more than a mere private trouble.

caused by the immediate milieu, and in the control, if not of the personal will of the suffering individual, at least of those concerned with his welfare. Such an approach might well be extended to deal with conditions in industry or in urban community.

We do not, however, always have such direct control of situations, and in any case, while the individual case might be treatable by a social worker, the problem of the recurrence of such cases has to be dealt with on a different level of social intervention. It is here that Mills introduces his notion of *public issues*. These, he tells us (1959b, p. 8):

> have to do with matters that transcend these local
> environments of the individual and the range of his inner life.
> They have to do with the organization of many such milieux
> into the institutions of an historical society as a whole,
> with the ways in which various milieux overlap and inter-
> penetrate to form the larger structure of social and
> historical life. An issue is a public matter: some value
> cherished by publics is felt to be threatened. Often there
> is a debate about what that value really is and about what
> it is that really threatens it. The debate is often without
> focus if only because it is the very nature of an issue,
> unlike even widespread trouble, that it cannot very well be
> defined in terms of the immediate or everyday environments
> of ordinary men. An issue in fact, often involves a crisis in
> institutional arrangements, and often too it involves what
> Marxists call 'contradictions' or 'antagonisms'.

Now, despite what we have said about the heritage of sociology from the Enlightenment, and the naïve optimism about the new institutional arrangements of industrial society which this engendered, it is worth noting that, not merely Mills, but all the classical figures of sociology's second wave, Durkheim, Weber, and Marx, were cautious and anxious about the direction industrial society was taking. All saw it as beset by public issues; Durkheim analysing them on a high level of generality as anomie; Weber, though he might have accepted the direction of history as inevitable, none the less drawing attention to some of the distress caused by the rational-calculating spirit taken to its extreme; and Marx, of course, seeing the alienation of man as lying, not merely in his exploitation by another man, but by another man who was a part of a whole system of exploitation. Moreover, there was a special reason why Durkheim should have seen these public issues as causing private troubles. Because he had sought the causes of individual phenomena in social structure, his account of that social structure bore directly on individual pathologies, cases and problems.

210

Part of the thesis of this book is that we now face private troubles on an increased scale and range because we are faced with new kinds of public issues. But before we turn to our own account of these we would do well to consider what the classical sociologists, as well as more recently, Mills, had to say. What we shall discover is that, because of the level of generality on which they considered problems, they were not simply concerned with the old classical type of social problem, but that they were, at least in part, aware of the kind of problems which we now wish to discuss.

Durkheim raises in *Suicide* the question of the limits of human need fulfilment. Unlike, say Malinowski, who simply sees the satisfaction of biological needs as the prime determinant of social structure, Durkheim immediately points out (1963, p. 247):

> Strictly speaking, we may consider that the quantity of
> material supplies necessary to the physical maintenance of
> human life is subject to computation, though this be less
> exact than [in the case of other animals] and a wider margin
> left for the free combinations of the will; for beyond the
> indispensable minimum which satisfies nature when instinctive,
> a more awakened reflection suggests better conditions,
> seemingly desirable ends craving fulfillment.

But 'human nature' places no limits on needs, and these 'constantly and infinitely surpass the means at their command'. Thus if men are not to be placed in an unbearable state, they must be subject to controls external to themselves, yet respected by them. In general Durkheim believes that it is in the nature of any true 'society' that it is accepted as a moral authority by the individual, but he does also see that in some cases this may be in question.

There are really two questions here. One is the question of a human situation in which human beings seek to satisfy their needs without limit. This Durkheim believed to be a morbid state which occurred in times of economic booms and in the anomic world of divorced and separated persons. But surely such is the very nature of contemporary capitalism. Demands must be stimulated all the time to keep the system going, and an ever-rising standard of life is the promise of every political party. Moreover, the so-called permissive society, which we have seen as the intrusion of commercial activity into spheres once held to be sacred and private, encourages individuals, not merely to seek personal and sexual fulfilment to some degree outside the family, but promiscuously and to the final degree. More generally than in the simple case of sex, one finds that it is a feature of our society that many people do many things, as the slang phrase has it, just for kicks.

All of this is an indication of the existence of a society in which

211

acceptable moral controls have broken down. And the state of affairs which this induces on a psychological level leads, so Durkheim believed, to life itself becoming intolerable. But what of the possibility of moral controls? Durkheim believes that this lies, above all, in the occupational system. There must be some shared appreciation of the worth of occupations (ibid., p. 249).

> The different functions are graded in public opinion and
> a certain coefficient of well-being assigned to each, according
> to its place in the hierarchy.

But there must also be a rule which declares who is entitled to occupy social positions (p. 250):

> The workman is not in harmony with his social position if
> he is not convinced that he has his deserts. If he feels
> justified in occupying another, what he has would not satisfy
> him. So it is not enough for the average level of needs for
> each social condition to be regulated by public opinion, but
> another, more precise, rule, must fix the way in which these
> conditions are open to individuals.

When one reads these carefully chosen words, it is possible to see how far existing capitalist society is from achieving Durkheim's ideal. It is not, as some British industrial relations experts have sought to argue, that an implicit sense of the relative worth of occupations, and an implicitly accepted wages policy have broken down. That may be partially true, but there is still, for better or worse, a recognition of some kind of status hierarchy of occupations. Neither is it simply the case that we now have a meritocracy in which everyone aspires to have a job in accordance with his merit or skill, although this is a strongly held social ideal in certain quarters. What matters most is that capitalist corporations looking for markets must induce men to seek higher and higher standards of living. Thus Merton (1957a, p. 131) was right in saying that anomie was the product of social structure. What may be at issue is which social structures are responsible for inducing it. Durkheim imagined a world in which industrial corporations, morally integrated with one another, set limits to anomie. In fact, what we find is that it is precisely industrial corporations which encourage it, being compelled by their own need for continuing profit to create an ever-growing demand.

Curiously, while Durkheim noted that what modern societies lacked were controls on, and limits to, human need-fulfilment, both Weber and Marx saw the limitations on human freedom as lying in the controls which actually existed. There can be little doubt that for Weber the long-term product of the rational-calculating spirit lay in the bureaucratic corporation, but it is also clear that the rationality of the corporation was dependent upon the partial dehumanisation of the men who staffed it. Only in so far as they saw themselves as fulfilling a supra-human duty without any concept of the end of the activity, or of gaining pleasure from participating in it, could men be expected to go on working in this way. When, however, as we have seen, belief in that kind of duty was lost, work within the organisation became purposeless. At the same time, home life was rigorously separated from work, and one has only to add to Weber's concept the notion that fulfilment through work is central to the meaning of human life to see that life within the leisure-based home became meaningless too. Thus, while work in a calling was rendered meaningless, social life divorced from work was so by definition.

Curiously, we may note in passing, the shadow of Immanuel Kant falls over the work of both Durkheim and Weber. Durkheim rejects the eternal increase of happiness or pleasure as an acceptable human goal, and calls for external restraints on the individual. Weber does not see private pleasure as even a possibility for men in industrial society, and suggests first a duty to an inscrutable God, and then duty for its own sake, as the principal motivating force on which social organisation relies. Clearly, the categorical imperative has to work for its living in the modern world!

Of course, one interpretation which might be put on this notion of moral duty is that it operates, not simply through external forces or from some abstract moral sense, but through that curious internalised external psychological mechanism, Freud's superego, or Mead's 'me' or generalised 'other'. But is the family by itself, or the family in conjunction with other educational agencies, really capable of fitting out the individual atoms of modern society with this control mechanism properly fitted and tuned so that they function efficiently? Even Parsons recognised (Parsons 1951, ch. 8) that it might not be so and that the sociologist, even of the most stable social system, must expect deviance. We must agree, but point out that the failures of the socialisation process which Parsons discusses are not merely problems for the society. They are problems for the individual, whose superego overwhelms him on the one hand, or fails him on the other. Yet at the very time when society depends so much on the family for supplying it with individuals, it also impoverishes family life, or puts so much strain on it by isolating it, that it is bound to produce failures. The psychologically disturbed are, of course, in one sense the consequence of family failure, but they are the consequence of family failure in producing an individual of a very particular type.

It may perhaps be noted that the survival of the modern social order seems, in both Durkheim and Weber, to depend upon the Protestant religion. True, Durkheim may argue that individual needs must be limited by an external power, and he has in mind here the occupational order of organic solidarity. But it is not organic solidarity which is contrasted, in *Suicide*, with the no longer tenable world of mechanical solidarity, which is associated with altruistic suicide. It is a kind of socialised or indoctrinated individualism. So Durkheim might have said, not that the human individual must subject himself to an external power with moral authority, but rather an internalised power. Thus the individual was, as Parsons puts it, forced to be free. He is the characteristic product of Protestant society. It is the same individual whom Weber sees as staffing modern bureaucracy.

The same general problem of the alienation of man from himself was the main theme of the whole Young Hegelian school of which Marx was a member. Why did spirit and the spirit of man suffer in the world of nature, history and culture? The answer was that the individual was dominated by forces external to himself. Sometimes they were simply figments of his imagination, like religious concepts described in the work of Feuerbach. Sometimes they were human creations which now controlled their creators, like money and the state. But, for Marxism, there was one source of alienation from which all other forms of the phenomenon arose. That source he found in the social relations of production, which deprived man of the product of his labour, of his labour itself, of his relationship with his fellow-men, but above all of his species being.

Thus, although the main theme in Marx was the economic exploitation of man by man, and that itself is for the exploited a private trouble, there is an individual and psychological dimension to his sociological theory, just as much as there is in Durkheim's. Alienation, like anomie, invades the individual soul. For Durkheim the sickness induced by society is the release of the individual from a balancing social order. For Marx it is the capture and control of a human being, who would otherwise be able to fulfil himself by working and loving and shaping his society in conditions of freedom. It was in this special way that Erich Fromm sought to explain the species being of man, in accordance with his own Marxist and Hegelian leanings. He did not, however, prove, any more than Marx did, that that loss of species being occurred in industry. Rather he saw it, because of his Freudian heritage, as occurring through an inadequate family system. Perhaps Weber's concept of bureaucracy, involving both the impoverishment of work and of family life, has some bearing here. So also does Durkheim's conception of the need for meaningful occupational associations.

We have been emphasising here that all of the classical sociologists were, in one way or another, concerned with the private troubles created by public issues. Durkheim, Freud and Marx were bound to be because of the philosophical anthropology which was built into their approach. Each of them was concerned, in his own way, about the loss by men of their true humanity or species being. Weber, on the other hand, simply left the matter implicit, but, given his methodologically individualist approach to the description of social structures, he was, in the course of describing these structures, also describing the human condition.

But we are concerned to be more specific than were the sociologists of the nineteenth and early twentieth centuries, in two respects. First, we want to consider, not generally the effect of modern social structures on the human condition, but the effect of specific public issues on specific troubles. Second, we want to carry the story forward, not confining ourselves to the dehumanising side effects of capitalism and industrialism in its pure form and in its heyday, but with all the additional side effects, experienced as new private troubles of a system in decay. Mills is very clear on the first of these, and what he says also covers some of the ground in the second.

The private troubles which relate to public issues are, for Mills, those which relate to employment, war, the metropolis, and marriage.

On unemployment, Mills distinguishes between the case of a single man unemployed in a city of a hundred thousand, and the case of a nation in which fifteen million out of fifty million are unemployed. Here (1959b, p. 9)

the very structure of opportunities has collapsed. Both
the correct statement of the problem and the range of
possible solutions require us to consider the economics
and political institutions of the society, and not merely
the personal situation and character of a scatter of
individuals.

On war, there is an individual problem of personal survival (ibid.).

But the structural issues of war have to do with its
causes; with what types of men it throws up in command;
with its effects upon economic and political, family and
religious institutions, with the unorganised irresponsibility
of a world of nation-states.

On the metropolis the question is not simply a private one of finding a nice home. The questions are (ibid.):

What should be done with this wonderful monstrosity? Break
it all up into scattered units, combining residence and work?
Refurbish it as it stands? Or after examination, dynamite

215

it, and build new cities according to new plans in new
places? What should those plans be? And who is to decide
and to accomplish them whatever choice is made?

On marriage, apart from personal matrimonial strain, what of
a society in which one marriage in four fails within the first four
years? Here there is a structural issue having to do with the institution of marriage and the family, and other institutions which bear
on them.

Now these *are* highly salient structural issues which produce
private problems. Let us look at each of them to see what can be
said about them fourteen years after the publication of *The Sociological Imagination*. Then let us go on to look at other structural
issues which emerge from our analysis, and look at the private
troubles to which they are likely to give rise. Our total analysis
should be in line with that of Mills, who saw his own society as on
the edge of an abyss, but further along that line, because we do really
envisage a new dark age in which life will be, relatively speaking,
poorer, nastier, more brutish and more brief. Certainly more so than
in those 'civilised' social systems where men savoured named wines
and cheeses in peace and ignored the world outside the metropolis.

Unemployment clearly is a problem today as much as it was in
the 1930s. But it is also a different kind of problem. In the 1930s a
large section of what had been the organised working class were laid
off indefinitely by their employers because capitalism was in crisis,
and the men either lived without hope or hoped for the ending of the
system. Now the curious thing is that capitalism is apparently in
good heart. There is overall economic growth and, on the technological level, there is a new industrial revolution. But this by no
means implies an overall gain for everyone. Technological change
implies the disappearance of many jobs, as machines take the place
of men, and the staff who remain are less like bureaucrats and workers
with varying degrees of skill. They tend to be professionals or
clever men who mend machines on the one hand, and others who
read coloured comics as they mind them. While these are well paid,
however, and join in the new prosperity, those who used to do simple
decision making, or those who sold their manual skill and labour,
are likely to be excluded from the labour process and will get any
subsistence which they do get by retirement settlements from their
firms, from the kindness and charity of their relatives, or from the
state. To be in this situation is to be deeply in private trouble, with
the sense of not knowing how debts are to be met, even if there is
enough food, and in the sense of role uncertainty, of continually
asking oneself what one is for.

War, for Mills (1960), meant the ever-present danger in his later

216

lifetime of World War Three. That danger still exists, even though the present industrial and military weakness of China, and the detente between the USSR and the USA conceals the fact. Even continued *preparation* and *testing* of nuclear weapons has led to bilateral agreement on arms control because of the terrible known consequences for individuals of radiation, and hazards still arise from the small-scale activities of countries like France. But if there is a steady statistical rate of nuclear deaths in the world through the testing of weapons, there is also the ever-present possibility of the actual use of these weapons in small-scale war. The European powers might well, out of respect for their own civilised cities, refrain from using them to settle their own disputes, but a gambler's throw to settle an Asian war seems quite on the cards. There would then be at least as many people suffering private troubles as suffer them in Hiroshima and Nagasaki.

For the moment, however, most wars – and it should be noted that we speak this way because war is a permanent phenomenon of the twentieth century – are colonial wars in which peoples who have suffered varying periods of colonial subordination fight to free themselves, either by fighting the colonial power directly, or by fighting amongst themselves because colonialism has forced them to live with other ethnic groups in an unnatural union, or because law and order have simply collapsed. So one has the series of wars in which Britain and France have engaged since the 'peace' of 1945, where for a while metropolitan interests had to be preserved and young Englishmen and Frenchmen were forced to fight the 'terrorists'. But then those 'terrorists' who survived became patriots and English and French mothers looked at the permanently youthful pictures of their soldier sons and wondered what they had died for. Then even after the last imperial soldiers went home, Greek fought Turk, Catholic fought Protestant, or even where no war occurred one ethnic group oppressed or expelled another, as in Guyana and Uganda.

In some cases, like that of the Arab Palestinians, their cause was a hopeless one if they fought according to all the laws of human decency. But those who cannot win can still hurt and terrorise those who win. That is the logic of the British and French nuclear weapons, which could perhaps destroy Leningrad or Kiev before Britain or France was eliminated. It is also the logic of the hijacker, the airport terrorist and the man who deals in letter bombs, car bombs and parcel bombs. There is a small structural difficulty here for the world of nations. There is an immense personal tragedy for the family of holiday-makers who see their child die in a pool of blood in the airport concourse, or the typist whose hand or head is blown off as she opens a parcel bomb in the mail.

217

But these acts of violence which horrify people and politicians alike in a democracy are small beer indeed compared with the sort of war which occurs when a former colonial nation comes apart and the mercenaries and gun-runners move in to keep it going to sustain the demand for their services. The ghastly little meaningless tragedy which happened in the Welsh village of Aberfan, when a coal tip slipped and buried a school, is magnified a thousand times as mothers try to keep their starving children alive with finger-fuls of Red Cross food, and where every service on which people rely for life in society has broken down, except that provided by the military, who are still on hand to kill their daily quota.

Did anyone think that Mills's private troubles referred only to middle-class Americans on psychiatrists' consulting couches? Such people may be in pain, for all suffering is ultimately mediated sub-jectively, but even more immediate than that sort of suffering is the actual fact of violence in the world. Moreover there is no pacifist short cut to an answer. The structure of the modern world was created through violence, even though those who suffered it were not in a position to write about it. It is unlikely, therefore, that an alteration of that structure will occur without at least equally violent redress. But when all that is said and done, the Catholic mother and the Protestant mother in Belfast look the same on the television when they are interviewed about their murdered children. So do communist and pro-American refugees.

Finally, it should be remembered that the lines between war and other forms of political violence, and between criminal and political violence, are hard to draw. Thus, in Birmingham, England, when a young half West Indian boy assaults and seriously injures a drunken Englishman and is sentenced to two concurrent sentences of twenty years imprisonment for what the newspapers call mugging, can this be wholly divorced from the question of colonialism, or the position of the colonial immigrant in British society? Yet that public issue is translated into a private trouble for an Englishman who may not be able to work again, and a young coloured man who may next emerge to freedom only when he is thirty-five.

We have engaged in an extended discussion of war and violence because these are the public issues which, more than any other, are going to provide a flow of private troubles, even for peaceful Europe, in the future. Let us, however, also note the other two types of prob-lem to which Mills refers. The first is that of the metropolis. One interesting point to notice here is how little the classical sociologists had to say about the city. Weber's interest was in the role of the late mediaeval city as the forcing-house of capitalist development. Durk-heim, although his concepts of mechanical and organic solidarity and anomie had application to the city (Rex, 1973b, ch. 4) none

218

the less did not develop his ideas in this direction. Engels, when he studied the city, was more concerned with the actual degradation of the workers by capitalism than with specifically urban processes. It was therefore left to Simmel (1971) to talk about the phenomenology and psychology of social relations in the city, and for Park and Burgess (1925), combining some of Simmel's insights with a theoretical social Darwinism, to lay the foundation of urban sociology.

The social Darwinist framework, however, was significant. It showed what was likely to happen in a city which was developed by unrestrained capitalism. The competitive process led ultimately to class segregation in a series of zones, and it may perhaps be noted that Burgess's analysis of life-styles in these zones has a greater degree of subtlety than some of the analyses which began from social relations in industry. What they could not have envisaged was that this process of urban segregation would provide an ideal terrain for the insertion of the race war and the revolution of the third world into the heart of metropolitan city life.

The race war, however, is not the sole problem of the cities. True, when white Americans say 'our cities are no longer fit to live in' they refer most often to the fact that the ghetto has taken control. But it is also arguable whether units of the size of New York are viable at all. They cannot guarantee elementary transport and refuse collection services and the life of the city is precariously dependent on services like these, so that if they fail, thousands could die. As yet, moreover, the art of town planning has not got further, in most capitalist societies, than guiding and influencing the forces of the market.

Lastly, Mills mentions the last citadel of *Gemeinschaft*, namely the family and marriage. There are two points to notice about this. One is Mills's reference to the institution itself and the plight of that institution. The other is his reference to the divorce rate as an instance of the use of pathological indices for sociological purposes.

Possibly the figures for marital breakdown, which Mills gave, are indicative of the fact that too much strain is placed, in a capitalist society or in a rational-bureaucratic society, on a single type of relationship to compensate for the dehumanisation of working life. Two things should be noticed about this, however. One is that when the modern family is compared with earlier social forms, like that of the working-class family in the industrial revolution, the rate of breakdown is not necessarily all that high. The other is that, all too often, proposals for a wider-based unit than the monogamous family have been caught up with different types of proposal for a free market in sex.

Unfortunately, capitalism is only too capable of invading even the attempts which are made to reform it. We should notice, however,

219

that the family as a social institution is far from perfect from the point of view of its members, however necessary it may be from the point of view of industry or society. It creates a precarious emotional environment for the children who grow up in it. It creates a relationship in which two individuals make excessive emotional demands on each other, yet are expected to go on responding for the rest of their lives. And finally, it creates a condition of bondage for women, which will hardly survive the development of contraceptive methods controlled by women.

One extreme view which has gained currency in recent years is that the family is a kind of lethal chamber for destroying human personalities (Cooper, 1961), and no one who has ever done any kind of pastoral or tutorial work can doubt that the kind of stresses and strains to which individuals are subject, not simply because of broken homes or incomplete families, but because their families are all too complete, are such that it must be seen as one of the most prolific of all sources of private troubles.

This, however, is not to say that the family can be reformed on its own. Parsons (1951, 1961, 1966) has produced a powerful theoretical argument to show that the kind of personal relationship involved in marriage is necessary to the maintenance of the impersonal world of work and that, together with the school and the peer group, they provide the means whereby, first the elementary socialisation of the child into an affective, diffuse, particularistic and ascriptive world, and then the secondary transition to its opposite, are achieved. Prima facie then it would appear that change in the structure of the family presupposes change in the larger industrial world. There is the interesting evidence of the development of the commune movement (Rigby, 1973) but it can still be asked whether this is not merely a subsidiary movement for those not closely involved with bureaucratic structures or those who are parasitic upon a family anyway. Our conclusion is that the family induces much pain but that it is none the less part of a wider network of social institutions.

Mills's reference to divorce rates, however, also reminds one of Durkheim's use of suicide rates. Such indices are often interesting for what they tell us, not merely about the institutions in which they occur, but something more general about the kind of social solidarity which exists, or about social facts which are 'unfixed'. There are, of course, grave difficulties about interpreting statistics relating to such matters as crimes of violence, mental illness and divorce, but it is worth noting that the capitalist industrial world has witnessed fairly steady increases in these since it began to keep statistics. This could, of course, be indicative of a society which becomes more concerned about its social problems. It could, however, also mean that one of the features of capitalist growth is a growth in the rate of private troubles.

So far, what we have been saying may be interpreted as meaning that most of our private troubles derive from capitalist rationality and capitalist rapacity, especially in its colonial forms. What then of the private troubles of the communist world? Are they the same or are they characteristically different from those of capitalism? And, so far as the colonial world is concerned, are all its private troubles to be explained in terms of capitalist neo-colonialism?

There clearly are certain aspects of communism, as we have seen, which represent the logical culmination of processes set in train under capitalism. Chief among these is the whole idea of commitment to a bureaucracy. It would seem, prima facie, that if this involves purpose-lessness and alienation, it should be more evident when bureaucracy is not merely a means of organisation within individual industry, but also the means of organising their relations one with another.

The answer to this, however, might well lie in the role of the communist party. Weber had seen that the Calvinist ideology could create the perfect bureaucrat as well as the perfect capitalist, and also that the future of bureaucracy without such ideological support was in jeopardy. The communist party, however, provides precisely this ideological support, precisely the kind of dedication, albeit to a human, rather than a divine, plan, which Calvinism did. More-over it also provides the kind of organisation which Calvinism lacked. It not merely produces dedicated individuals as Calvinism did, it also has its version of the Catholic confessional. It is a powerful combination.

The party, however, is itself bureaucratic. More than that, it is ultimately autocratic and has many of the features which had been noted under the heading of patrimonialism by Weber, and oriental despotism by Wittfogel. It cannot tolerate independent organisa-tions, and it cannot tolerate intellectual and political freedom. The cost, therefore, of living in a communist society is that one faces the possibility of such punishments as imprisonment in a labour camp for actions which would, in no sense, be criminal in a free capitalist society and, in so far as one lives, not in the communist metropolis, but in one of its satellites, one knows that moves towards greater economic and intellectual freedom are likely to be met with military force. Living in a communist society therefore means, either com-mitting oneself to the official belief system, including a belief in the legitimacy of the party's rule, or it means publicly conforming to a regime which one finds totally alien.

Given the structure of communist society, the question certainly arises whether a new form of exploitation by a new ruling class might not arise. Wherever the allocation of resources through the

H*   221 market is replaced by the allocation of these resources by office holders, the question must surely arise whether they may not be allocated to the office holders' own advantage. If this were the case one would have, additionally to everything else, a new exploiting class. In fact, in the communist world, such exploitation appears to exist only to a limited extent. Moreover, it should be noted that many of the other problems which arise from the breakup of capitalism are not evident under communism, because *its* break up has not even begun to occur. It has been checked by an iron discipline and, after years of discipline, the use of force may well drop more into the background.

The principal private troubles of communist societies, however, are those which arise from its iron discipline. Social stability is bought at a price of terror, murder, and labour camps, used not merely against the class enemy, but against anyone who might be deemed to be so. Moreover, since repression begets resistance, once enemies are persecuted, their numbers tend to multiply so that the whole process escalates and not solely because of the paranoia of those who rule.

Finally, so far as private troubles are concerned, the man in the third world seems to get the worst of all three worlds, or perhaps one might say all four. From the old colonialism he has learned to accept that he is regarded as inferior and even when his country is free, he encounters the indignities of racialism and racism when he deals with his former masters. From neo-colonialism he has to suffer the mediaeval brutality of neo-colonial, and possibly artificially engendered civil wars. From his own version of the one party state, taken over from communism, he runs all the risks of imprisonment and persecution. And, in his own world of the third world bourgeoisie, he encounters a party which, in most cases, *is* run by an exploiting class. The base-line of all this is one of poverty and near starvation, but the everyday world is also a world of military terror and of fetid tropical gaols.

What all this means is not simply that we are saying 'a plague on all three of your worlds', we are, however, seeking to demystify and de-ideologise. The picture we have given here, of private troubles, therefore, may help to rectify the facile idealism of more orthodox political ideology. Men suffer, we are saying, and the direction of the world opened up by capitalism and the Enlightenment is to ensure an increase in that suffering. But the suffering is not due simply to the wickedness of individuals. It is not even due to the evils of one system as against another. The fact is that, having escaped from the pre-capitalist, pre-industrial world, this is where we are. Before we begin to project utopias we need to take a cold look at the social systems with which we have to deal.

222

15 The vocation of a sociologist in a collapsing civilisation

Early in this book we provocatively embraced the label which had been given to earlier work of this kind, namely that which dubbed it 'morally nihilistic'. Subsequently, however, we may have appeared on the face of it, either by use of big generalisations as in chapters 8 to 11, or by writing with a degree of moral passion, as in the last chapter, to be producing a sociology which was anything but value-free. In fact, had it not been for these preparatory words, many would have read the later chapters of this book as advocating a committed and radical sociology. How shall we explain this paradox?

The crux of the matter lies in the way in which the term 'morally nihilist' is used. As we see it, it is used by men who are on the inside. In British terms we are talking of men in the Higher Civil Service, in, say the Home Office or the Department of Health and Social Security. We do not wish to berate them, as the radical sociologist Martin Nicolaus (Blackburn, 1972, p. 45) did when he heaped on the spokesman of the Department of Health, Education and Welfare, who was to have spoken to the American Sociological Association, responsibility for every evil committed by his political masters. Only in a very extended sense would this be true. But what is true is that there are men who, by their very profession, cannot open up a problem too much. They cannot throw it back to those who formulate it and say that it could be formulated in a different way. Rather they have to address themselves to the narrow task of solving it; and, when they do this, they have the enormous moral justification that they are getting on with helping people, and not sitting around talking airy fairy theory.

Unfortunately, sociology in Britain did not, from its inception, escape from this perspective. It was founded as a subject in the London School of Economics within the perspective of Fabianism. This meant that it had a natural predilection for social statistics, or

223

for what we have called the book-keeping of social reform. The problem was clear. It was a problem of finding out how much inequality there was, whether in terms of income or equality of educational opportunity, so that it could be reduced. This did involve a radical posture, a posture of criticism based upon a non-Establishment value-judgment, for the Treasury dominated Civil Service was concerned with its major task of guiding and managing the economy, and could not be concerned with questions like equality. To ask such questions was to speak, not on behalf of the economy, but on behalf of the man in the street, the man in his union, indeed on behalf of the political economy of the working class. It was only a matter of time, however, before these very values were assimilated into the social utilitarianism of the Treasury, to become the new indices of welfare economics.

When Sir William Harcourt said 'we're all socialists now', this surely was his central meaning. For, if Sidney Webb and his spiritual descendants had rejected utilitarianism and individualism, they had done so only to do what the more enlightened establishment was doing anyway, namely looking at the population as a set of administrative units, and seeing whether, by the use of the most precise quantitative methods possible, these units were adequately serviced and functioning.

To this perspective, sociological theorising was a nuisance and a trouble. A probably apocryphal story is that one of the most distinguished early teachers of sociology in Britain once said of his work 'we give our students the facts and, so far as theory is concerned, we leave them to trust to their Marxist intuitions'. So far as other theory was concerned it was introduced only to be castrated. Durkheim appeared, of all things, as the sociologist who had made sociology scientific by turning to the statistics of suicide, while Weber's greatest achievement, setting aside what was assumed to be simply a justification of capitalism and the Prussian bureaucracy, was seen as lying in his recognition that class was a matter of relative life chances. Even the one non-insular perspective, namely that of Hobhouse's social evolutionism, was channelled in a similar direction. While his work arrayed something of the variety of cultures and social systems which mankind had known, the real crux of the human story lay in the discovery of the left-liberal values of a humane gentleman scholar before the First World War. History is seen as leading up to the values of the welfare state (Hobhouse, 1925).

This style of sociologising produced its own philosophy of social science, and a very distinguished philosophy it was too. Karl Popper, who had argued for science against mere ideology on the grounds that the latter, embodied above all in the works of Freud and Marx, was not subject to the test of falsification, now began to advocate a political philosophy of piecemeal social engineering (Popper, 1957). Such a philosophy purported, like Habermas's notion of analytical-empirical science, to simply be concerned with the control of things and to be value free. In fact, however, by narrowing its focus to the study of measurable relationships and causal sequences, it remained blind to the political values which it served. The same is true of most positivist philosophies of social science.

In America, in the early years, sociology played a somewhat similar role. True, in the work of W. G. Summer, there was a thundering social conservatism, but the work of all the more forward looking sociologists at the beginning of the century was concerned with social reform, and it was only later that anti-Communist paranoia was to push America's own theorists into justifying their own social system as integrated or as pluralist. In Europe, Weber's colleagues in the *Verein für Sozialpolitik* were once again socially concerned men, who had no time to stop and separate out their self-evident value-judgments from their factual social research and, so far as France was concerned, the traditions of positivism as well as the institutional set up of research and teaching in Paris almost demanded a Durkheim who could see social facts as things, even as hard quantifiable things.

Most recently, both American and British sociology has reacted to the problem of racial violence by producing a new kind of problem-oriented research. In America the earnestly-posed problem was this: Lloyd Warner has shown that though the colour line tilted it never disappeared. Compensatory welfare and employment problems had been expected to achieve just this breakthrough. When they did not all men of goodwill had to address themselves to the problem of why this was so. The upshot of this was that extraordinary document, The Moynihan Report, which became the central political instrument of two administrations and, for many, the standard analysis of the cause of the deprivation of black America. The problem of social engineering was no longer simply that of channelling money to the blacks. It was the anthropological one of dealing with the incomplete American family. More generally, however, the problem of race riots was identified as a problem of the cities.

In Britain, a similar story was unfolding. Immigrants were arriving in large numbers from the black Commonwealth and, given not merely a free housing market, but also a public sector in which the native working class were left free to discriminate in their own favour, these black immigrants were very soon visibly concentrated in the 'twilight' or lodging house zones of British cities (Rex and Moore, 1967). There was a political panic (Deakin *et al.*, 1970; Rex,

225

1968), and the election of 1964 was fought on the issue of the problems posed by immigration. The political leader who was to win that election promised, during his campaign, to give special aid to areas affected and, in due course, such aid was given. The idea that there was specifically a racial problem was systematically played down, and a new ideology developed to the effect that the problems of the blacks were only, after all, the problems of the poor (see Runnymede Trust, 1970, 1971). The various panels of the National Committee for Commonwealth Immigrants met and as the racial element was squeezed out of the discussion, the universal solution was to deal with areas of special social need (NCCI, 1967). These programmes were soon to be reflected in the academic world.

At this stage, sociology had come haltingly to the ancient élite universities and earliest of all to Oxford. There some more esoteric aspects of the subject did develop, including a growing interest in sociological questions by political theorists of the more philosophic kind and some study of the sociology of religion. For the most part, however, what Oxford had to do was to pick up the problems of the Fabianised establishment and continue to pursue them with suitable earnestness and energy. Oxford provided a retreat for politicians who wanted to think, and those who dined with them quickly became attuned to their problems and applied their sociological skills to solving them.

Many of the problems which emerged in these discussions were the old ones, namely those of social mobility, equality and educational opportunity, but even some of these now had a new ring. Social mobility was studied against a background of argument concerned with the question of whether the voting behaviour of the working class showed that that class was breaking up (Goldthorpe et al., 1968), thus putting the whole discussion on to a more sophisticated footing. The question of wages policy was sharply posed and discussed, surprisingly, in terms of the theory of relative deprivation derived from Stouffer's 'American Soldier' studies (Stouffer et al., 1949; Merton, 1957a; Runciman, 1966) and in terms of Durkheim's theory of anomie (Fox and Flanders, 1969; Goldthorpe, 1967). There was thus an inflow of middle-level theoretical insights into the old problem-oriented research.

More perplexing, however, were the new problems. Those centred on educational deprivation which, in a dozen different ways, had emerged as a problem in its own right and, of course, more generally on the notion of areas of special need. The Department of Education and Science had created a number of educational priority areas, and the Home Office a number of community development areas. These two sets of schemes were sometimes referred to as the urban programme. Sociologists were called upon to service the exercise. An opportunity existed, such as had scarcely ever existed before, for sociologists to influence social policy, not merely by writing blue books and talking to ministers, though they might do that, but by actually designing schemes for change and monitoring their implementation.

All of this could be accomplished within an overall framework of values which assumed that increasing equality was a good thing, and very quickly the assumption grew that these values did hold in government quarters. But, as in America, so here in England, it was seen that there were institutional obstacles to the attainment of that equality which all enlightened men desired. Goldthorpe drew attention to some of these as they related to the working class, while Halsey, concerned with the deprived areas of cities, including the problem of immigrant children in schools, found himself in the role of Britain's Moynihan. He had to show, it seemed, not merely how the 'caste line' could be made to tip further, but how it could be breached. But since, however, there was no recognised caste line in Britain, the problem had to be posed in a different way. The drive towards equality had been implicit in all Fabian thinking and in empiricist sociology generally. But, this assumed that reform was possible. Now what threatened was a great social divide and the possibility that the coming of 'the coloureds' would 'tear the political fabric apart', so social research into deprivation had to take place against the background of an urgent and compelling question 'will the coloureds revolt?' (Halsey, 1970).

That agonised question signalled, more than any other before, the breaking point which empiricist sociology had reached. There was no intention here of encouraging racism. Indeed, the opposite was the case. But, in fact, the whole framework of empiricist sociology, based as it was on the assumption that reform was possible, was going on, and could be quantitatively measured, was now challenged by a new type of problem. The 'coloureds' were therefore conceived, not as a political threat, but essentially as an academic one. It was not the political fabric which they would tear apart so much as the whole set of assumptions lying behind policy-oriented research.

The specific problem to which we are referring here is one which we have discussed before (1973b, 1973c, 1973d). We raise it here again to point to its more general significance. We wish now to make a contrast, first and above all, between policy-oriented research and our own notion of a critical sociology, which we have called 'morally nihilistic'. We see sociology as far more than a tool for social engineering, for solving practical problems. We would say, in fact, that from the point of view of government it is literally useless. This, however, has very wide implications indeed, which we must now consider.

The position which we took on this question in an earlier work (1961) was a more modest and a more moderate one. It derived from Myrdal (1958) and it was, in a sense, a version of the social engineering thesis. The criticism which Myrdal makes of both policy-oriented empiricism and of functionalism, is that neither of them makes its value standpoint explicit. Policy-oriented empiricism simply claims to talk about the facts, but what facts it looks at and how these facts are assembled depends upon the undisclosed policy objective of the researcher or his employer, so that there really is no such thing as looking, for instance, at the facts of the American 'Negro problem'. Myrdal might have gone further than this and pointed out that when policy-oriented research is undertaken, the researcher does sometimes 'disclose a value standpoint', but this may be a falsehood, an unconscious or deliberate attempt to conceal the real standpoint from which the research is undertaken. Thus, governments often do not have morally respectable goals, and the piecemeal social engineering in which they engage may be quite nefarious, but it is often convenient, from a propaganda point of view, to bridge this moral gap by a loose and unoperationalisable definition of goals. Policy-oriented research can then go on with its concealed value standpoints, but also with a cloak of moral respectability. A great deal of research which goes on on behalf of governments had this character. On the other hand, of course, the researcher may, in order to get government support, have to pretend to be doing his research in order to show how more morally questionable goals confessed to by government departments can be attained, whereas he actually has quite different goals. This is equally reprehensible and often leads to extremely confused research.

The critique of functionalism implicit in Myrdal's work raises fewer problems. In one sense, of course, he is a functionalist, because, unlike the empiricist, he always asks of facts whether they are necessary and if so from what point of view. This means that he must trace functional interconnections between one institutional area and another. Like Weber, however, and unlike the anthropological functionalists and structural functionalists, he does not accept the notion of a closed system of mutually sustaining institutions, each of which has no purpose other than that of maintaining the whole. What is necessary can be looked at from different institutional points of view, from different class points of view and from different value standpoints.

In our earlier discussion of these questions (1961) we suggested that there was a line of methodological thinking here connecting Myrdal with both Karl Mannheim and Max Weber. The argument was that Mannheim (1954) had also shown that apparent sociological truths could be looked at from a number of different class points of view, or from the point of view of maintaining the *status quo*, or changing it, while Weber had argued, in his essay on objectivity, that socio-cultural reality could be studied from an infinitude of different standpoints. In fact, we now want to say that neither Mannheim, before he settled in England at least, nor Max Weber, was a social engineer, still less a piecemeal one.

In the case of Mannheim, there is clearly no sense in which he can be taken to be saying simply that facts are relative to a value standpoint, and that all that one has to do is to disclose this standpoint. What he is saying is much more negative than this. It is that no partial standpoint has validity, however much one may confess to one's values. Thus, what we are urged to do is to transcend this partiality either by putting together and contrasting a number of different perspectives, or by a social rather than an intellectual act, detaching ourselves from all limited perspectives. The second of these techniques may be the precondition of the first, and it is certainly close to the position taken here. We too insist that we should detach ourselves from all immediate limited value standpoints in terms of which ideologies and popular sociologies discuss problems. Therein lies our moral nihilism. The question is whether, having done this, we are able to do more than a reflexive sociology which studies the limitation on the sociologist's perspective, but fails to say anything about that which he has a perspective on. Mannheim does not seem to have thought this was possible. Nor do our latter-day phenomenologists. Max Weber and Georg Simmel, however, believed that we could.

The difficulty of understanding Max Weber's position on these points is a twofold one. On the one hand he discusses the question of value standpoints on a number of different logical and methodological levels. On the other, his actual position changed over time from an original one in which he seemed to deny the possibility of an objective and a formal sociology, to his last one, in which he had transcended his own cultural relativism and, via an enriched comparative and historical perspective, was giving life to Simmel's programme and concepts.

The problem of logical and methodological levels we have discussed in the first two chapters of this book, but it is as well that we should recall our conclusions at this point. There is undoubtedly a problem involved in the simple apprehension of socio-cultural reality and it is one way of putting the matter to say that only if we start with a system of values and meaning are we able to apprehend that reality at all. But it is still the case that the 'givens of sociological analysis', as we called them, can and do simply take many of these issues for granted, that is to say, having noted that they exist, we may accept as facts propositions which involve cultural meanings

229

and valuations. Unfortunately, when Weber was discussing this problem, that is to say the problem of observation, he also discussed a number of other questions like that of Marxism and the functional relationship between one institution and another, so that he appeared to be saying that the study of structures was inseparable from that of values in a more far-reaching way. But, however much he may have confused his levels, he did always remain clear that once we had located our problems and our facts there was what he was always inclined to call a 'causal', that is a scientific and objective, analysis to be made. This is the basis of his transition to his final methodological position (Rex, 1971).

What Weber means by causal and scientific, of course, is full of difficulty as we have seen, but it does lead him to the notion of patterns of action-orientation and structures of social relations as implicit in and determining behaviour, quite apart from the plausible accounts which actors might give of their own behaviour or that of others. Thus we arrive at the notion of objective social forms or structures, and an implicit recantation of Weber's earlier denunciation (1949, p. 68) of Simmel's programme for formal sociology.

We also arrive at the same position by another route. This is by the use of the comparative and historical method. Thus Weber starts with a very particular study of Protestantism and the capitalist spirit (1962) and also insists, in his methodological writings (1949), that one cannot and should not seek to transcend the concrete historical case. But this leads him to make comparisons none the less, and those comparisons lead, not merely to looking at the equivalent relationship between the two institutions concerned in other cultures, but looking also at a wide range of cultural forms in all of them (1964, 1967, 1968b). Comparison turns out to be possible because, on a structural level, the forms are comparable and, quite apart from local meanings and value standpoints, a general language of the social forms emerges in actual historical studies. Later it is only necessary to systematise it (1968a).

Functionalism, even of Myrdal's kind, has concealed the extent to which it is possible to be detached and objective here. For functionalism does always raise the questions 'what is the purpose of this institution?' and 'how is it purposively connected with other institutions?' Such questions also arise for Weber. They are implicit in the sectional organisation of his systematic work and explicit in the examples which he gives of the actual operation and changes in the nature of formal structures. None the less the corpus of Weber's major work would not have been possible if he had not been able to elaborate a typology of forms apart from questions of function of possible structures, divorced from a discussion of purpose.

The connection which we once recognised between Weber and

Mannheim and Myrdal is, of course, a real one and all have it in common that, in so far as they are called upon to work for governments or other political authorities, they are recalcitrant and even subversive. Myrdal says that he will choose his own value standpoint and make it explicit whether the powers that be like it or not; Mannheim exposes the relativity of the truth sought or proclaimed, not only by the government, but by the forces of revolution, and Weber, confronted with demands for petty advice steps outside of his own society and looks at it from the long view of history.

Here then are some models of sociological detachment, of withdrawal, that is to say from the limited perspectives and value-judgments which our own society imposes on us. They are the more impressive because they emerge in the work of scholars who are not stridently campaigning for a radical sociology. Perhaps because they are not, they never are in danger of getting caught up in ephemeral, cheapjack and insular perspectives.

Mannheim's is a somewhat interesting case. Maybe his strength lay in the fact that he was not on the radical left of the school to which he gave leadership. Maybe, for all we know, he did the right thing for the wrong reason, simply seeking to evade political commitment. But the consequence of this is that Mannheim urged us to detach ourselves from the forces of revolution as much as those of reaction, from those of utopia as well as of ideology. Moreover, he believed that only a displaced person could do this.

We are inclined to share Mannheim's view that only a displaced person is capable of doing real sociology. Our experience of the insularity of British sociologists, whether of the right or of the left, reinforces this view. They are concerned with equality or with the problems of organised labour as they occur internally in British society, and find it difficult to take an interest in any wider issue or to look critically at their own value standpoints in making their studies. The same also seems to be true of other national traditions. America certainly offers a case in point in its extreme insularity of approach to the sociology of race relations, a point which is as true of radicals as it is of conservatives. Similar considerations probably apply in Europe. But while we share Mannheim's view in practice, we do not necessarily do so in theory. When we speak of a posture of moral nihilism we are calling upon sociologists not to rely upon the accident of becoming displaced persons, but of deliberately displacing, dislodging and detaching themselves, intellectually, and perhaps practically and politically, from the sacred values of their society.

Weber, of course, was very far indeed from being a displaced person. He was a core member of his society. But he was a civilised man with a sense of history. He came to have the gift of never

231

looking at a social or cultural object without asking whether it might not be otherwise, and in what directions it could be otherwise. Sometimes this meant detecting surprising similarities, such as seeing Roman social forms in recent American history. Sometimes it involved seeing sharp differences and potentiality for change.

If, in fact, we cannot rely upon the accidents of history to train sociologists, we must perhaps introduce them to history. No one should pretend to be a sociologist who has not studied and lived spiritually within less than three or four separate cultures widely separated from each other in time and place. It is only from this kind of experience that worthwhile theory and worthwhile questions to put to the facts of our own society can be generated. The point is well made by Glaser and Strauss in their thought-provoking book, *The Discovery of Grounded Theory* (1968). But it is a sign of the impoverishment of American sociological culture that the point has to be made. Had sociology kept its links with the comparative method and with history, rather than getting tied down to questions of statistical sampling and control groups, 'grounded theory' would not have needed discovering. It would have been there as clearly as it is in the work of Weber.

We have now reached a point at which it makes sense to say that living in a collapsing civilisation is not only a problem for the sociologist, although, as we shall see, it is that. It is also an advantage. When Mannheim wrote, the archetypal displaced person was the European Jew. Today, far more people are displaced, not merely as refugees, though there are many kinds of those, but all those people, young and old, who have lost faith in the civilisation which bred them. They are capable of standing outside the limited perspectives of their own culture. The danger, however, is that their counter-culture will trap them. That is why it is more than ever necessary that those who wish to understand their society today should read sociology historically and history sociologically. To become aware of the historical relativity of one's position is not simply to lose faith in that position. It is to enrich it by understanding its historical significance.

Much of the most provocative sociology of recent years has been produced by those who study deviance, because they are in some degree deviant themselves. But really they are only an insignificant group in the sort of world which we have described in chapters 8 to 11 and in chapter 14. On the whole they are a small group of middle-class children who have lost faith in their parents' culture, or have simply been given the possibility of deviance by their indulgent and liberal seniors.

Nor surprisingly, the insights of the kind of sociology which is produced in this way are limited. They involve little in the way of alternative structures because, indeed, they have no real notion of structure. And they have no notion of structure because the structures within which they live are taken for granted. So what they think is at issue is a question of labels. They shouldn't be called naughty, or criminal, or deviant, and they make this point by calling attention to the fact that naughtiness or criminality involves someone who labels an act as such, as well as an act and an actor which is so labelled.

We parody the work of the labelling theorists and the new criminologists in order to make the point that what is involved here is cultural, or moral, or aesthetic disagreement and discussion rather than revolution. And this is all the more true of those radicals amongst the new criminologists, who claim to see crime as a political act. If they were, like Durkheim, seeing the criminal as pioneering a new type of social *structure* (which was what Durkheim always saw as lying behind statistical facts) this notion would be important, but what they tend to do is to concentrate on types of *action* as though these, and the labels attached to them, were the whole of social structure (see Taylor, Walton and Young, 1973).

What we are trying to discuss is a range of social structures with taken-for-granted values and meanings built into them, which are now in crisis, and which hurt the people who live in them. The deviants are among those who are hurt, but what we are trying to ask is what sorts of new structural alternatives are available to men and which of these are coming into being. It is perhaps by extending the term deviant to cover the political innovator rather than by extending the term political to cover the deviant that the new criminology will best relate itself to what we are doing.

The sociologist today has to deal with social structures and conflicts, both internal to particular societies, and as operating between them, of a kind he has not known before. And he has to deal with private troubles created by these structures, of an enormity not recently experienced in European society. The insular structural models which most sociology provides, however, are derived from the culture and the intellectual activity of that society, so that the sociologist must, if he is to understand the world we live in, get outside of these models and set them against a much wider range of historical possibilities.

Of course, any attempt in this day and age to define the vocation of the sociologist in purely technical terms must be wide of the mark. For the sociologist to pretend to offer such a service to governments or industry is, in fact, to provide a guarantee that he will *not* perform his true role, in fact that he will not be doing sociology. For, in a world in which any sense of moral and social direction is lacking, but in which none the less there are moral and social purposes built into institutions, what sociology will be about will be the location of these goals and purposes. If it pretends that it has technical information to offer, it *must* be fraudulent, since, if ends are not known, there can be no intellectual problem of the discovery of means.

What we are saying here is, in many ways, not new. It is of the essence of the original style of functional analysis. When Merton spoke of institutions as having manifest and latent functions, he could not surely have meant that we simply had two sets of data to describe. Surely the problem was this. Manifest functions were publicly declared and therefore researchable. The means to the performance of these functions were also accessible to observation. The problem, however, lay in the disparity between effects actually occurring as a result of these 'means' and the effects which they were expected to produce. When these other unintended consequences were discovered, the sociologist actually claimed to be making a double demonstration. One was that certain unintended effects occurred. The other was that this was in the logic of the situation (see Jarvie, 1967).

The notion of the logic of the situation is, of course, different from that which is in accordance with the purposes or intentions of a particular actor. In terms of methodological individualism, it refers to the purposes of a hypothetically constructed actor, who is invented to explain the situation. But this notion usually only makes sense if we say that the particular situation is conceived of as caught up in a larger means-ends chain, and that the 'latent function' can be understood best by looking further along it.

Sociologists will certainly never be particularly popular if they expose latent functions. They will certainly find it difficult to get jobs, except where a higher authority who is capable of taking the larger view, or looking further along the means-ends chain, wishes to review or criticise or blame a too insular underling (Gouldner, 1973). That this is so is particularly clear if we take Malinowski's terms of 'charter' and 'functions' rather than Merton's milder distinction between manifest and latent functions. No sociologist who arrives in a respectable social situation and says 'alright, that's what you say you are doing. Let's find out what you're really up to' is likely to get much backing from those in power. It might work in the context in which Malinowski proposed it, for the tribesman whose 'charters' are exposed rarely gets a chance to read the anthropologist's report. But to make such a report to a town council or a government department is to invite dismissal. Let us look briefly at some examples of how this works.

Town planning is a sphere in which the sociologist is often called upon to provide technical knowledge about means and ends. But if he looks critically at the problem which is posed to him, he will find that it has some curious features. 'How large', he may be asked, 'should the neighbourhood unit be?' Now, if he is asked such a question, he should then ask, 'by what standard or in terms of what end must I judge the issue?' The answer given will be 'human happiness'. But this is so unspecific an end that the discerning sociologist will then ask to see what goals, say, the new town was set up to subserve. These turn out to be a rather curious set of statements. They tend to be highly utopian, but do refer to such matters as the achievement of balance between the social classes. These matters refer to measurable states of affairs. What then appears, however, is that there is an almost total lack of relationship between the disclosed aims and what the town is achieving, not merely in the size of its neighbourhood units, but in almost every direction in relation to which aims were set down.* The task which the sociologist would then set himself would be to look at the logic of the situation and see what 'latent functions' the new towns were serving. This would not be what the town planner wanted, however. These are precisely the issues which he would want hushed up. On the other hand, some higher authority, conducting a review of town planners and planning, perhaps with an open mind on the question of sacking some of the staff, might be very interested in these findings.

Very similar problems arise with industrial consultancy of any kind. There, usually, once economic policies have been decided, a whole lot of questions of technical rationality are posed, including many about social structure. Quite often, although not as often as in a public service like town planning, where there is no ultimate test, like profitability, to which all things are subject, one may find that social structures are being preserved or destroyed for reasons quite different from those which appear in the 'charters' or lists of 'manifest functions'. For instance, it may be found that the real reason for a policy is class bias or prejudice or sheer traditionalism. The factory manager will not be particularly interested in receiving this news, though his company chairman might. The finding may also be of interest to those more liberal capitalists whom Mills recognised as being capable of taking the wider view because they were men of many interests. Finally, it should be of interest to those concerned with economic planning in the government, to whom local interests and privileges should be of little account (though we are well aware, from experience, that governments in these matters are all too often concerned with the politics of the matter, not really

---

* I have in mind here unpublished studies which were carried out in the University of Durham by Ken Patton, on new towns in County Durham. On the specific point of class balance there is an interesting study of Crawley by Brian Heraud (1968).

promoting industrial efficiency, but appearing to by actually supporting the most powerful political forces involved).

When we turn from local government and industry to national
governments, however, our problems become even more acute. One
can direct one's report on town planning over the planner's head
to his bosses and one can bypass the management and go to the
board or the group chairman. But usually, when one is dealing with
government departments, there is no more ultimate authority to
whom one can turn. This is clear enough in the case of race relations
in Britain. Here policy-oriented research has quite widely adopted
Roy Jenkins's definition of 'integration' as the standard in terms of
which the functioning of government policy should be measured
(Deakin *et al.*, 1970). But this definition has the curious quality of
being adaptable to the justification of segregationist and dis-
criminatory policies, as well as egalitarian ones. Research cannot,
therefore, be carried out in these terms at all. What has to be done
is to discover actually operative 'charters' akin to those of the
'charters' of the new towns and then to submit those 'charters' to
critical functional analysis with a view to discovering the real
purposes or functions of government policy in this sphere.

It should be clear enough from what has been said that there will
be many office-holders in a capitalist industrial society, or indeed in
a communist one, who will see sociology as a dangerously subversive
activity to be suppressed if at all possible. Fortunately, however, the
independent corporate status of universities, in some societies, has
made it possible for the kind of independent critical study of social
functions, outlined here, to be undertaken. Moreover, simple
utilitarian arguments can be used to show that any society will be
wise to build into its structure independent sociological research
agencies, who can keep the actual functioning of structures continually under review. It is, after all, a better way than using secret
police to carry out the review, and was actually tried, *ex post facto*,
by the Polish government when it employed sociologists, rather
than policemen, to discover the causes of the Poznan riots.

There are, however, two reasons why the problems of defining
the role of the sociologist in the modern world are more difficult
than this. The first is that a great many of the problems which face
us are understandable only in terms of a logic of the situation which
knows no national boundaries. Such is the logic of the nuclear
situation between the super powers. Another is the ending of the
colonial era. But, more than this, the logic of these situations is, in a
sense, no logic at all, for it is the logic of a world which is coming
apart.

The first task, of course, of the sociologist, is to try to understand
this world, in order that the more immediate structural issues and,

within these, the private troubles of individuals, might be looked at in perspective. To do this, however, he will have to encounter conceptual, as well as political, difficulties.

So far as conceptual problems go, one thing he can be sure of is that he will get little help from traditional European ideologies, including ideologies of revolution. (We say ideologies rather than utopias of revolution, because the notion of revolution has become part of the conservative thinking of the first and second worlds.) But what one can do in a world which is coming apart is to begin to look at the bits and the way in which they are fitting together, or not fitting together in systems. This takes us back to the questions which we raised in chapters 5, 6 and 7. It seems clear that one of the things which happens in a world of chaos is the emergence of a feudal order of protectors and protected. That is one way in which the bits may be ordered. Another is the imposition of an alien or autocratic rule. Neo-colonialism is a social system which lives by coming to terms with chaos and using it to its own advantage. Similarly, as consequential chaos emerges in the advanced countries, it will be necessary to look at the new types of forced order which arise there too. It goes without saying that to try to deal with all these ways in which the bits are fitted together in terms of some kind of generalised systems theory is to say nothing at all and to miss the specificity of the problem. That is the ultimate condemnation of Parsonian structural-functionalism.

Politically, the problems of the sociologist appear at first to be acute. In addition to being unemployable, if he thinks too hard and always looks for further latent functions, which engulf even his ultimate employer, he will be accused of subversion and treason.

But it is also important to notice that he will have an audience. Those who encourage petty power and have their charters to defend, together with the ideologists who work for them, will, of course, do all that they can to suppress any true understanding of the world. They will, for instance, have their discussions of the problem of violence in the abstract, without any serious attempt to grasp the contexts in which it occurs. They will continually redefine public issues in terms of purely private troubles. In all likelihood, too, they will turn more and more to psychology as their intellectual guide, because psychology specifically looks at man divorced from meaningful social contexts and is therefore precluded from offering solutions to social problems. Even more, they may turn to biological theories such as racism.

The bombs, however, will continue to go off in the supermarket, those puzzling bombs which are a symbol of the social world we do not understand. And, because of the bombs and because of the puzzlement, serious sociological analysis will begin, more and more,

237

to get a hearing. We may not be able to influence the powerful. We *may* be able to help the alienated and puzzled young to self and social understanding, not merely, that is, to achieving strategies of personal survival through cheating by role playing or by learning to manipulate the immediate social milieu, but by enabling them to see the flow of horror about them, not simply as something shocking, but as part of the world in which they are destined to live. Such an audience, however, in rejecting ideological views of the world, will also reject the nation. It will approximate to the stoic ideal of an international community of the wise. The function of sociology, in being morally nihilistic about ideological values, is to bring such a community into being.

Mere stoic acceptance of the world, however, is *not* what we recommend. Stoic indifference to the values of the polis or the nation is simply the starting point from which men may go on to act. Moreover, action itself is a source of knowledge. But we would not accept the real wisdom of Marx's eleventh thesis, that 'hitherto philosophies have only interpreted the world, the point is to change it', without adding 'politicians and ideologies have too often tried to change the world without first interpreting it and understanding it'. The sociologist could do well to keep both of these ideals firmly in mind.

16 Some utopian perspectives for a distant future

The ending of the *ancien régime* in Europe, modernisation of social institutions and rationalisation of technology, the conquest of the socially 'backward' parts of the world, the liberation of their peoples from superstition and the modernisation and rationalisation of their world so that, either through private initiative and free trade, or through rational planning, all men everywhere would increase their wealth and happiness – these were the *utopian* goals of the European Enlightenment. For many they still provide an *ideological* view of what is happening in the world. Having done what we can to demystify ideological images of what is happening in the first, second and third worlds separately, let us now try to de-ideologise this picture and then, having diagnosed the actual processes which are at work in their world, consider what issues are posed, and what could be done about them, in order to avert certain ultimate disasters which appear to face mankind.

The actual social processes which have been at work in the world for the last five hundred years, as distinct from those referred to in the opening sentence of the paragraph above, are these: the unleashing of capitalist rapacity so that every unsatisfied want represented an opportunity for profit, the rationalisation and disenchantment of the world, the creation of the disciplined party to mobilise all men for action on a national scale, and the conquest of the third world by the first so that capitalism and/or rationalisation would know no bounds. Before these processes, ancient civilisations were to crumble, all traditional moral and aesthetic values were to be set aside in favour of those involved in rational calculation, and people everywhere were to be shaken out of their traditional roles and structures to be ejected into the void as the social atoms of a new future.

The political theorists of the Enlightenment had imagined that what was happening in the world was clearly for the good in the best of all possible worlds. Their sociological successors looked more closely at the institutions which they had created and cautiously or anxiously pointed to what lay on their underside. Yet they too still believed that the processes which they were observing could be controlled for the good, would still lead to some morally acceptable function or, through a great revolutionary negation, which would itself be the product of the new social system's inherent dialectic, achieve utopia. What we are saying is that these things are not likely to occur. The process has got out of hand and no one knows where it will lead. The best men can do is to talk about economic growth rates if they are capitalists, and socialism separately in one, two, three or four countries if they are communists.

The first thing which we have to say in this debate is that we do not accept the assumption that the only way in which the world can achieve release from poverty is by abandoning all earlier forms of social order in favour of the disorderly and uncontrolled processes of rational capitalism or communist planning. Clearly we do hold that poverty and the precarious dependence of pre-industrial man on nature are things to be overcome. But we do not believe that all traditional social orders are simply to be described as 'traditional' and nothing more, involving a kind of iron cage which, though it serves to prevent social disorder, also locks man into a limited subsistence and a limited happiness.

It is true that most non-Western civilisations which are not based upon the rational-calculating spirit do embody values which are lacking in the modern West. Whatever else is lacking, and whatever tyranny and superstition there might be, there is also an enjoyment of the immediate, the personal and the tangible in human relations, which is entirely lost in a rationalistic world whose sole hopes lie in the future. This is apparent in the very faces of untouched tribesmen when they are 'discovered' by anthropologists and their photographs. The pity is perhaps that cannibalism is so rare, for otherwise they would eat the anthropologist and the photographer, civilised men would not know about them, and no one would ever try to develop them.

But let us not make idle jokes about tribesmen and cannibals. Occasionally, our television journalists, probably cursing the local hotels for their inadequate sanitation and so on, as they make their films, stray beyond the mountains and deeper into the jungle and find palaces and temples there which are embellished by an art which makes modern man seem almost a total barbarian. And the art is almost always embodied in a social context. We are not going to pretend that the whole of what we see does not very often involve exploitation also. Manifestly it does, and the social context of the art is all too often a social context which glorifies the king at the cost of his people. But what is not true is that there is no cumulative cultural achievement here. Men have advanced their ideas and worked out the logic of cultural meanings. In the most important sense of all, therefore, we may say they have 'progressed'. What they lack is simply the sense that there lies before them a never-ending future in which one form after another has to be torn down in the name of progress and that future progress lies in an indefinite increase in the number of units of something measurable, called pleasure. Seen in this context, rather than against its relatively immediate background of reactionary counter-revolutionary political theory, Durkheim's notion of anomie becomes startlingly relevant. Many of the ancient civilisations knew both progress and psychological and cultural peace before the explorers, the conquerors, the newsmen and the salesmen from 'the West' tore them apart. Moreover, we are not talking here simply of a few proto-civilisations standing out in seas of tribal barbarism. Much of what is said about tribal barbarism is the product of colonialist legitimising myths. There are peoples for whom the unit of social organisation was based upon kinship, it is true, and some of these with a low level of technology, but there was also an enormously valuable social and cultural heritage, which was ruthlessly set aside and destroyed. It could be and should be one of the prime tasks of the universities of 'the West' to rediscover what remains of this heritage. Outrageous as the idea may seem to many, this is an intellectual task which has become essential to our own survival. It is now an entirely rational matter to devote funds to this purpose, instead of to the development of computers, whose social effect, in substituting calculation for values in human relations, can only be disastrous.

What we want to see is a rediscovery of the substantive rationality of pre-capitalist socio-economic formations, which is as different from the substantive rationality of communism as it is from the formal rationality of the capitalist world. We should stop and pay attention, therefore, whenever we learn that in a third world country there is, along with the parties of capitalism, socialism and modernising rationalism, also a traditional party. Its actual members and its policies may have little to commend them in an immediate sense. They may well represent only residual vested interests derived from traditional society. Still worse, they may be vested interests of a modern kind in disguise. But by their very existence they remind us of another possible line of development, or rather other possible lines of development than those with which our parties of progress have made us familiar.

If, however, the values of these civilisations are to be defended, and the resources available to them used to raise living standards, the resources themselves, and the political forms through which they will be developed, must be saved from the plunderers and the conquerors from 'the West' who have set upon them. There are those who talk in 'the West' nowadays about conservation, and the conservation of the world's resources as a whole is a problem for mankind. But the doctrine as it is commonly preached takes some very curious forms. The most absurd of these is that, since industrialisation by all nations is impossible without an ecological catastrophe, it should not happen in the third world. From the point of view from which we are writing here, the first task which faces us is to stop 'the West' plundering the world for *its* industrialisation.

The means to this end, of course, is the liberation and self-defence of the countries of the third world as against Western colonialism and neo-colonialism. One cannot see the forces of a political and military kind necessary for this task being mobilised very easily, however. That is why there is a temptation to third world politicians to take short cuts, to sell themselves to capitalist developers or to Cold War powers, in order to get the wherewithal to buy arms. But all that this can lead to is the bloody mediaeval butchery of the neo-colonial civil war.

It is the problem of neo-colonialism, more than any other, which leads us to refer, in the title of this chapter, to utopian perspectives only in a distant future. It is not easy to see how one can talk about the mobilisation of political and military forces in the third world when so many of those forces are paid for by the forces of neo-colonialism and deployed only in their interests. One may be impressed by the capacity of a Moise Tshombe to command the largest army in Africa, or by the guerrillas of Frelimo to supply their forces with the smartest and most efficient weapons and uniforms. But what happens to these nations and movements if they no longer appear to be acting in the interest of their capitalist or communist arms suppliers? Further, is it not certain that, if China can provide military advisers to one party or liberation movement, America or Russia is likely to supply them to another? Thus one starts by importing into one's country the means to colonial liberation, and one ends by importing only the Cold War.

Since there is money to be made for political leaders in the business of neo-colonialism, it is not to be expected that it will be easily halted by any genuine liberation movements and politicians working for liberation who survive. In any case, politicians of the apparent moral and political integrity of a Julius Nyerere are rare, even though the principles of his Arusha Declaration are quite in line with all we are arguing for here. What is the most likely line of development is that, out of the war of all against all which neo-colonial wars will eventually produce, there will emerge a kind of feudalism. At least then there will be peace within the state and the daily butcheries will stop. It will then be the task of communities of the people to build up a new society within the peace, just as the mediaeval merchants created bourgeois society under the protection of European feudalism. What will be produced here, however, will not be the social order of the merchants. It will be a communal movement drawing on traditional values as much as on modern ones, but directing itself in terms of its own substantive rationality, internally towards the growth of its own welfare, and externally to political and cultural independence.

So far we have been talking about the internal social structures of the exploited nations and of what they can do for themselves. But, both politically and economically, they remain subordinate to the countries of the West and, as Gundar Frank (1971) has taught a generation of sociologists of 'development', there is little hope that economic growth can occur in these circumstances. The problem then is how they are to change the balance of power and the balance of trade in their own favour. Militarily speaking, it would appear that their chances are small. In any head-on confrontation, the smaller powers would, at best, be in a position to fight defensive wars on their own terrain. They could certainly not afford to get involved in the kind of conflict abroad which would strengthen their position. Their best hope, in fact, in this sphere, appears to be in playing off one great power against another, but this could mean risking becoming a proving ground for a nuclear war which the super powers avoided fighting in their own territory. Neither is there any real hope that the smaller powers could join the 'nuclear club' in any significant way. Their principal hope, therefore, must lie in using their control of raw materials, especially oil, as a means of driving hard bargains with the great powers. There thus appears to be a slight possibility that some countries might experience real inflows of wealth, enabling economic development to take place.*

In fact, national control of raw materials is one of the few means, at present, by which these materials are conserved, and thus must raise the question of the establishment of agencies to control their use on an *international* basis. How far does this depend upon the existence of central economic planning and how far does it depend upon the establishment of world government?

Clearly the answer of capitalism to the question of the control of raw material supplies is to leave it to the working of the market. If supplies are threatened, prices should rise and the use of materials be restricted, but it is doubtful if this is what will occur if either the

---

* This was written before the Arab-Israeli war of 1973. Events since then have confirmed our predictions at a quite unexpected rate.

users or sellers of the materials have complete control of them. Their unborn children are not in a position to compete for their use in the market. In the case of third world political élites, what may appeal is a quick profit in the here and now, and in the case of private capitalists there will be a rational calculation of market opportunities.

What may lead to the establishment of controls is international competition, which may mean that the super powers are concerned with retaining suppliers in the third world, or that they will service each other on a *quid pro quo* basis, each side undertaking to sustain supplies which the other needs. The problems of setting up international agencies are, however, immense, and it must be assumed that any international agency at all will only be effective in so far as the great powers want it to be so, and that every few years it will come under pressure as one or other of the powers seeks to use it to its own advantage. So far as resource control is concerned, the one positive fact compelling the powers to respect the agency is the threat which the disappearance of world resources implies.

One further aspect of this problem, at an international level, is that resource control also suggests the notion of resource development. For the most part, people and governments threatened with the cutting-off of essential industrial supplies reassure themselves by arguing that, in all such cases in the past, substitutes have been found, and it is, of course, true that even private capitalist undertakings have invested capital, on a very large and speculative scale, in exploration. But there is no reason why such investment should be responsible or systematic unless it is subject to political control at international level. Sooner or later, then, one may expect regional and international agencies emerging, not just to conserve, but to develop, resources.

This theme will have to be followed through as we come to consider the internal problems of the advanced societies. In the meanwhile, however, we should notice that, while international control of resources is forced upon the great powers by shortage of, and loss of access to, materials, particularly in the third world, international control of armament development and testing is forced upon them through the development of the destructive potential of military weapons. Nuclear war between the great powers is now, if not totally unthinkable, at least sufficiently so to rule out an all-out direct confrontation. The most that can happen, as between the great powers, is the attempt to win a conventional war by the introduction of nuclear weapons, or by their use by one power against the satellites of another. Even these policies, however, are fraught with risks and are only likely to be embarked upon if there is some tacit agreement, at least as to the limits of the exercise. The hot-line between Washington and Moscow is the ultimate check on this. It is a precarious social connection, of course, and the possibility of nuclear war by accident is still very real. But it is this kind of reality which makes it realistic to imagine that the great powers will find other means of settling their differences in the future than by resort to war.

Agencies of international government are, in fact, emerging, rather as the fact of state intervention does in a pure type of capitalist economy. Just as chaos is avoided and the operation of private capitalist corporations made possible by the emergence of a state to hold the ring, so the international power system, within which nations pursue their policies, is eventually subjected to rules. It might, however, be pointed out that in the case of the regulation of power on an international level, the very growth in the scale of power, and the impossibility of its use, makes an ultimate dependence on world government inevitable. What prevents us at the moment is the myth of a nuclear war. This may last until there is an actual small-scale war, but really the most likely scenario for the international drama of the future is that *after* this war, the great powers will recognise that some form of international arbitration of disputes has to be accepted. This may then have consequential effects for the use of power between nations, although, as was shown in the case of the events in Budapest in 1956, it is possible for the great powers to use their force within their own area of dominance without outside intervention.

What we are talking about here may not seem to some to be part of the legitimate subject matter of sociology at all. Yet surely it is not possible to confine that subject matter any longer solely to the internal affairs of states, whether in the first, second, or third world. What we are saying here is that there is some realistic hope that conflicts between nations, and the allocation of resources between nations may come to be regulated to some degree by international organisations. This then will provide the first growth point for other aspects of international co-operation.

International organisation does not, as yet, challenge national organisation as the prime focus of human loyalty, or the prime way in which men carry on their affairs. This is true of governmental activity opposed from above, and it is true of international working-class or revolutionary activity. It is less true, however, of the workings of capitalist corporations, which exist more and more on an international basis and require at least regional regulation of the market to supplement what happens at national level. A most interesting review of the relations between these and other types of international organisation, from a Marxist point of view, is contained in Robin Jenkins's book *Exploitation* (1970). Jenkins's position is probably a utopian one in Mannheim's sense, however, since he tends to overestimate the extent to which the forces of

I

international class conflict are already organised and the conflict unavoidable. All that we would claim is that, in a world of national units and of international conflicts which transcend national boundaries, there is a growing degree of international organisation.

What then of the national units? We have depicted each of them as subject to considerable internal strain and conflict. The question is now whether they are likely to change, and whether there are realistic prospects of change in directions which might actually reduce private troubles. We begin with the capitalist countries. Here we have to consider change coming about through conflict between labour and capital, change which is forced on the system by its own need to adapt to contingencies, and finally change arising from revolt against the dehumanising effects of the capitalist corporation and capitalist rationality.

So far as revolutionary change, along the lines suggested by Marx's model, is concerned, we clearly do not have any example of this happening in the most advanced countries. Organised labour has either developed on the lines of business unionism arranging contractual relationships between its members and the capitalist bureaucracies which employ them, or it has developed a political arm which wins for them the basic concessions of welfare services provided from progressive taxation, a degree of public ownership and of planning for full employment, and the continuance of the right to collective bargaining. The latter type of system has achieved a certain degree of stability in most West European countries and in the white Commonwealth countries, and is quite commonly referred to as though it were a distinct type of society, known as the Welfare State.

One hesitates to accept the notion that this is a distinct type of society, because its basic institutions rest upon a somewhat fragile truce, and hardly provide the basis of a new sort of social system and social consensus into which the young can be socialised. What tends to happen instead is that, from time to time, the system tends to revert to type. The capitalist class, or rather capitalist-based political parties, seek to undermine collective bargaining, to replace welfare financed from taxation with privately financed services, and to reduce the overall amount of public ownership. What this tends to do, however, is to goad the working class into corporate activity once again and so to restore the equilibrium.

When we speak of utopias, of course, we should remember that the existence of trade unionism already represents a utopia achieved, because it carves out for the worker a degree of freedom and welfare which capitalism of its own nature would not provide. What we should note under the title of this chapter, however, is the possibility that this utopia, already gained, may be lost, and unfree labour, in some form, instituted. There are those, no doubt, like Thomas Carlyle, who argued that slave labour or militarised labour represented a superior human condition, for whom this loss of labour's freedom would be a utopia, but this would be an unusual use of the term.

The real issue is whether the capitalist class, or their political allies, will necessarily be forced, in the future, to end labour's freedom and, if so, whether this will provoke a revolutionary class consciousness and a working class which seeks hegemony. In the twentieth century it has usually been the case, however, either that working-class activity has forced the system to return to state, or that, given conditions of crisis induced by such factors as the decline of imperialism and authoritarian government, the destruction of free trade unionism has been carried through. What does seem clear is that, in such testing circumstances, the working class rarely has the means to take political, as distinct from trade union, action, and the political party of the working class fails to organise political forces, and particularly extra-parliamentary forces, to prevent the establishment of authoritarian rule. The classic case of such resistance, moreover, in Spain of the 1930s, led eventually to the military defeat of the workers and their allies.

The second possibility which we mentioned was change induced in the system through adaptations made by the capitalist class to the total economic situation. Now it does seem to be the case that, more and more, the maintenance of that sort of market situation in which capitalist corporations can operate at all requires some degree of state intervention, if not centralised planning. This may take the form of increased availability of statistical forecasting and the setting of targets for production as the basis of rational and quantitative data rather than on the basis of guesswork. It may take the form of government action, either to persuade or legally to compel firms to control prices and incomes. It will involve the control of the supply of money through fiscal methods and the control of interest rates. It will mean using the control exercised over the public sector of industry to affect the operation of the economy as a whole. It will also involve taking into public ownership, and subsidising the operation of, more key industries. And, apart from these responses to *economic* difficulties, it is bound to organise its own response to the crisis of resources, arranging, on a public basis, for their conservation and development.

Many will see in this that kind of peaceful transition to socialism which Fabianism all along envisaged. It by no means solves the kind of problems which we talked about in chapter 12, however. If some argue that a kind of national planned capitalism gets the best of both worlds, we may also argue that it gets the worst. For, when public socialised organisation comes into being only in order to allow a

247

core of capitalist enterprises to seek profit in the old way, then the logic of the system as a whole is the logic of formal rationality and there can be no guarantee of substantively rational goals being achieved. Moreover, at this stage of development, capitalist society moves on to an even more rationally bureaucratic basis, involving that combination of the impoverishment of work and impoverishment of private life which we have seen, not merely as the source of ennui, but of anomie, the social sickness.

Apart from, or in addition to, the crises of the market which capitalism has to face, we saw that it posed real social and personal crises, both in the world of work and in the world of home and community. In the world of work, the meaninglessness of filling an office becomes clearer and clearer as the religious notion of a calling is forgotten, but in any case the long-term fulfilment of capitalist rationality replaces man with computers and really has work to offer only to a select section of the population. In home and community life, privatisation and alienation produce an intolerable world and leave the privatised individual open to manipulation as consumer and citizen.

When we spoke of the moral disintegration of Western capitalist society, we had all these points in mind. The question is whether the very depth of the crisis might not force men to act and to change the world in which they live. Is there perhaps in this sphere an equivalent of the increasing 'immiseration' of the proletariat which Marx noted as the long-term trend within relations of employment, or is it the case that, crisis or no crisis, capitalism will find ways of accommodating, or soothing, or isolating, or defeating its dissidents? It is by no means easy to say. What can be said at the moment, however, is that the moral legitimacy of the Western capitalist way of life is now much in question and that the growth of a dissident counter-culture, along with the more violent challenges of crime and race war in the cities, may yet shake it to its foundations. Certainly if we are talking about 'a distant future' one cannot imagine that present stratagems for maintaining the *status quo* will continue to be effective.

The crisis in the nature of working life means that two developments are likely. One is that men at work will be less and less called upon to work as bureaucrats. That kind of work will be done by machines. The motivations of those at work will therefore have to be quite different. Professionalisation may be one consequence of this. Another may be a greater concentration on, and acceptance of, the business of social interaction at work for its own sake, as sheer drudgery becomes a less common feature of work. Such developments might help to move the centres of moral control over men at work out of the factory itself, and undermine the moral autocracy of the capitalist. Moreover, in the larger political community, the goals of men at work will intersect with those of the unemployed. This could mean simply a new class relationship of privileged and underprivileged. But it could also lead to a dissociation of the question of the standard of life which a man has from the work which he does. That is to say, income would be shared and an increasing proportion of all men's income would come from welfare benefits. This could be associated with work-sharing, but what is now called leisure, including the leisure of unemployment, might itself become enriched. The routine business of production being in the hands of machines, men could pursue meaningful goals, other than those which we currently list under the heading of earning a living.

In this situation more concern might be shown for the non-profit-making corporations, such as schools or hospitals. It will be remembered that we suggested earlier that this area tended to be invaded by, and exploited by, capitalism. But we also raised the question as to whether these organisations could not flex *their* muscles and subordinate capitalism to their purposes. Might one not imagine, for example, that one day community complexes providing for the education of adults and children, for positive as well as preventive and curative health services, as well as for creative work and art not oriented to the market, might be established and their substantially rational goals become the main determinant of the system as a whole?

Here too, it would seem, would lie the answer to some of the problems of privatisation. In a larger world of communal activity, men would not be confined to minding their own gardens, and social relationships would be increased, both in number and in quality. The family, with its remote television of the larger world, would assume a much less important role in men's lives than it now does. And if the new centres of communal activity became also centres of adult information and education, they might provide just that pluralistic check on the manipulative society which the optimistic theorists of the mass society envisaged.

Of course, one should beware here of the danger of substituting one form of privatisation for another. Communal activity of an intimate and local kind is undoubtedly enriching, as is evident in those enclaves of corporate communal life where isolated working-class communities survive. But there are positive things about life in the metropolitan city too, which should not be ignored. A city is not simply a world of cold impersonal relations. That framework of impersonal relationships is there, it is true. But it provides the opportunity for men to see what is socially available and, given a range of choice, to savour some things and to pass others by. But, in any case, the choice in social relations is not merely one between complete intimacy and complete impersonality. In between these

249

two, life for the urban and urbane man is infinitely enriched by those social contacts he makes with people, which are significant yet not intimate. Living in a street or enjoying the life of a particular urban quarter are not necessarily intimate experiences of a human kind, but they do allow for an intermediate perception of the social world which is neither intimate nor totally impersonal, and this itself means an enormous enrichment of life. The tragedy of capitalism's present crisis is that it now sees its cities as battlefields. They could be a civilisation's finest expression.

The hope of a transformation of capitalism, then, would appear to be not so much in a revolution of the workers or of the left, since this 'revolution' is more than likely to end in compromise or defeat. It may lie in the fact that, in the ultimate development of rationality, production in industry will become the work of machines and the focus of human life will move outside the factory. At the same time, and as a consequence of this, it may be possible for the public and welfare sector to 'flex its muscles' and impose its rationality on that of profit-seeking corporations. This is the constructive goal which the growing numbers of the politically and culturally alienated might set themselves. The first task will be the emancipation of man from work. The second will be the subordination of all corporate activity to human purposes.

In this conception of social change the object is not simply to subordinate private corporations to centralised state planning. There may be much to be said for this, at least in terms of re-achieving substantive rationality in economic and productive life. But the clear road of revolution which leads from capitalism to state planning is apparently not easily available to us. At best, it is historically unlikely. But none the less, there are in existence today centrally planned societies, and whether they are as they are because they are simply alternative forms of organisation for industrialisation and modernisation, rather than structures born out of a revolution which has also revolutionised man, or simply because it is inherent in state planning, it is clear that these centrally planned societies today have their own crises.

The central institution, through which communism seeks both to subordinate all human activity to the substantively rational goals of the plan, and at the same time to moralise or socialise men, is the disciplined party. That party, however, has become an instrument based upon an iron discipline, and this iron discipline has meant the suppression of intellectual freedom through the threat of corrective labour at home, and the suppression of political freedom through armed might abroad. The result has been a travesty of the communist ideal, for, at its worst, Stalinism competes with the worst sort of right-wing authoritarianism in brutality and violence.

250

The overthrow of Stalinism may well have been due to little more than a palace revolution. In so far as it was, it may be expected that, without real institutional changes, the amnesty and the thaw will not last and the system will revert to type. Maybe it will simply become more sophisticated, putting its dissidents into mental hospitals rather than prisons or labour camps. But there are at least some signs that a more permanent change has occurred. The attempt to re-impose the iron discipline has met with some resistance and, indeed, heroic defiance. If this continues, it might well be possible that dissent will find its place within the party rather than out of it. At the moment, the dissenters seem to have no other resource available to them than a despairing appeal to the free capitalist West. But, in a communist one-party state, this must be regarded as treason. The hope must be that if the defiance is repeated and the work of the defiant intellectuals really opens up issues of socialist humanism, the party will begin to treat its members, not as automatons and bureaucrats, but as adult human beings who can be trusted to explore new thoughts and feelings and, in fulfilling themselves, create the new socialist world.

It will be noticed that, in both the capitalist world and the communist world, one central problem is the reconquest of the bureaucracy which has conquered man. In the one case the centre of the struggle is in the individual capitalist corporation. In the other it is in the ruling party. On the other hand, the difference lies in the fact that capitalism has to be made responsible to substantively rational goals, whereas communism has to rediscover concepts of justice and humanism, which are in part recognised in the liberal and libertarian traditions of the capitalist world. Is there, finally, any equivalent of these problems and these solutions in the third world?

What we said about the third world, it will be remembered, was that its suffering was fourfold. Its institutions of production involved forms of labour, compared with which the situation of the exploited proletariat under capitalism would certainly count as liberation. Politically, it still suffered from neo-colonial intervention. In so far as it did resist colonialism, its basic instrument for doing so was the disciplined party based upon the communist model, and sharing its deformities. And finally, this party involved the additional deformity that it produced a new exploiting political class, unencumbered by any socialist or humanist ideology.

The hope for the third world, on the other hand, was seen to lie, as we said earlier in this chapter, in the growth of communal developments within the social system which the party imposes. If it is granted that most governments will be primarily concerned with neo-colonial development which provides an apparent short-cut to economic growth, while at the same time enriching the élite, and that

251

the political situation will be one of colonial civil war terminated by feudalism, real and fundamental change can only come at the grass-roots. This will take the form of peasant communes, involving both agricultural and industrial production. Clearly much can be gained here from a consideration of the Chinese experience, but it must also be the case that the people of each new third world country must apply their own traditions and their own substantive rationality. This, after all, is what the Chinese themselves have tried to do.

In the neo-colonial world with its one-party state, such peasant-based communes will be the means of subverting neo-colonialism, the power of the new élite, and the autocratic single party. It should be noticed, however, that there are both political and economic forces running strongly against such communes. Countries like Tanzania, in which government and party encourage such developments, are the exception rather than the rule. Even in China there is tension between the communes and the party bureaucracy. Thus it may well be that the notion of communal development going on peacefully within neo-colonial society and subverting it is likely to remain a utopian myth, unless it is recognised that eventually it is bound to lead to political confrontation with the party and neo-colonial corporations.

It will be noticed that there is an inherent similarity about what we are suggesting as to the way in which each of the three kinds of society will be transformed. In capitalist society it is the divorcing of meaningful social life from the control of capitalist bureaucracy, and the imposition of the substantive rationality of the communal and social sector on capitalism, so that the latter becomes subordinate to the former. In communist society, the party which started as a means of implementing substantively rational goals of the people has to be humanised again so that it guarantees the civil rights of its members and provides for their education in a real socialist humanist sense. And, in the third world, we see some hope as lying in humble communal enterprises, which embody traditional culture at the same time as involving a substantially rational commitment to increasing welfare. In each case one is calling for communal forms which involve, not simply rationalistic domination of man by man, but a kind of moral integration. Durkheim saw the importance of this in his critique of conceptions of the division of labour in his own time, but he paid all too little attention to the actual social forces which were at work and which ensured that the domination of the market and of market power had to be ended before one could begin to envisage his ideal society. On the other hand, his realistic critics have too often forgotten that the mere act of political revolution does not make a utopia.

Let us now conclude by considering both the limitations and the real importance of this chapter on utopias. We started our ideal typical account of contemporary social structures by noting that most early sociological accounts of the new industrial social order had implicitly posited some kind of theory of progress. They were optimistic that the new social forces, which the political and industrial revolutions had unleashed, would in some way, and in the foreseeable future, create a more humane world in which men would not merely be better off, but freer and more at home. By the end of the nineteenth century the sociological picture of the world had become more gloomy. So, picking up themes from Weber, Marx and Durkheim, we were led to ask the question whether the new social forces, which had been welcomed by the Enlightenment, were not in fact leading to a new Dark Age, an age of chaos and anomie. We suggested that it was important for the sociologist to divorce himself from the naïve optimism of the sort of policy-oriented research which avoided thinking about this possibility and, to emphasise this point, we described our approach as morally nihilistic.

In subsequent chapters we discussed some of the inherent stresses and strains of capitalist, communist, and third world societies, and then pointed to their inherent tendencies to disintegration and to the ways in which, as they developed, they would lead, not to ever increasing human happiness, but to an increase in 'private troubles'. To emphasise these possibilities is by no means to delight in them, however. All that we wished to do was to demystify the world and bring both structural issues and private troubles, which ideology and policy-oriented sociology cover up or evade, into the clear light of day. Having done this, and avoiding all facile solutions, we asked what developments might occur in each of the three worlds, which would at least arrest the processes of exploitation, dehumanisation and tyranny which the Enlightenment had bequeathed to us. We have tried, then, to show that within these Dark Ages there are social changes which, in the long run, may produce the basis of a new civilisation.

It should not be thought that we are seeking a more sophisticated analysis in order to avoid the tiresome necessity of associating ourselves with man's fight against exploitation. We see, as central to what we have been saying, the ending of inequalities and exploitation, both as between the third world and the advanced countries, and within the advanced countries themselves. But we want the revolution against such exploitation to be thoroughgoing and complete. That is why we wish to demystify the ideology of revolution as well as the ideology of the *status quo*. Against that background of demystification it becomes more possible for men to set themselves utopian perspectives, but also realistically to work to achieve them.

Bibliography

ADORNO, T. *et al.* (1950), *The Authoritarian Personality*, Harper & Row, New York.

ALTHUSSER, LOUIS (1969), *For Marx*, trans. with a glossary by Ben Brewster, Allen Lane, Penguin Press, London.

BECKER, HOWARD, JNR (1963), *Outsiders*, Free Press, New York.

BERNSTEIN, BASIL (1971), *Class, Codes and Control*, vol. 1, Routledge & Kegan Paul, London.

BERNSTEIN, BASIL (1973), *Class, Codes and Control*, vol. 2, Routledge & Kegan Paul, London.

BLACKBURN, ROBIN (ed.) (1972), *Ideology in Social Science*, Fontana/Collins, London.

BLAUNER, ROBERT (1972), *Racial Oppression in America*, Harper & Row, New York.

BOTT, ELIZABETH (1957), *Family and Social Network; Roles, Norms and External Relationships in Families*, Tavistock, London.

BOXER, CHARLES RALPH (1963), *Race Relations in the Portuguese Colonial Empire (1415–1825)*, Oxford University Press, London.

BRAMSON, LEON (1961), *The Political Context of Sociology*, Princeton University Press.

BROOM, LEONARD AND GLENN, NORVAL D. (1967), *The Transformation of the Negro American*, Harper & Row, New York.

BUELL, RAYMOND LESLIE (1965), *The Native Problem in Africa*, 2 vols, Frank Cass, London. Reprint of edition first published by The Bureau of International Research of Harvard University in 1928.

CARR-SAUNDERS, ALEXANDER MORRIS and JONES, DAVID CARADOG (1927), *Social Structure in England and Wales 1927, as illustrated by Statistics*, Oxford University Press, London.

CICOUREL, AARON (1963), *Method and Measurement in Sociology*, Free Press, New York.

CICOUREL, AARON (1968), *The Social Organization of Juvenile Justice*, Wiley, New York.

CICOUREL, AARON (1973), *Cognitive Sociology*, Penguin Books, Harmondsworth.

254

COHEN, PERCY (1968), *Modern Social Theory*, Heinemann Educational, London.

COMTE, AUGUSTE (1858), *The Positive Philosophy of Auguste Comte*, 2 vols, trans. and condensed by H. Martineau, Chapman & Hall, London.

COOPER, DAVID (1961), *The Death of the Family*, Allen Lane, Penguin Press, London.

COSER, LEWIS (1956), *The Functions of Social Conflict*, Routledge & Kegan Paul, London.

COSER, LEWIS and ROSENBERG, BERNARD (eds)(1969),*Sociological Theory*,3rd edition, Collier-Macmillan, New York.

COX, OLIVER CROMWELL (1970), *Caste, Class and Race: A Study in Social Dynamics*, Monthly Review Press, New York.

DAHRENDORF, RALF (1959), *Class and Class Conflict in Industrial Society*, Routledge & Kegan Paul, London.

DAHRENDORF, RALF (1968a), 'Homo Sociologicus' in *Essays in the Theory of Society*, Routledge & Kegan Paul, London.

DAHRENDORF, RALF (1968b), 'Out of Utopia' in *Essays in the Theory of Society*, Routledge & Kegan Paul, London.

DAVIS, ANGELA (1971), *When They Come in the Morning*, Orbach & Chambers, London.

DAVIS, KINGSLEY and MOORE, WILBERT (1964), 'The functions of social stratification' in Coser and Rosenberg (eds) (1969).

DAWE, ALAN MARTIN (1971), 'The relevance of values' in Sahay (ed.) (1971), pp. 37–67.

DAWE, ALAN MARTIN (1973), 'The underworld of Erving Goffman', *British Journal of Sociology*, vol. 24, no. 2, pp. 246–53.

DEAKIN, NICHOLAS, COHEN, BRIAN and MCNEAL, JULIA (1970), *Colour, Citizenship and British Society*, Panther, London.

DEBRAY, REGIS (1967), *The Revolution in the Revolution?* Monthly Review Press, New York.

DICKIE-CLARK, HAMISH (1966), *The Marginal Situation: A Sociological Study of a Coloured Group*, Routledge & Kegan Paul, London.

DILTHEY, WILHELM (1957), *Dilthey's Philosophy of Existence, Introduction to Weltanschauungslehre*, trans. William Kluback and Martin Weinbaum, Vision, London.

DOBB, MAURICE (1946), *Studies in the Development of Capitalism*, Routledge & Kegan Paul, London.

DURKHEIM, EMILE (1956), *Education and Sociology*, Free Press, New York.

DURKHEIM, EMILE (1959), *Socialism and Saint Simon*, Routledge & Kegan Paul, London.

DURKHEIM, EMILE (1962), *The Rules of Sociological Method*, Chicago University Press.

DURKHEIM, EMILE (1963), *Suicide*, Routledge & Kegan Paul, London.

DURKHEIM, EMILE (1964a), *Division of Labour in Society*, Free Press, New York.

DURKHEIM, EMILE (1964b), *The Elementary Forms of Religious Life*, Allen & Unwin, London.

EASTON, LLOYD and GUDDATT, KURT H. (eds) (1967), *Writings of the Young Marx on Philosophy and Revolution*, Doubleday Anchor, New York.

ELKINS, STANLEY (1959), *Slavery: A Problem in American Institutional and Intellectual Life*, Chicago University Press.

FANON, FRANZ (1965), *The Wretched of the Earth*, MacGibbon & Kee, London.

FERNANDES, FLORESTAN (1969), *The Negro in Brazilian Society*, Columbia University Press, New York.

FEUERBACH, LUDWIG (1957), *The Essence of Christianity*, Harper & Row, New York.

FILMER, PAUL, PHILLIPSON, MICHAEL, SILVERMAN, DAVID and WALSH, DAVID (1972), *New Directions in Sociological Theory*, Collier-Macmillan, London.

FLORENCE, PHILIP SARGENT (1961a), *The Logic of British and American Industry*, Routledge & Kegan Paul, London.

FLORENCE, PHILIP SARGENT (1961b), *Ownership, Control and Success of Large Companies*, Sweet & Maxwell, London.

FOX, ALAN and FLANDERS, ALAN (1969), 'The reform of collective bargaining from Durkheim to Donovan', *British Journal of Industrial Relations*, July.

FRANK, ANDRE GUNDAR (1971), *The Sociology of Underdevelopment and the Underdevelopment of Sociology*, Pluto Press, New York.

FROMM, ERICH (1955), *The Sane Society*, Holt, Rinehart & Winston, New York.

FROMM, ERICH (1960), *The Fear of Freedom*, Routledge & Kegan Paul, London.

GALBRAITH, JOHN KENNETH (1962), *The Affluent Society*, Penguin Books, Harmondsworth.

GARFINKEL, HAROLD (1967), *Studies in Ethnomethodology*, Prentice-Hall, New York.

GENOVESE, EUGENE D. (1965), *The Political Economy of Slavery*, Pantheon Books, New York.

GENOVESE, EUGENE D. (1969), *The World the Slave-Holders Made*, Pantheon Books, New York.

GENOVESE, EUGENE D. and FONER, LAURA (eds) (1969), *Slavery in the New World*, Prentice-Hall, New York.

GERTH, HANS and MILLS, C. WRIGHT (1959), *Character and Social Structure: The Psychology of Social Institutions*, Routledge & Kegan Paul, London.

GIDDENS, ANTHONY (ed.) (1972), *Emile Durkheim: Selected Writings*, Cambridge University Press, London.

GIDDENS, ANTHONY (1973), *The Class Structure of Advanced Societies*, Hutchinson, London.

GLASER, BARNEY G. and STRAUSS, ANSELM L. (1968), *The Discovery of Grounded Theory*, Weidenfeld & Nicolson, London.

GOFFMAN, ERVING (1969), *The Presentation of Self in Everyday Life*, Allen Lane, Penguin Press, London.

GOLDMANN, LUCIEN (1969), *The Human Sciences and Philosophy*, Cape, London.

GOLDTHORPE, JOHN (1967), 'Social integration and social inequality in Great Britain', Presidential Address to Section N of the British Association Meeting, Exeter.

256

GOLDTHORPE, JOHN, LOCKWOOD, DAVID, BECHHOFER, FRANK and PLATT, JENNIFER (1968), *The Affluent Worker: Political Attitudes*, Cambridge University Press, London.

GOODE, WILLIAM (1956), *After Divorce*, Free Press, New York.

GOODE, WILLIAM (1963), *World Revolution in Family Patterns*, Free Press, New York.

GOULDNER, ALVIN (1973), *For Sociology*, Allen Lane, Penguin Press, London.

HABERMAS, JURGEN (1972), *Knowledge and Human Interests*, Heinemann, London.

HALSEY, A. H., FLOUD, JEAN and ANDERSON, C. ARNOLD (eds) (1961), *Education, Economy and Society*, Free Press, New York.

HALSEY, A. H. (1970), 'Race relations – the lines to think on', *New Society*, no. 390, 19 March, pp. 472–4.

HEGEL, GEORG WILHELM FRIEDRICH (1962), *The Philosophy of Right*, Clarendon Press, Oxford.

HEGEL, GEORG WILHELM FRIEDRICH (1964), *The Phenomenology of Mind*, Allen & Unwin, London.

HERAUD, BRIAN J. (1968a), 'Social class and the new towns', *Urban Studies*, vol. 5, no. 1, pp. 33–58.

HERAUD, BRIAN J. (1968b), 'New towns: the end of a planner's dreams', *New Society*, no. 302, 11 July, pp. 46–9.

HESS, MOSES (1921), *Sozialistische Aufsätze 1841–47*, Welt Verlag, Berlin.

HININGS, CHRISTOPHER ROBIN *et al.* (1967), 'An approach to the study of bureaucracy', *Administrative Science Quarterly*.

HOBHOUSE, LEONARD TRELAWNY (1925), *Morals in Evolution*, Chapman & Hall, London.

HOETINK, HAROLD (1967), *The Two Variants in Caribbean Race Relations*, Oxford University Press, London.

HOGGART, RICHARD (1957), *The Uses of Literacy*, Chatto & Windus, London.

JARVIE, IAN (1967), *The Revolution in Anthropology*, Routledge & Kegan Paul, London.

JENKINS, ROBIN (1970), *Exploitation*, Paladin, London.

JUDSON, T., LANDIS, P. H. and LANDIS, M. G. (eds) (1957), *Readings on Marriage and the Family*, Prentice-Hall, New York.

KORNHAUSER, WILLIAM (1960), *The Politics of Mass Society*, Routledge & Kegan Paul, London.

KUHN, THOMAS (1962), *The Structure of Scientific Revolutions*, Chicago University Press.

LAZARSFELD, PAUL (1970), 'The place of empirical research in the map of contemporary sociology' in McKinney and Tiryakian (eds) (1970), pp. 301–18.

LAZARSFELD, PAUL and OBERSCHALL, ANTHONY R. (1965), 'Max Weber and empirical social research', *American Sociological Review*, vol. 30, no. 2, pp. 185–98.

LAZARSFELD, PAUL and ROSENBERG, M. (eds) (1962), *The Language of Social Research*, Free Press, New York.

LE BON, GUSTAVE (1909), *The Crowd*, Fisher Unwin, London.

LEMERT, EDWIN MCCARTHY (1951), *Social Pathology: A Systematic Approach to Human Behaviour*, McGraw-Hill, New York.

LEMERT, EDWIN MCCARTHY (1967), *Human Deviance, Social Problems and Social Control*, Prentice-Hall, New York.

LEVINE, DONALD N. (ed.) (1971), *Georg Simmel on Individuality and Social Forms*, Chicago University Press.

LÉVI-STRAUSS, CLAUDE (1963), *Structural Anthropology*, Basic Books, New York.

LÉVI-STRAUSS, CLAUDE (1967), *The Scope of Anthropology*, Cape, London.

LÉVI-STRAUSS, CLAUDE (1968), *The Savage Mind*, Weidenfeld & Nicolson, London.

LICHTHEIM, GEORGE (1970), *Lukács*, Fontana/Collins, London.

LIPSET, SEYMOUR MARTIN (1963), *Political Man*, Mercury Books, Heinemann, London.

LIPSET, SEYMOUR MARTIN and TROW, MARTIN (1970), *Union Democracy*, Free Press, New York.

LOCKWOOD, DAVID (1964), 'Social integration and system integration' in Zollschan and Hirsch (ed.) (1964).

LUKES, STEVEN (1973), *Emile Durkheim*, Allen Lane, Penguin Press, London.

LUNDBERG, GEORGE (1939), *Foundations of Sociology*, Macmillan, New York.

MACIVER, ROBERT and PAGE, CHARLES (1969), *Society*, Macmillan, New York.

MACKENZIE, ROBERT (1963), *British Political Parties*, Heinemann, London.

MCKINNEY, JOHN and TIRYAKIAN, EDWARD A. (eds) (1970), *Theoretical Sociology*, Appleton-Century-Crofts, New York.

MALINOWSKI, BRONISLAW (1944), *A Scientific Theory of Culture*, University of North Carolina Press, Chapel Hill.

MANNHEIM, KARL (1940), *Man and Society in an Age of Reconstruction*, Routledge & Kegan Paul, London.

MANNHEIM, KARL (1954), *Ideology and Utopia*, Routledge & Kegan Paul, London.

MANSUR, FATMA (1962), *Process of Independence*, Routledge & Kegan Paul, London.

MARCUSE, HERBERT (1954), *Reason and Revolution*, Routledge & Kegan Paul, London.

MARCUSE, HERBERT (1955), *Eros and Civilization*, Beacon Press, Boston.

MARCUSE, HERBERT (1964), *One Dimensional Man*, Routledge & Kegan Paul, London.

MARSH, DAVID CHARLES (1965), *The Changing Social Structure of England and Wales*, Routledge & Kegan Paul, London.

MARTINDALE, DON (1961), *The Nature and Types of Sociological Theory*, Routledge & Kegan Paul, London.

MARX, KARL (1959), *Economic and Philosophical Manuscripts*, Lawrence & Wishart, London.

MARX, KARL (1962a), 'Inaugural address of the Working Men's International Association' in Marx and Engels (1962), vol. 1.

MARX, KARL (1962b), 'Address to the Communist League' in Marx and Engels (1962).

MARX, KARL (1967a), 'Toward the critique of Hegel's Philosophy of Law: Introduction' in Easton and Guddatt (eds) (1967).

MARX, KARL (1967b), 'On the Jewish question' in Easton and Guddatt (eds) (1967).

MARX, KARL and ENGELS, FRIEDRICH (1962), Selected Works, 2 vols, Lawrence & Wishart, London.

MEAD, GEORGE HERBERT (1934), Mind, Self and Society, Chicago University Press.

MERTON, ROBERT (1957a), Social Theory and Social Structure, revised and enlarged edition, Free Press, New York.

MERTON, ROBERT (1957b), 'The role-set: problems in sociological theory', British Journal of Sociology, vol. viii, no. 2, June, pp. 106–21.

MERTON, ROBERT and NISBET, ROBERT ALEXANDER (1963), Contemporary Social Problems, Rupert Hart-Davis, London.

MICHELS, ROBERT (1958), Political Parties, Free Press, New York.

MILLS, CHARLES WRIGHT (1959a), The Power Élite, Oxford University Press, New York.

MILLS, CHARLES WRIGHT (1959b), The Sociological Imagination, Oxford University Press, New York.

MILLS, CHARLES WRIGHT (1960), The Causes of World War Three, Ballantine Books, New York.

MILLS, CHARLES WRIGHT (1967), White Collar, Oxford University Press, New York.

MOSCA, GAETANO (1939), The Ruling Class, McGraw-Hill, New York.

MYRDAL, GUNNAR (1944), An American Dilemma, Harper, New York.

MYRDAL, GUNNAR (1958), Value in Social Theory, Routledge & Kegan Paul, London.

NATIONAL COMMITTEE FOR COMMONWEALTH IMMIGRANTS (1967), Areas of Special Housing Need, NCCI, London.

NETTLEFORD, REX (1971), Mirror, Mirror, Collins, London.

NICHOLS, THEO (1969), Ownership, Control and Ideology, Allen & Unwin, London.

NICOLAUS, MARTIN (1972), 'The unknown Marx' in Blackburn (eds) (1972).

NISBET, ROBERT ALEXANDER (1962), Community and Power, Oxford University Press, New York.

NISBET, ROBERT ALEXANDER (1965), Emile Durkheim, Prentice-Hall, New York.

NISBET, ROBERT ALEXANDER (1967), The Sociological Tradition, Heinemann, London.

NISBET, ROBERT ALEXANDER (1970), The Social Bond, Knopf, New York.

PACKARD, VANCE (1957), The Hidden Persuaders, Longmans, London.

PARETO, VILFREDO (1963), The Mind and Society, 4 vols, Dover, New York.

PARK, ROBERT and BURGESS, ERNEST (1925), The City, Chicago University Press.

PARSONS, TALCOTT (1947), Introduction to Weber (1947).

PARSONS, TALCOTT (1951), *The Social System*, Routledge & Kegan Paul, London.

PARSONS, TALCOTT (1961), 'The school class as a social system' in Halsey, Floud and Anderson (eds) (1961), pp. 434–55.

PARSONS, TALCOTT (1966), *Essays in Sociological Theory*, Collier-Macmillan, New York.

PARSONS, TALCOTT (1965), *The Structure of Social Action*, Free Press, New York.

PARSONS, TALCOTT (1974), *The Sociology of Knowledge and the History of Ideas*, Routledge & Kegan Paul, London.

PARSONS, TALCOTT and BALES, ROBERT (1956), *Family; Socialization and Interaction Process*, Routledge & Kegan Paul, London.

PARSONS, TALCOTT and SHILS, EDWARD (1962), *Towards a General Theory of Action*, Harper & Row, New York.

PATTERSON, SHEILA (1953), *Colour and Culture in South Africa*, Routledge & Kegan Paul, London.

PERHAM, MARJORIE (1956–60), *Lugard*, 2 vols, Collins, London.

POPPER, KARL (1957), *The Poverty of Historicism*, Routledge & Kegan Paul, London.

PUGH, DEREK *et al.* (1963), 'A conceptual scheme for organizational analysis', *Administrative Science Quarterly*.

PUGH, DEREK *et al.* (1968), 'Dimensions of organizational studies', *Administrative Science Quarterly*.

RADCLIFFE-BROWN, ALFRED REGINALD (1956), *African Systems of Kinship and Marriage*, Oxford University Press, London.

RADCLIFFE-BROWN, ALFRED REGINALD (1964), *The Andaman Islanders*, Free Press, New York.

RADCLIFFE-BROWN, ALFRED REGINALD (1968), *Structure and Function in Primitive Society*, Cohen & West, London.

REX, JOHN (1961), *Key Problems of Sociological Theory*, Routledge & Kegan Paul, London.

REX, JOHN (1968), 'The race relations catastrophe' in Burgess, T. (ed.) *Matters of Principle*, Penguin Books, Harmondsworth.

REX, JOHN (1971), 'Typology and objectivity: a comment on Weber's four sociological methods' in Sahay (ed.) (1971).

REX, JOHN (1972), 'The reserve, the compound and the location', unpublished paper delivered to the British Sociological Association, York.

REX, JOHN (1973a), *Discovering Sociology*, Routledge & Kegan Paul, London.

REX, JOHN (1973b), *Race, Colonialism and the City*, Routledge & Kegan Paul, London.

REX, JOHN (1973c), 'The future of race relations research in Britain. Sociological research and the politics of racial justice', *Race*, vol. xiv, no. 4, April.

REX, JOHN (1973d), Correspondence with A. H. Halsey, in *Race*, vol. xv, no. 1, July.

REX, JOHN and MOORE, ROBERT (1967), *Race, Community and Conflict*, Oxford University Press, London.

RIGBY, ANDREW (1973), *Alternative Realities*, Routledge & Kegan Paul, London.

ROCHE, MAURICE (1973), *Phenomenology, Language and the Social Sciences*, Routledge & Kegan Paul, London.

ROSE, ELLIOT JOSEPH BEN et al. (1969), *Colour and Citizenship*, Oxford University Press, London.

RUNCIMAN, WILLIAM GARRISON (1966), *Relative Deprivation and Social Justice*, Routledge & Kegan Paul, London.

RUNNYMEDE TRUST (1970), *Race in the Inner City: A Report on Handsworth, Birmingham*, Runnymede Trust, London.

RUNNYMEDE TRUST (1971), *Here to Live*, Runnymede Trust, London.

SAHAY, ARUN (ed.) (1971), *Max Weber and Modern Sociology*, Routledge & Kegan Paul, London.

SCHUTZ, ALFRED (1964), *Collected Papers*, Martinus Nijhoff, The Hague.

SCHUTZ, ALFRED (1967), *The Phenomenology of the Social World*, Northwestern University Press, Evanston, Ill.

SEGAL, RONALD (1966), *The Race War*, Cape, London.

SHAW, GEORGE BERNARD (ed.) (1889), *Fabian Essays in Socialism*, Fabian Society, London.

SHILS, EDWARD (1956), *The Torment of Secrecy*, Heinemann, London.

SHILS, EDWARD (1957), 'Daydreams and nightmares: reflections on the criticism of mass culture', *Sewanee Review*, vol. 65, pp. 587–608.

SHILS, EDWARD and YOUNG, MICHAEL (1953), 'The meaning of the Coronation', *Sociological Review*, new series, vol. 1, no. 2, pp. 63–81.

SIMEY, THOMAS (1965), 'Weber's sociological theory of value: an appraisal in mid-century', *Sociological Review*, vol. 13, pp. 45–64.

SIMEY, THOMAS (1966), 'Max Weber: man of affairs or theoretical sociologist?', *Sociological Review*, vol. 14, pp. 303–27.

SIMMEL, GEORG (1959), 'How is society possible?' in Wolff (ed.) (1959).

SIMMEL, GEORG (1969), *The Sociology of Georg Simmel*, ed. K. Wolff, Free Press, New York.

SIMMEL, GEORG (1971), 'The metropolis and mental life' in Levine (ed.) (1971).

SMELSER, NEIL (1962), *The Theory of Collective Behaviour*, Routledge & Kegan Paul, London.

SMITH, MICHAEL GARFIELD (1965), *The Plural Society in the British West Indies*, University of California Press, Berkeley and Los Angeles.

SMITH, MICHAEL GARFIELD and KUPER, LEO (1971), *Pluralism in Africa*, University of California Press, Berkeley and Los Angeles.

SOREL, GEORGE (1970) *Reflections on Violence*, Collier-Macmillan, New York.

SPENCER, HERBERT (1967), *Principles of Sociology*, 2 vols, Chicago University Press.

SPIEGELBERG, H. (1965), *The Phenomenological Movement: A Historical Introduction*, 2 vols, Martinus Nijhoff, The Hague.

STOUFER, SAMUEL et al. (1949), *The American Soldier*, Princeton University Press.

TAYLOR, IAN, WALTON, PAUL and YOUNG, JOCK (1973), *The New Criminology*, Routledge & Kegan Paul, London.

261

BIBLIOGRAPHY

TENBRUCK, FRIEDRICH (1959), 'Formal sociology' in Wolff (ed.) (1959).

THOMAS, WILLIAM ISAAC and ZNANIECKI, FLORIAN (1958), *The Polish Peasant in Europe and America*, Dover, New York.

TÖNNIES, FERDINAND (1955), *Community and Association*, trans. and supplemented by Charles P. Loomis, Routledge & Kegan Paul, London.

TYLOR, EDWARD BURNETT (1929), *Primitive Culture*, 2 vols, 5th edition, Murray, London.

WALLWORK, ERNEST (1973), *Emile Durkheim: Morality and Milieu*, Harvard University Press, New York.

WARNER, W. LLOYD (1936), 'American class and caste', *American Journal of Sociology*, vol. xlii, pp. 234–7.

WEBB, SIDNEY (1889), 'The historic basis of socialism', in Shaw (ed.) (1889).

WEBB, SIDNEY and WEBB, BEATRICE (1941), *Soviet Communism: A New Civilization*, Longmans, London.

WEBER, MAX (1947), *The Theory of Social and Economic Organization*, Free Press, New York.

WEBER, MAX (1949), *The Methodology of the Social Sciences*, Free Press, New York.

WEBER, MAX (1961), *General Economic History*, Collier Books, New York.

WEBER, MAX (1962), *The Protestant Ethic and the Spirit of Capitalism*, Allen & Unwin, London.

WEBER, MAX (1963), *The Sociology of Religion*, Beacon Press, New York.

WEBER, MAX (1964), *The Religion of China*, Macmillan, London.

WEBER, MAX (1967), *Ancient Judaism*, Free Press, New York.

WEBER, MAX (1968a), *Economy and Society*, 3 vols, Bedminster Press, New York.

WEBER, MAX (1968b), *The Religion of India*, Free Press, New York.

WHYTE, WILLIAM HOLLINGSWORTH (1957), *The Organization Man*, Cape, London.

WILLIAMS, RAYMOND (1960), *Culture and Society*, Chatto & Windus, London.

WILLIAMS, RAYMOND (1961), *The Long Revolution*, Chatto & Windus, London.

WINCH, PETER (1963), *The Idea of a Social Science*, Routledge & Kegan Paul, London.

WITTFOGEL, KARL (1957), *Oriental Despotism*, Yale University Press, New Haven.

WITTGENSTEIN, LUDWIG (1968), *Philosophical Investigations*, Macmillan, London.

WOLFF, KURT (ed.) (1959), *Georg Simmel 1858–1918*, Ohio State University Press.

WOLFF, KURT (1960), *Emile Durkheim 1858–1917*, Harper, New York.

YANCEY, WILLIAM L. and RAINWATER, LEE (1967), *The Moynihan Report and the Politics of Controversy*, Massachusetts Institute of Technology Press.

ZOLLSCHAN, GEORGE K. and HIRSCH, WALTER (eds) (1964), *Explorations in Social Change*, Houghton Mifflin, Boston.

Index

263

trade unions—*continued*
  communism, 154–6
  traditional society, 240–1, 243
Treasury, 224
Tricontinental Conference in
  Havana (1966), 195
Trinidad, 201–2
Trow, Martin, 135, 145
True Socialists, 149
Tshombe, Moise, 242
Tylor, Edward, 100
types: average, 62–3; ideal, 15, 35,
  37–41, 43–4, 45, 46–7, 49–50,
  52–3, 60, 62–5, 71, 72, 82, 93,
  95, 101–2, 119
Typographical Union (USA), 135

unemployment, 215, 216, 249
urban *see* cities
USA: blacks, 171–2, 189, 192, 194,
  201, 202–3, 204–5, 228; cities,
  189, 219; coloured population,
  168; political corruption, 128,
  183; primitive accumulation,
  161; relations with Russia 217;
  sociology in, 10, 13, 134–7, 162,
  225, 232
utilitarianism, 87, 89, 179, 224
utopianism, 87, 93, 146, 149, 160,
  181, 239–53

value, 23, 75, 92, 101, 139–40, 145,
  229, 231, 233; assumptions, ix,
  50; judgments, 3–5, 9, 24, 25,
  49, 90–1, 93; orientation, 11–12,
  70, 107, 138
variate language, 52
Verein für Sozialpolitik, 92, 225
verstehen, 42, 49
Vietnam war, 163, 194, 199, 204,
  205
violence, 218, 237; political, 190,
  190–2, 222
voluntarism, 11, 19

Wallwork, Ernest, 60, 88

Walton, Paul, 233
war, x, 215, 216–18; (neo-)
  colonial, 162, 198, 217–18, 222,
  252; nuclear, 243, 244–5
Warner, W. Lloyd, 172, 225
Watergate tribunal, 192
Watts, 204
Webb, Sidney, 89, 149, 224; and
  Beatrice, 89–90
Weber, Max, x, 4, 5, 9, 11, 13–15,
  20, 21, 29, 30, 33, 35, 36–47, 49,
  50, 53–4, 61–5, 69, 71–6, 77,
  78–81, 90, 91–8, 99, 101–2, 106,
  109, 112, 122–3, 126, 132, 148–9,
  150, 159, 163–4, 165, 174, 179,
  180, 185, 210, 212–14, 218, 221,
  224–5, 228–32, 253; *Economy
  and Society*, 36, 39; *General
  Economic History*, 93; *Methodology of Social Science*, 39
welfare *see* social services
West, the *see* Europe
West Indies, 201–2
Whyte, William H., 122
William, Raymond, 139, 140, 141
Winch, Peter, 26, 35, 41, 53
Wittfogel, Karl, 96, 158–9, 221
Wittgenstein, Ludwig, 25
Wolff, Kurt, 88
women, status of, 220
working class, 82, 83, 87, 104–5,
  109, 123–4, 129, 130–2, 139–40,
  145, 149, 154, 180–1, 187–8, 193,
  226, 227, 246–7; colonial, 162,
  170–1

Yancey, William L. and Rain-
  water, L., 171
Young, Jock, 233
Young, Michael, 135

Znaniecki, Florian, 7
Zollschan, George K. and Hirsch,
  Walter, 102

International Library of Sociology

Edited by
John Rex
University of Warwick

Founded by
Karl Mannheim
as The International Library of Sociology
and Social Reconstruction

*This Catalogue also contains other Social Science
series published by Routledge*

Routledge & Kegan Paul   London and Boston
68-74 Carter Lane London EC4V 5EL
9 Park Street Boston Mass 02108

Contents

● *Books so marked are available in paperback*
All books are in Metric Demy 8vo format (216 × 138mm approx.)

GENERAL SOCIOLOGY

Belshaw, Cyril. The Conditions of Social Performance. *An Exploratory Theory. 144 pp.*

Brown, Robert. Explanation in Social Science. *208 pp.*

● Rules and Laws in Sociology.

Cain, Maureen E. Society and the Policeman's Role. *About 300 pp.*

Gibson, Quentin. The Logic of Social Enquiry. *240 pp.*

Gurvitch, Georges. Sociology of Law. *Preface by Roscoe Pound. 264 pp.*

Homans, George C. Sentiments and Activities: *Essays in Social Science. 336 pp.*

Johnson, Harry M. Sociology: *a Systematic Introduction. Foreword by Robert K. Merton. 710 pp.*

Mannheim, Karl. Essays on Sociology and Social Psychology. *Edited by Paul Keckskemeti. With Editorial Note by Adolph Lowe. 344 pp.*
Systematic Sociology: *An Introduction to the Study of Society. Edited by J. S. Erös and Professor W. A. C. Stewart. 220 pp.*

Martindale, Don. The Nature and Types of Sociological Theory. *292 pp.*

● **Maus, Heinz.** A Short History of Sociology. *234 pp.*

Mey, Harald. Field-Theory. *A Study of its Application in the Social Sciences. 352 pp.*

Myrdal, Gunnar. Value in Social Theory: *A Collection of Essays on Methodology. Edited by Paul Streeten. 332 pp.*

Ogburn, William F., and **Nimkoff, Meyer F.** A Handbook of Sociology. *Preface by Karl Mannheim. 656 pp. 46 figures. 35 tables.*

Parsons, Talcott, and **Smelser, Neil J.** Economy and Society: *A Study in the Integration of Economic and Social Theory. 362 pp.*

● **Rex, John.** Key Problems of Sociological Theory. *220 pp.*

Urry, John. Reference Groups and the Theory of Revolution.

FOREIGN CLASSICS OF SOCIOLOGY

● **Durkheim, Emile.** Suicide. *A Study in Sociology. Edited and with an Introduction by George Simpson. 404 pp.*
Professional Ethics and Civic Morals. *Translated by Cornelia Brookfield. 288 pp.*

● **Gerth, H. H.,** and **Mills, C. Wright.** From Max Weber: *Essays in Sociology. 502 pp.*

Tönnies, Ferdinand. Community and Association. *(Gemeinschaft und Gesellschaft.) Translated and Supplemented by Charles P. Loomis. Foreword by Pitirim A. Sorokin. 334 pp.*

SOCIAL STRUCTURE

Andreski, Stanislav. Military Organization and Society. *Foreword by Professor A. R. Radcliffe-Brown. 226 pp. 1 folder.*

Coontz, Sydney H. Population Theories and the Economic Interpretation. *202 pp.*

Coser, Lewis. The Functions of Social Conflict. *204 pp.*

Dickie-Clark, H. F. Marginal Situation: *A Sociological Study of a Coloured Group. 240 pp. 11 tables.*

Glass, D. V. (Ed.). Social Mobility in Britain. *Contributions by J. Berent, T. Bottomore, R. C. Chambers, J. Floud, D. V. Glass, J. R. Hall, H. T. Himmelweit, R. K. Kelsall, F. M. Martin, C. A. Moser, R. Mukherjee, and W. Ziegel. 420 pp.*

Glaser, Barney, and **Strauss, Anselm L.** Status Passage. *A Formal Theory. 208 pp.*

Jones, Garth N. Planned Organizational Change: *An Exploratory Study Using an Empirical Approach. 268 pp.*

Kelsall, R. K. Higher Civil Servants in Britain: *From 1870 to the Present Day. 268 pp. 31 tables.*

König, René. The Community. *232 pp. Illustrated.*

● **Lawton, Denis.** Social Class, Language and Education. *192 pp.*

McLeish, John. The Theory of Social Change: *Four Views Considered. 128 pp.*

Marsh, David C. The Changing Social Structure of England and Wales, 1871-1961. *288 pp.*

Mouzelis, Nicos. Organization and Bureaucracy. *An Analysis of Modern Theories. 240 pp.*

Mulkay, M. J. Functionalism, Exchange and Theoretical Strategy. *272 pp.*

Ossowski, Stanislaw. Class Structure in the Social Consciousness. *210 pp.*

SOCIOLOGY AND POLITICS

Hertz, Frederick. Nationality in History and Politics: *A Psychology and Sociology of National Sentiment and Nationalism. 432 pp.*

Kornhauser, William. The Politics of Mass Society. *272 pp. 20 tables.*

Laidler, Harry W. History of Socialism. *Social-Economic Movements: An Historical and Comparative Survey of Socialism, Communism, Co-operation, Utopianism; and other Systems of Reform and Reconstruction. 992 pp.*

Mannheim, Karl. Freedom, Power and Democratic Planning. *Edited by Hans Gerth and Ernest K. Bramstedt. 424 pp.*

Mansur, Fatma. Process of Independence. *Foreword by A. H. Hanson. 208 pp.*

Martin, David A. Pacificism: *an Historical and Sociological Study. 262 pp.*

Myrdal, Gunnar. The Political Element in the Development of Economic Theory. *Translated from the German by Paul Streeten. 282 pp.*

Wootton, Graham. Workers, Unions and the State. *188 pp.*

FOREIGN AFFAIRS: THEIR SOCIAL, POLITICAL AND ECONOMIC FOUNDATIONS

Mayer, J. P. Political Thought in France from the Revolution to the Fifth Republic. *164 pp.*

CRIMINOLOGY

Ancel, Marc. Social Defence: *A Modern Approach to Criminal Problems. Foreword by Leon Radzinowicz. 240 pp.*
Cloward, Richard A., and **Ohlin, Lloyd E.** Delinquency and Opportunity: *A Theory of Delinquent Gangs. 248 pp.*
Downes, David M. The Delinquent Solution. *A Study in Subcultural Theory. 296 pp.*
Dunlop, A. B., and **McCabe, S.** Young Men in Detention Centres. *192 pp.*
Friedlander, Kate. The Psycho-Analytical Approach to Juvenile Delinquency: *Theory, Case Studies, Treatment. 320 pp.*
Glueck, Sheldon, and **Eleanor.** Family Environment and Delinquency. *With the statistical assistance of Rose W. Kneznek. 340 pp.*
Lopez-Rey, Manuel. Crime. *An Analytical Appraisal. 288 pp.*
Mannheim, Hermann. Comparative Criminology: *a Text Book. Two volumes. 442 pp. and 380 pp.*
Morris, Terence. The Criminal Area: *A Study in Social Ecology. Foreword by Hermann Mannheim. 232 pp. 25 tables. 4 maps.*
● **Taylor, Ian, Walton, Paul,** and **Young, Jock.** The New Criminology. *For a Social Theory of Deviance.*

SOCIAL PSYCHOLOGY

Bagley, Christopher. The Social Psychology of the Epileptic Child. *320 pp.*
Barbu, Zevedei. Problems of Historical Psychology. *248 pp.*
Blackburn, Julian. Psychology and the Social Pattern. *184 pp.*
● **Brittan, Arthur.** Meanings and Situations. *224 pp.*
● **Fleming, C. M.** Adolescence: Its Social Psychology. *With an Introduction to recent findings from the fields of Anthropology, Physiology, Medicine, Psychometrics and Sociometry. 288 pp.*
● The Social Psychology of Education: *An Introduction and Guide to Its Study. 136 pp.*
Homans, George C. The Human Group. *Foreword by Bernard DeVoto. Introduction by Robert K. Merton. 526 pp.*
Social Behaviour: *its Elementary Forms. 416 pp.*
Klein, Josephine. The Study of Groups. *226 pp. 31 figures. 5 tables.*
Linton, Ralph. The Cultural Background of Personality. *132 pp.*
Mayo, Elton. The Social Problems of an Industrial Civilization. *With an appendix on the Political Problem. 180 pp.*
Ottaway, A. K. C. Learning Through Group Experience. *176 pp.*
Ridder, J. C. de. The Personality of the Urban African in South Africa. *A Thematic Apperception Test Study. 196 pp. 12 plates.*
● **Rose, Arnold M.** (Ed.). Human Behaviour and Social Processes: *an Interactionist Approach. Contributions by Arnold M. Rose, Ralph H. Turner, Anselm Strauss, Everett C. Hughes, E. Franklin Frazier, Howard S. Becker, et al. 696 pp.*

Smelser, Neil J. Theory of Collective Behaviour. *448 pp.*
Stephenson, Geoffrey M. The Development of Conscience. *128 pp.*
Young, Kimball. Handbook of Social Psychology. *658 pp. 16 figures. 10 tables.*

SOCIOLOGY OF THE FAMILY

Banks, J. A. Prosperity and Parenthood: *A Study of Family Planning among The Victorian Middle Classes. 262 pp.*
Bell, Colin R. Middle Class Families: *Social and Geographical Mobility. 224 pp.*
Burton, Lindy. Vulnerable Children. *272 pp.*
Gavron, Hannah. The Captive Wife: *Conflicts of Household Mothers. 190 pp.*
George, Victor, and **Wilding, Paul.** Motherless Families. *220 pp.*
Klein, Josephine. Samples from English Cultures.
 1. Three Preliminary Studies and Aspects of Adult Life in England. *447 pp.*
 2. Child-Rearing Practices and Index. *247 pp.*
Klein, Viola. Britain's Married Women Workers. *180 pp.*
 The Feminine Character. *History of an Ideology. 244 pp.*
McWhinnie, Alexina M. Adopted Children. *How They Grow Up. 304 pp.*
Myrdal, Alva, and **Klein, Viola.** Women's Two Roles: *Home and Work. 238 pp. 27 tables.*
Parsons, Talcott, and **Bales, Robert F.** Family: Socialization and Interaction Process. *In collaboration with James Olds, Morris Zelditch and Philip E. Slater. 456 pp. 50 figures and tables.*

SOCIAL SERVICES

Bastide, Roger. The Sociology of Mental Disorder. *Translated from the French by Jean McNeil. 260 pp.*
Carlebach, Julius. Caring For Children in Trouble. *266 pp.*
Forder, R. A. (Ed.). Penelope Hall's Social Services of England and Wales. *352 pp.*
George, Victor. Foster Care. *Theory and Practice. 234 pp.*
 Social Security: *Beveridge and After. 258 pp.*
● **Goetschius, George W.** Working with Community Groups. *256 pp.*
Goetschius, George W., and **Tash, Joan.** Working with Unattached Youth. *416 pp.*
Hall, M. P., and **Howes, I. V.** The Church in Social Work. *A Study of Moral Welfare Work undertaken by the Church of England. 320 pp.*
Heywood, Jean S. Children in Care: *the Development of the Service for the Deprived Child. 264 pp.*
Hoenig, J., and **Hamilton, Marian W.** The De-Segration of the Mentally Ill. *284 pp.*
Jones, Kathleen. Mental Health and Social Policy, 1845-1959. *264 pp.*

King, Roy D., Raynes, Norma V., and **Tizard, Jack.** Patterns of Residential Care. *356 pp.*
Leigh, John. Young People and Leisure. *256 pp.*
Morris, Mary. Voluntary Work and the Welfare State. *300 pp.*
Morris, Pauline. Put Away: *A Sociological Study of Institutions for the Mentally Retarded. 364 pp.*
Nokes, P. L. The Professional Task in Welfare Practice. *152 pp.*
Timms, Noel. Psychiatric Social Work in Great Britain (1939-1962). *280 pp.*
●   Social Casework: *Principles and Practice. 256 pp.*
Young, A. F., and **Ashton, E. T.** British Social Work in the Nineteenth Century. *288 pp.*
Young, A. F. Social Services in British Industry. *272 pp.*

SOCIOLOGY OF EDUCATION

Banks, Olive. Parity and Prestige in English Secondary Education: a Study in Educational Sociology. *272 pp.*
Bentwich, Joseph. Education in Israel. *224 pp. 8 pp. plates.*
● **Blyth, W. A. L.** English Primary Education. *A Sociological Description.*
  1. Schools. *232 pp.*
  2. Background. *168 pp.*
Collier, K. G. The Social Purposes of Education: *Personal and Social Values in Education. 268 pp.*
Dale, R. R., and **Griffith, S.** Down Stream: *Failure in the Grammar School. 108 pp.*
Dore, R. P. Education in Tokugawa Japan. *356 pp. 9 pp. plates*
Evans, K. M. Sociometry and Education. *158 pp.*
Foster, P. J. Education and Social Change in Ghana. *336 pp. 3 maps.*
Fraser, W. R. Education and Society in Modern France. *150 pp.*
Grace, Gerald R. Role Conflict and the Teacher. *About 200 pp.*
Hans, Nicholas. New Trends in Education in the Eighteenth Century. *278 pp. 19 tables.*
●   Comparative Education: *A Study of Educational Factors and Traditions. 360 pp.*
Hargreaves, David. Interpersonal Relations and Education. *432 pp.*
●   Social Relations in a Secondary School. *240 pp.*
Holmes, Brian. Problems in Education. *A Comparative Approach. 336 pp.*
King, Ronald. Values and Involvement in a Grammar School. *164 pp.*
  School Organization and Pupil Involvement. *A Study of Secondary Schools.*
● **Mannheim, Karl,** and **Stewart, W. A. C.** An Introduction to the Sociology of Education. *206 pp.*
Morris, Raymond N. The Sixth Form and College Entrance. *231 pp.*
● **Musgrove, F.** Youth and the Social Order. *176 pp.*
● **Ottaway, A. K. C.** Education and Society: An Introduction to the Sociology of Education. *With an Introduction by W. O. Lester Smith. 212 pp.*
Peers, Robert. Adult Education: *A Comparative Study. 398 pp.*

7

Pritchard, D. G. Education and the Handicapped: *1760 to 1960. 258 pp.*
Richardson, Helen. Adolescent Girls in Approved Schools. *308 pp.*
Stratta, Erica. The Education of Borstal Boys. *A Study of their Educational Experiences prior to, and during Borstal Training. 256 pp.*

SOCIOLOGY OF CULTURE

Eppel, E. M., and **M.** Adolescents and Morality: *A Study of some Moral Values and Dilemmas of Working Adolescents in the Context of a changing Climate of Opinion. Foreword by W. J. H. Sprott. 268 pp. 39 tables.*
● **Fromm, Erich.** The Fear of Freedom. *286 pp.*
The Sane Society. *400 pp.*
Mannheim, Karl. Essays on the Sociology of Culture. *Edited by Ernst Mannheim in co-operation with Paul Kecskemeti. Editorial Note by Adolph Lowe. 280 pp.*
Weber, Alfred. Farewell to European History: *or The Conquest of Nihilism Translated from the German by R. F. C. Hull. 224 pp.*

SOCIOLOGY OF RELIGION

Argyle, Michael. Religious Behaviour. *224 pp. 8 figures. 41 tables.*
Nelson, G. K. Spiritualism and Society. *313 pp.*
Stark, Werner. The Sociology of Religion. *A Study of Christendom.*
Volume I. *Established Religion. 248 pp.*
Volume II. *Sectarian Religion. 368 pp.*
Volume III. *The Universal Church. 464 pp.*
Volume IV. *Types of Religious Man. 352 pp.*
Volume V. *Types of Religious Culture. 464 pp.*
Watt, W. Montgomery. Islam and the Integration of Society. *320 pp.*

SOCIOLOGY OF ART AND LITERATURE

Jarvie, Ian C. Towards a Sociology of the Cinema. *A Comparative Essay on the Structure and Functioning of a Major Entertainment Industry. 405 pp.*
Rust, Frances S. Dance in Society. *An Analysis of the Relationships between the Social Dance and Society in England from the Middle Ages to the Present Day. 256 pp. 8 pp. of plates.*
Schücking, L. L. The Sociology of Literary Taste. *112 pp.*

SOCIOLOGY OF KNOWLEDGE

Mannheim, Karl. Essays on the Sociology of Knowledge. *Edited by Paul Kecskemeti. Editorial Note by Adolph Lowe. 353 pp.*
Remmling, Gunter W. (Ed.). Towards the Sociology of Knowledge. *Origins and Development of a Sociological Thought Style.*
Stark, Werner. The Sociology of Knowledge: *An Essay in Aid of a Deeper Understanding of the History of Ideas. 384 pp.*

URBAN SOCIOLOGY

Ashworth, William. The Genesis of Modern British Town Planning: *A Study in Economic and Social History of the Nineteenth and Twentieth Centuries. 288 pp.*
Cullingworth, J. B. Housing Needs and Planning Policy: *A Restatement of the Problems of Housing Need and 'Overspill' in England and Wales. 232 pp. 44 tables. 8 maps.*
Dickinson, Robert E. City and Region: *A Geographical Interpretation. 608 pp. 125 figures.*
The West European City: *A Geographical Interpretation. 600 pp. 129 maps. 29 plates.*
● The City Region in Western Europe. *320 pp. Maps.*
Humphreys, Alexander J. New Dubliners: *Urbanization and the Irish Family. Foreword by George C. Homans. 304 pp.*
Jackson, Brian. Working Class Community: *Some General Notions raised by a Series of Studies in Northern England. 192 pp.*
Jennings, Hilda. Societies in the Making: *a Study of Development and Re-development within a County Borough. Foreword by D. A. Clark. 286 pp.*
● **Mann, P. H.** An Approach to Urban Sociology. *240 pp.*
Morris, R. N., and **Mogey, J.** The Sociology of Housing. *Studies at Berinsfield. 232 pp. 4 pp. plates.*
Rosser, C., and **Harris, C.** The Family and Social Change. *A Study of Family and Kinship in a South Wales Town. 352 pp. 8 maps.*

RURAL SOCIOLOGY

Chambers, R. J. H. Settlement Schemes in Tropical Africa: *A Selective Study. 268 pp.*
Haswell, M. R. The Economics of Development in Village India. *120 pp.*
Littlejohn, James. Westrigg: *the Sociology of a Cheviot Parish. 172 pp. 5 figures.*
Mayer, Adrian C. Peasants in the Pacific. *A Study of Fiji Indian Rural Society. 248 pp. 20 plates.*
Williams, W. M. The Sociology of an English Village: *Gosforth. 272 pp. 12 figures. 13 tables.*

9

SOCIOLOGY OF INDUSTRY AND DISTRIBUTION

Anderson, Nels. Work and Leisure. *280 pp.*
● **Blau, Peter M.,** and **Scott, W. Richard.** Formal Organizations: *a Comparative approach. Introduction and Additional Bibliography by J. H. Smith. 326 pp.*
Eldridge, J. E. T. Industrial Disputes. *Essays in the Sociology of Industrial Relations. 288 pp.*
Hetzler, Stanley. Applied Measures for Promoting Technological Growth. *352 pp.*
Technological Growth and Social Change. *Achieving Modernization. 269 pp.*
Hollowell, Peter G. The Lorry Driver. *272 pp.*
Jefferys, Margot, *with the assistance of Winifred Moss.* Mobility in the Labour Market: *Employment Changes in Battersea and Dagenham. Preface by Barbara Wootton. 186 pp. 51 tables.*
Millerson, Geoffrey. The Qualifying Associations: *a Study in Professionalization. 320 pp.*
Smelser, Neil J. Social Change in the Industrial Revolution: *An Application of Theory to the Lancashire Cotton Industry, 1770-1840. 468 pp. 12 figures. 14 tables.*
Williams, Gertrude. Recruitment to Skilled Trades. *240 pp.*
Young, A. F. Industrial Injuries Insurance: *an Examination of British Policy. 192 pp.*

DOCUMENTARY

Schlesinger, Rudolf (Ed.). Changing Attitudes in Soviet Russia.
2. The Nationalities Problem and Soviet Administration. *Selected Readings on the Development of Soviet Nationalities Policies. Introduced by the editor. Translated by W. W. Gottlieb. 324 pp.*

ANTHROPOLOGY

Ammar, Hamed. Growing up in an Egyptian Village: *Silwa, Province of Aswan. 336 pp.*
Brandel-Syrier, Mia. Reeftown Elite. *A Study of Social Mobility in a Modern African Community on the Reef. 376 pp.*
Crook, David, and **Isabel.** Revolution in a Chinese Village: *Ten Mile Inn. 230 pp. 8 plates. 1 map.*
Dickie-Clark, H. F. The Marginal Situation. *A Sociological Study of a Coloured Group. 236 pp.*
Dube, S. C. Indian Village. *Foreword by Morris Edward Opler. 276 pp. 4 plates.*
India's Changing Villages: *Human Factors in Community Development. 260 pp. 8 plates. 1 map.*

Firth, Raymond. Malay Fishermen. *Their Peasant Economy. 420 pp. 17 pp. plates.*
Gulliver, P. H. Social Control in an African Society: a Study of the Arusha, Agricultural Masai of Northern Tanganyika. *320 pp. 8 plates. 10 figures.*
Ishwaran, K. Shivapur. *A South Indian Village. 216 pp.*
Tradition and Economy in Village India: *An Interactionist Approach. Foreword by Conrad Arensburg. 176 pp.*
Jarvie, Ian C. The Revolution in Anthropology. *268 pp.*
Jarvie, Ian C., and **Agassi, Joseph.** Hong Kong. *A Society in Transition. 396 pp. Illustrated with plates and maps.*
Little, Kenneth L. Mende of Sierra Leone. *308 pp. and folder.*
Negroes in Britain. *With a New Introduction and Contemporary Study by Leonard Bloom. 320 pp.*
Lowie, Robert H. Social Organization. *494 pp.*
Mayer, Adrian C. Caste and Kinship in Central India: *A Village and its Region. 328 pp. 16 plates. 15 figures. 16 tables.*
Smith, Raymond T. The Negro Family in British Guiana: *Family Structure and Social Status in the Villages. With a Foreword by Meyer Fortes. 314 pp. 8 plates. 1 figure. 4 maps.*

SOCIOLOGY AND PHILOSOPHY

Barnsley, John H. The Social Reality of Ethics. *A Comparative Analysis of Moral Codes. 448 pp.*
Diesing, Paul. Patterns of Discovery in the Social Sciences. *362 pp.*
Douglas, Jack D. (Ed.). Understanding Everyday Life. *Toward the Reconstruction of Sociological Knowledge. Contributions by Alan F. Blum. Aaron W. Cicourel, Norman K. Denzin, Jack D. Douglas, John Heeren, Peter McHugh, Peter K. Manning, Melvin Power, Matthew Speier, Roy Turner, D. Lawrence Wieder, Thomas P. Wilson and Don H. Zimmerman. 370 pp.*
Jarvie, Ian C. Concepts and Society. *216 pp.*
Roche, Maurice. Phenomenology, Language and the Social Sciences. *About 400 pp.*
Sahay, Arun. Sociological Analysis.
Sklair, Leslie. The Sociology of Progress. *320 pp.*

International Library of Anthropology
General Editor Adam Kuper

Brown, Raula. The Chimbu. *A Study of Change in the New Guinea Highlands.*
Van Den Berghe, Pierre L. Power and Privilege at an African University.

International Library of Social Policy

General Editor Kathleen Jones

Holman, Robert. Trading in Children. *A Study of Private Fostering.*
Jones, Kathleen. History of the Mental Health Services. *428 pp.*
Thomas, J. E. The English Prison Officer since 1850: *A Study in Conflict.*
   258 pp.

Primary Socialization, Language and Education

General Editor Basil Bernstein

Bernstein, Basil. Class, Codes and Control. *2 volumes.*
   1. *Theoretical Studies Towards a Sociology of Language. 254 pp.*
   2. *Applied Studies Towards a Sociology of Language. About 400 pp.*
Brandis, Walter, and **Henderson, Dorothy.** Social Class, Language and
   Communication. *288 pp.*
Cook-Gumperz, Jenny. Social Control and Socialization. *A Study of Class
   Differences in the Language of Maternal Control.*
Gahagan, D. M., and **G. A.** Talk Reform. *Exploration in Language for Infant
   School Children. 160 pp.*
Robinson, W. P., and **Rackstraw, Susan, D. A.** A Question of Answers.
   2 volumes. 192 pp. and 180 pp.
Turner, Geoffrey, J., and **Mohan, Bernard, A.** A Linguistic Description and
   Computer Programme for Children's Speech. *208 pp.*

Reports of the Institute of Community Studies

Cartwright, Ann. Human Relations and Hospital Care. *272 pp.*
   Parents and Family Planning Services. *306 pp.*
   Patients and their Doctors. *A Study of General Practice. 304 pp.*
● **Jackson, Brian.** Streaming: *an Education System in Miniature. 168 pp.*
Jackson, Brian, and **Marsden, Dennis.** Education and the Working Class:
   *Some General Themes raised by a Study of 88 Working-class Children
   in a Northern Industrial City. 268 pp. 2 folders.*
Marris, Peter. The Experience of Higher Education. *232 pp. 27 tables.*
Marris, Peter, and **Rein, Martin.** Dilemmas of Social Reform. *Poverty and
   Community Action in the United States. 256 pp.*
Marris, Peter, and **Somerset, Anthony.** African Businessmen. *A Study of
   Entrepreneurship and Development in Kenya. 256 pp.*
Mills, Richard. Young Outsiders: *a Study in Alternative Communities.*

Runciman, W. G. Relative Deprivation and Social Justice. *A Study of Attitudes to Social Inequality in Twentieth Century England. 352 pp.*

Townsend, Peter. The Family Life of Old People: *An Inquiry in East London. Foreword by J. H. Sheldon. 300 pp. 3 figures. 63 tables.*

Willmott, Peter. Adolescent Boys in East London. *230 pp.*

The Evolution of a Community: *a study of Dagenham after forty years. 168 pp. 2 maps.*

Willmott, Peter, and Young, Michael. Family and Class in a London Suburb. *202 pp. 47 tables.*

Young, Michael. Innovation and Research in Education. *192 pp.*

● Young, Michael, and McGeeney, Patrick. Learning Begins at Home. *A Study of a Junior School and its Parents. 128 pp.*

Young, Michael, and Willmott, Peter. Family and Kinship in East London. *Foreword by Richard M. Titmuss. 252 pp. 39 tables.*

The Symmetrical Family.

Reports of the Institute for Social Studies in Medical Care

Cartwright, Ann, Hockey, Lisbeth, and Anderson, John L. Life Before Death.

Dunnell, Karen, and Cartwright, Ann. Medicine Takers, Prescribers and Hoarders. *190 pp.*

Medicine, Illness and Society

General Editor W. M. Williams

Robinson, David. The Process of Becoming Ill.

Stacey, Margaret. *et al.* Hospitals, Children and Their Families. *The Report of a Pilot Study. 202 pp.*

Monographs in Social Theory

General Editor Arthur Brittan

Bauman, Zygmunt. Culture as Praxis.

Dixon, Keith. Sociological Theory. *Pretence and Possibility.*

Smith, Anthony D. The Concept of Social Change. *A Critique of the Functionalist Theory of Social Change.*

Routledge Social Science Journals

The British Journal of Sociology. *Edited by Terence P. Morris. Vol. 1, No. 1, March 1950 and Quarterly. Roy. 8vo. Back numbers available. An international journal with articles on all aspects of sociology.*

Economy and Society. *Vol. 1, No. 1. February 1972 and Quarterly. Metric Roy. 8vo. A journal for all social scientists covering sociology, philosophy, anthropology, economics and history. Back numbers available.*

Year Book of Social Policy in Britain, The. *Edited by Kathleen Jones. 1971. Published Annually.*

Printed in Great Britain by Lewis Reprints Limited
Brown Knight & Truscott Group, London and Tonbridge

1373